PEAK EXPERIENCES

UNDER THE SIGN OF NATURE

Explorations in Ecocriticism

PEAK EXPERIENCES

Walking Meditations
on Literature, Nature, and Need

IAN MARSHALL

UNIVERSITY OF VIRGINIA PRESS
CHARLOTTESVILLE AND LONDON

University of Virginia Press

© 2003 by the Rector and Visitors of the University of Virginia

All rights reserved

Printed in the United States of America on acid-free paper

First published 2003

9 8 7 6 5 4 3 2 1

LIBRARY OF CONGRESS CATALOGING-IN-PUBLICATION DATA

Marshall, Ian, 1954–

    Peak experiences : walking meditations on literature, nature, and need / Ian Marshall.

       p.   cm. — (Under the sign of nature)

    Includes bibliographical references and index.

    ISBN 0-8139-2167-8

    1. American literature—History and criticism.   2. Nature in literature. 3. Maslow, Abraham H. (Abraham Harold)—Influence.   4. Psychology in literature.   5. Need. (Psychology)   6. Mountaineering.   I. Title.   II Series.

    PS163 .M37 2003

    810.9'36—dc21

                                       2002013490

Again,

And Always,

For Jacy and Kira

I only went out for a walk,
and finally concluded to stay out till sundown,
for going out, I found,
was really going in.

—John Muir

Encouraged, I set out once more to climb the mountain of the
earth, for my steps are symbolical steps, and in all my walking
I have not reached the top of the earth yet.

—Henry David Thoreau

CONTENTS

ACKNOWLEDGMENTS

For their company, conversation, and friendship on the trail, heartfelt thanks to my hiking companions—Julie Davis, David Taylor, Peter Rogers, Sean O'Grady, Michael P. Cohen, John Calderazzo, Susan Rosen, Scott Slovic, Tim Palmer, and Ann Viliesis. You made the view a little clearer and the uphill breath easier to catch. David, thanks too for the songs. Julie, thanks for the songs, the stories, and the lessons on weaving. For scholarly companionship and inspiration, my thanks to friends and colleagues in the Association for the Study of Literature and Environment. Some scholarly organizations are a testing ground for ideas. ASLE (to use a more earth-friendly metaphor) has been a seedbed. It is a true community (as opposed to simply an academic community), where people share themselves and not just their ideas. For moral support and occasional advice on style, literary theory, or biology, thanks to my colleagues Carolyn Mahan, Sandy Petrulionis, Steve Sherrill, Michael Wolfe, and Ken Womack.

Pattiann Rogers, "Suppose Your Father Was a Redbird," "On the Existence of the Soul," "Till My Teeth Rattle," "The Family Is All There Is," "Justification of the Horned Lizard," "The Hummingbird: A Seduction," "Geocentric," and "Supposition" in *Song of the World Becoming: New and Collected Poems, 1981–2001* (Minneapolis: Milkweed Editions, 2001). Copyright ©2001 by Pattiann Rogers. Reprinted with permission from Milkweed Editions.

PEAK EXPERIENCES

A WANDERING INTRODUCTION

Meeting the Sun . . . First day of winter. I write this at the moment of meeting the sun, on the ridgeline of Bald Eagle. Heading up, my heart thumping like the sudden, rising wing-flurry of the grouse I disturbed in the rhododendron just below the first stream crossing, I thought of my walk as a race with the sun. But I remembered the tortoise and the hare, and how that race turned out. The sun is a tireless tortoise. Besides, what kind of race would have the contestants approach the finish line from different directions? So I recast my metaphor. We're *meeting* here, not racing, and we'll walk together on the ridgeline, and maybe the sun will accompany me back down the mountain.

It wasn't really predawn on the way up. I could see blue overhead. But I had been in the mountain's shadow. Now, the sun has risen several spans of itself above Tussey Ridge.

I can hear a porcupine chomping on something in the woods behind me, where I sit, stumped—on a stump, that is.

On the way up, crossing several separate streamlets angling down different slopes of my side of the ridge, I thought of them as threads of narrative. The streamlets do all manage to conjoin eventually, and they make their way as one down a crease in the mountain to Bald Eagle Creek, which makes its way to the West Branch of the Susquehanna, which makes it to the Susquehanna and then the Chesapeake Bay. On the eastern side of the mountain, the rills descend to Buffalo Run, to Spring Creek and then Bald Eagle, the West Branch, and the Susquehanna.

Lots of paths to follow. Bear with me.

Deconstructing Hercules . . . Hercules, I see (or last night I saw), has his own TV show. "The Legend Continues," says the show's subtitle. In his latest incarnation Hercules fights for Truth, Justice, and the Athenian (or Roman) way, a democratic hero standing up for the little guy against the tyrannous gods. The introduction to the show announces that "only one man dares to challenge the gods," who are described as petty and cruel. Last week there was a surprise birthday party for Hercules. Amid the preparations we hear the classic line, "You know, Hercules is not the easiest person to shop for." In last night's show Hercules decided he wants to marry the Golden Hind. But his brother Aries, god of war, warns Hercules that if he does so he'll lose his great strength. I gather that the idea now is that his strength is like Superman's, a special power granted him by the gods—not just world's-strongest-man kind of strength, but locomotive-stopping strength. Before Hercules marries and loses his strength, though, he has a good rip-roaring fight with some soldiers. He seems to have learned karate in the last two millennia. When he kicks, his foes sail clear over the roofs of nearby shanties.

The episode seems intended to demonstrate the humanity, the virtue of Hercules for giving up his godlike attributes, his supernatural strength, for love. He's against war, and he wants to marry the Hind, a spirit of nature.

But here's what has me thinking. In the original myths the gods, too, were associated with the forces of nature—Zeus of the thunder and lightning, Poseidon of the sea, windy Aeolus, sunny Apollo, Diana of the moon, and so on. Back then, rather than being some sort of Mr. Natural with muscles, Hercules actively resisted the forces of nature.

Consider the famous twelve labors of Hercules, assigned him as penance for killing his family in a fit of madness brought on by Hera, who was jealous of Hercules because he was the product of one of Zeus's philanderings. Hercules killed a lion, a flock of birds, and a nine-headed swamp creature called the Hydra (surely some sort of endangered species); he captured a stag, a boar, a bull, and a herd of horses; and he stole the girdle of Hippolyta, Queen of the Amazons—necessity dictating of course that he first kill her. Then he stole the Golden Apples of the Hesperides, which had been a wedding present from Gaia to

Hera. Well, actually, Hercules had Atlas steal the apples while he agreed to hold the world on his shoulders. Then when Atlas said he was tired of holding the world up, Hercules said OK, I'll do it, but just hold it again for a moment while I readjust my position. Then he split, leaving Atlas still holding up his end of the bargain. So Hercules is not just a murderer and thief, he's deceitful to boot.

My favorite is the part about cleaning the Augean stables. Hercules rerouted a river or two to run through the stables. Hooray for Hercules, the Hero/God of Direct Discharge Sewage!

But what about the rivers? In celebrating Hercules as a hero, even to this day, aren't we glorifying the slaughter of wild creatures and the kind of human arrogance that says nature, on no matter how grand a scale, is subject to our control, existing to serve our needs, even if that leads to the ruination and despoliation of nature? In Shakespeare's *Henry IV, Part One,* Hotspur and his co-conspirators, in plotting their rebellion, discuss how to divide up the country once their revolution succeeds. To make the parts come out even, they decide that they'll have to reroute the Trent River. In the play, the idea suggests the supreme arrogance of the rebels, not just because they're divvying up the country before they've even won the battle, but because they dare to imagine that they can control the very forces of nature. Is not Hercules a type of Hotspur? Is his not the same kind of hubris and chutzpah? Why then the continued glorification of Hercules?

But of course we glorify Hercules. He symbolizes the way of our culture—the control of nature, the use of nature, the defeat of nature. Technology is the musculature of our Herculean culture, damming and rerouting rivers, eradicating the threat of wildness. Once, when he was too hot, Hercules threatened to shoot the sun with an arrow. When his boat was being rocked, he threatened to punish the waves if they did not calm down.

The epitome of the Herculean is his wrestling match with Antaeus, the son of Poseidon, god of the sea, and Gaia, Mother Earth. While Hercules was searching for the Golden Apples of the Hesperides, he wandered into the country of Antaeus (usually considered Libya). Antaeus, a giant who challenged all who entered his country to a wrestling match, was undefeated, because his strength was renewed whenever he touched the earth. Hercules threw Antaeus to the ground three times and figured out that Antaeus came back stronger every time. He finally defeated Antaeus by holding him up in the air and crushing him to death.

Here we are, two thousand years later, held aloft by the power of technology, desperate to touch the earth, being crushed. Except most of us seem to be enjoying the view from up there, caught in the grasp of Hercules, barely conscious of the tightening in our chests, not all that concerned about our distance from the earth.

It is the purpose of this book to remind us why we need the earth, why we need to make contact with earth, why we experience renewal there. For the Antaean impulse never really died. Hercules had to put the lifeless body of Antaeus down at some point, and we know how the earth likes to make new life from old bones. There are those who have reminded us of the way of Antaeus from time to time. I think of people like Benton MacKaye, the visionary of the Appalachian Trail, who said that as our culture becomes increasingly civilized, we more than ever need some contact with the "primeval."[1] I think too of poets like Homer, or Walt Whitman, or the contemporary poet Pattiann Rogers; of environmentalist writers like John Muir, Aldo Leopold, and Rachel Carson; of contemporary nature writers like Annie Dillard, Gary Snyder, Scott Russell Sanders, and David Quammen; of architects like Frank Lloyd Wright or painters like Thomas Cole—they too have touched the earth, gained strength from it, and told us of what is to be gained from the experience.

Climbing Mount Maslow . . . In a journal entry for October 29, 1857, Henry Thoreau wrote about the mountain of his dreams. It lay, he said, "in the easterly part of our town (where no high hill actually is)," and he talked of climbing it:

> My way up used to lie through a dark and unfrequented wood at its base,—I cannot now tell exactly, it was so long ago, under what circumstances I first ascended, only that I shuddered as I went along (I have an indistinct remembrance of having been out overnight

alone),—and then I steadily ascended along a rocky ridge half clad with stinted trees, where wild beasts haunted, till I lost myself quite in the upper air and clouds, seeming to pass an imaginary line which separates a hill, mere earth heaped up, from a mountain, into a superterranean grandeur and sublimity. What distinguishes that summit above the earthy line, is that it is unhandselled, awful, grand. It can never become familiar; you are lost the moment you set foot there. You know no path, but wander, thrilled, over the bare and pathless rock, as if it were solidified air and cloud.

A few lines later Thoreau asks, "And are there not such mountains, east or west, from which you may look down on Concord in your thought, and on all the world? In dreams I am shown this height from time to time, and I seem to have asked my fellow once to climb there with me, and yet I am constrained to believe that I never actually ascended it."[2]

A couple of weeks later, as he was writing to his friend H. G. O. Blake, Thoreau's dream mountain was still in his mind's eye. "I keep a mountain anchored off eastward a little way," he wrote, "which I ascend in my dreams both awake and asleep. Its broad base spreads over a village or two, which do not know it; neither does it know them, nor do I when I ascend it. . . . I find that I go up it when I am light-footed and earnest. It ever smokes like an altar with its sacrifice. I am not aware that a single villager frequents it or knows of it. I keep this mountain to ride instead of a horse."[3]

I know this mountain Thoreau speaks of, this floating, galloping geologic entity. I have clambered over its rocks. I've sweltered in the sun on it, sipped from its springs, peed on its laurel. I've been caught in a whiteout there, have gotten lost and left my tracks. I've camped on its slopes and exulted on its summit. I have even counted Thoreau himself among my companions in climbing it, pausing to pick huckleberries, all the while moving further and further off the trail as we are lured by the mother lode of berries just a bit further on, and Henry making such a big transcendental deal out of everything, like saying the search for ever-bigger and juicier berries is just like life, or asking everyone if they'd seen some hound and bay horse and turtledove that he seemed to have misplaced.

More often, I've gone alone, looking for myself, and have seen the mountain from vantage points atop other peaks—from here on Bald Eagle, from Mont St. Hilaire, Mount Marcy, and High Point; Wawayanda, Lions Head, October Mountain, Saddle Ball, Greylock; Pico Peak, Killington; Moosilauke, the Kinsmans, and the Presidentials; Mahoosuc Arm, Baldpate, and the Chairbacks; Nesuntabunt and Katahdin; Hawk Mountain, the Pinnacle; Mount Tamalpais; Bear Fence, Hightop, and Humpback; the Priest, Spy Rock, Tar Jacket Ridge; Punchbowl and Apple Orchard and High Cock Knob; Springer Mountain, Blood Mountain, Standing Indian; Wine Spring Bald, Wayah Bald, and Cheoah; Thunderhead and Clingmans Dome; Big Bald and Big Butt, Max Patch and Roan High Knob; yes, even from Shasta and Rainier and Logan, and from El Rucu Pichincha. The Taconics, the Berkshires, the Greens, the Whites, the Nantahalas and Smokies, Grayson Highlands and the Hudson Highlands and the Blue Ridge, Kittatinny Ridge, the Catskills, the Adirondacks, the Coastal Range, the Cascades, the Rockies, the Andes—the names alone seem to make solid my footing, saying them is a deep breath from the uphill climb—from all these, that mountain Thoreau speaks of has been visible off in the distance, or sometimes looming as if it's a few steps away.

At its base lie bog and savanna. Ferns in the shady spots, pond lilies in the wetlands, grasses in the open. Then on the lower slopes deciduous forests rise. Oak, hickory, and beech, mostly, with a few chestnuts mixed in that somehow escaped the blight. Higher up, maples and birches mixed in with pine, then higher up still spruce and fir, gradually diminishing in size and thinning in density. Then alpine meadows, with low-lying krummholz and spongy mosses and lichens and delicate alpine flowers. Then snow and ice, wrapped in cloud most of the time. This mountain does not appear on any known maps, so I've taken the Adamic liberty of naming it myself—Mount Maslow.

On Nature Writing as Preposition . . . My route up Bald Eagle: I go out the door, across the deck, down the steps, over the gravel of the driveway, onto the lawn, around Greg's house, past the old-fashioned hand pump, and into the trees on the old woods road that leads down to the stream. I follow the road for about a hundred yards, then turn off to the left, along the edge of the hemlock stand at first, then through it, leaning low under branches. Then over a fallen log, around the trunk of a pine, through brambles, and across the road. I step over a cable, avert my eyes from the "No Trespassing" sign (just in case, so I can say "what sign?"), cut away from the cell-phone relay tower and up an old logging road.

I recall a conversation with a friend once, one of those meandering conversations that unwinds over a day of hiking, about what part of speech nature writing would be if it were a part of speech. I suppose we were trying to understand the literary grammar with which we carry on our conversations with the world. What is the nature of human utterance, and how does the natural world fit into that sentence? My friend opted for the noun. She liked the idea that nature writing is about identifying the concrete things of this world, their verifiable presence. I played with the idea of verb for a while, thinking of nature writing as that which contains the essential energy and action of life, or conveys the action of the human subject upon the directly experienced objects of the world. Then I reconsidered, for I didn't want to perceive the world solely as object and ourselves as sole speaking subject. I considered the possibility of nature writing as a linking verb as opposed to a transitive one, that which builds an equivalency between subject and object (not we love or destroy nature, but we *are* nature) or turns nature into subject complement, completing our subjecthood. Ultimately I settled on the preposition, that part of speech which shows us the position of things in relation to one another. Anything a rabbit can do to a hill, I've heard prepositions described as. (And, to paraphrase Winston Churchill, a fine word to end a sentence with.) The rabbit can go over the hill, around the hill, under, through, into the hill; be behind, beyond, above, below, next to, atop, or on the hill; seem to be of the hill. You get the idea—a preposition shows position, tells us where we stand (or walk) in relation to the world.

I plod up the slope, no scampering rabbit I on the uphill, past the wasp nest on the side of a hickory—the nest is empty, torn, gray, the size of a bloated rugby ball—and up to the strewn rocks near the next trail junction, where in the winter you can just see the last house through the trees, and where sometimes the dog there will bark. Higher up I come to the first flat spot, the first stream crossing, where the stream exits a rhododendron thicket and passes under the trail in a fat pipe. From there I edge along the rhododenrons, step across a tributary rill where the water seeps year-round, never more than an inch deep and never requiring more than a single step to cross, a flat sandstone rock conveniently placed on either side, then up to the leaning, hollowed-out pine. A good-sized logging road heads off to the north there, angling along the side of the ridge, but I continue upward to the east, along the high bank above the stream, till I reach the meadowy patch, often wet, where the springseeps gather after spilling off the upper slopes and before falling into the well-defined stream banks just below the meadowy patch—high with weeds from mid-May on. From here I can branch off to the south and go up the steep trail and around the high knoll and then back to the north along the ridgeline path, or I can continue heading east, then take another trail up to the top of the knoll, or stay to its south and head directly to the big flat spot, which I think of as the summit because it is the most open spot on the ridge, even though it's not the highest point. Unless it's muddy or icy, I usually opt for the steep trail. First I look back the way I came and notice that already the road is out of sight, out of earshot.

Not far up the steep trail a dirt road branches off to the right and up and out of the glen. There's a house up there, a hunters' cabin. Their ATVs keep these old logging roads open. I stay on the upward slope, pass clumps of birch, a laurel thicket, striped maples encroaching on the trail, a hunter's tree stand (just a few horizontal planks about fifteen feet up in a tree), and then I'm up to the ridgeline. The trail follows it to the northeast. To the east, Tussey Mountain gives the sun an upward shove, Happy Valley glows in the morning sunshine. I look for Mount Maslow, then realize I'm standing on it.

On Maslow's Hierarchy and Literature . . . The name comes of course from the psychologist Abraham Maslow, of "The Hierarchy of Needs." That pyramid that looks like a mountain, complete with life zones labeled "physiological needs," "safety needs," "the need for love and belonging," "the need for esteem," and, ultimately, in the thin, rarefied air atop the hierarchy, "self-actualization." These are the needs that motivate our behavior, says Maslow's classic theory. As we satisfy one need, we are motivated by the next one up, until we reach the highest state of satisfaction: self-actualization. In my Intro to Psych notebook long ago I had drawn the pyramid, then doodled in trees on the slopes.

Why name my mountain for a diagram of human psychological needs? Because it is my contention that that mountain nobody knows about is where we need to go to satisfy our needs.

Maslow's theory, first propounded in a 1954 book called *Motivation and Personality*, remains a staple of psychology texts, and it continues to serve as the subject for further scholarly inquiry and professional applications not only in psychology, but in business, economics, political science, and education. Researchers in psychology continue to invoke Maslow in seeking to comprehend human behavior; often their invocation takes the form of challenge or modification. Researchers in other fields consider how Maslow's hierarchy can serve as a tool for teachers, managers, marketers, and politicians to use in understanding and motivating (or manipulating) students, employees, consumers, citizens. And yes, even literary critics have on occasion found ways to apply Maslow's ideas.[4]

Maslow termed his brand of psychology "humanistic" or "third-force" psychology, focusing less on psychological problems than did the dominant forces of twentieth-century psychology—psychoanalysis and behaviorism—and more on the means by which individuals pursue psychological health and develop their human potential. Maslow's hierarchy distinguishes between deficiency needs (physiological and safety needs) and being needs or meta-needs (the higher ones, as we strive for the fulfillment of self-actualization). The assumption is that, in general, lower needs must be fulfilled before you can move on to the next level.

To be sure, there have been challenges to Maslow's concept of the hierarchy of needs. Some have noted a cultural bias in the hierarchy, with one study pointing out that in Japanese culture, for instance, feelings of satisfaction and self-actualization are produced less by individual achievement than by social belonging (part of Maslow's level three need).[5] So, too, one can object that preoccupation with lower-level needs, as in a tribal culture where food may be scarce and danger often near, need not preclude the possibility of self-actualization.

Maslow has also been charged with making self-actualization seem like an elitist state of psychological grace denied to most of us. He suggests that self-actualization occurs only when other needs are generally satisfied and that it is fairly rare, attained by only about 1 percent of the population. On the one hand, that seems low. Surely just about everyone has experienced at least flashes of the state of achievement and satisfaction and well-being that qualify as self-actualization. On the other hand, I doubt that even 1 percent feel so free of angst that they find themselves in a state of self-actualization often enough to claim permanent residency there. It seems to me that loss of contact with the natural world is one of the factors in our psychological dissatisfaction—call it a deficiency of self-actualization—and that literature and nature can show us the way up the path to self-actualization, or better yet can show us how to find it at every step along the way.

Another criticism of Maslow's hierarchy is that he defined self-actualization by first deciding who the self-actualized are—identifying them by name and reputation—and then deciding on the basis of his self-selected sample what the *characteristics* of self-actualization are. That's not very scientific, is the charge, and his hypothesis about what constitutes self-actualization hardly lends itself to controlled testing. Well, maybe I'm not being very scientific either, but here's my hypothesis: that nature, if not the only means of meeting our psychological needs, is an important and way-too-neglected means of satisfying them—and that our excursions to the woods highlight the nature of our needs (and our need for nature, too, if you want to get cute about it)—and that literature shows us the way. I offer myself as test subject—recently divorced, a father sharing custody of two children, someone with a high regard for the written word (having read too much for my own good, I'm tempted to say, but in truth it's probably been not enough for my own good), a little too stressed-out these days, no more self-actualized than the next person but just as curious about it—and what I have going for me are a lot of well-read books, a good pair of broken-in hiking boots, and a thing for mountains.

Among the attractions of Maslovian psychology are his positive view of human nature and his sense that we seek and can find psychological health and satisfaction. Maslow thought a lot about those mystical moments of pure, intense, joyous transcendence, those moments "of great ecstasy and wonder and awe" that self-actualized people sometimes achieve. He called those moments "peak experiences."[6]

Maslow never elaborated on the geographic metaphor implicit in his thinking about peak experiences. In fact, he talked very little about nature's role in satisfying human psychological needs. The closest he came was in the preface to *Toward a Psychology of Being* (2nd edition), where he envisioned a "higher" psychology that would be "transpersonal, transhuman, centered in the cosmos rather than in human needs and interest." This sounds a lot like the attempt of deep ecologists to move beyond a human-centered view of the world toward biocentrism, a perspective that takes into account the perspectives of all living things, or toward ecocentrism, the perspective of the whole ecosystem. Only recently have psychologists begun to ponder such issues, exploring, in a blend of deep ecology and psychology called "ecopsychology," how our mental health is connected to the health of the natural world. A starting point for the development of ecopsychology was undoubtedly Paul Shepard's *Nature and Madness* (1982), a provocative look at the cultural history that has led to our current state of arrested development, both as individuals and as a culture. Shepard felt that as we have lost connections to wilderness, we have lost as well the arena for testing the self in the kinds of initiation rites that lead the way to maturity. One of my favorite titles in the genre is Chellis Glendinning's *My Name Is Chellis and I'm in Recovery from Western Civilization,* a study of our "addiction" to technology. Other "diagnoses" offered by ecopsychology include the suggestions that we suffer from mass narcissism, amnesia (essentially, we have forgotten our connection to the earth), repression, or a "dissociative split between human spiritual values and the realities of nature, the flesh, and the senses."[7] The remedy, of course, is simple: We need to get back in touch with nature. But if the psychological crises we face today are associated with the ecological crisis, then taking care of ourselves also means taking better care of the world, a connection suggested by the subtitle of a fine collection of essays on the subject, *Ecopsychology: Restoring the Earth, Healing the Mind.* Other titles make similar connections: Howard John Clinebell's *Ecotherapy: Healing Ourselves, Healing the Earth: A Guide to Ecologically Grounded Personality Theory, Spirituality, Therapy, and Education,* Jean Troy-Smith's *Called to Healing: Reflections on the Power of Earth's Stories in Women's Lives,* Deborah Du Nann Winter's *Ecological Psychology: Healing the Split between Planet and the Self,* and the one I recommend for an excellent introduction to the field, Ralph Metzner's *Green Psychology: Transforming Our Relationship to the Earth*—all published since the mid-1990s.[8]

Two related (and almost as recently developed) fields of psychology have given rise to ecopsychology. The more broadly defined field of environmental psychology seeks to identify and measure the restorative benefits of various sorts of contact with nature—aesthetic and recreational as well as spiritual or psychological benefits—and to identify environmental preferences. The classic works in this area are Rachel and Stephen Kaplan's *The Experience of Nature: A Psychological Perspective* and their edited collection *Humanscape: Environments for People.* Others in the field, notably Roger Ulrich, have studied the physiological effects that underlie the psychological or spiritual benefits, finding that contact with nature decreases heart rate and blood pressure and may increase the release of endorphins, thus reducing stress and giving us a feeling of well-being. Insights from this field have been applied in the fields of land management, park planning, landscape architecture—even in the medical field. In general, compared to the field of ecopsychology, environmental psychology, for better or for worse, seems broader in its range of inquiry (studying a variety of environments, for instance, and inviting applications from a variety of disciplines), more empirical, more interested in the built environment, more concerned with shaping environments in order to enhance their benefits to people, less concerned with the idea and appeal of wilderness, less philosophical, less spiritual, less focused on psychopathology, and less radical in calling for changes in our way of life.[9] But there is obviously a great deal of overlap in the concerns of the two fields.

Another related field is evolutionary psychology, which emerged from the controversial field of sociobiology (controversial for seeming, to some, to diminish the influence of culture in its emphasis on the genetic basis for behavior and to establish a single reified norm of human nature; for its apparent emphasis on biological determinism; and for its perceived association with the racist, classist, and elitist tendencies of the social Darwinism of the late nineteenth and early twentieth centuries). Concerned with the genetic grounding of the human mind, evolutionary psychologists point out the mismatch between the world we evolved to inhabit and the world we live in now. Since evolutionary change comes slowly, we are still genetically equipped for the hunter/gatherer culture of the Paleolithic, not our present technological society. We are happiest in the woods because that is where we are physically and psychologically equipped to live; our bodies, our senses, and our minds are adapted to the world outdoors. And our preference for parklike environments that include natural nooks and crannies dates back to our origins on the African savanna, where we sought the advantages of both prospect, which allowed us to see predators coming, and refuge.[10]

Since literature is an important means by which we seek to understand our relationship with the natural world, the ideas of all three branches of ecopsychology (to choose that as the all-embracing term that includes environmental and evolutionary psychology) seem promising in their potential relevance to literary ecocriticism. Ecopsychologists themselves have at times turned to literature to demonstrate their points; Metzner, for example, finds in mythology evidence of a once-closer human connection to the natural world and suggests that story is the means of reconnecting us to natural places. Herb Hammond and Stephanie Judy have suggested that "biblio-therapy," or "reading works by land use visionaries," might be a way of encouraging land managers to consider spiritual values in their decision-making processes.[11] As yet, however, literary ecocritics have made little use of psychological approaches, with the exception of Scott Slovic, whose thesis in *Seeking Awareness in American Nature Writing* is that nature writers "are not merely, or even primarily, analysts of nature or appreciators of nature—rather, they are students of the human mind, literary psychologists," concerned with the "phenomenon of 'awareness.'"[12]

My interest in Maslow derives from my sense that nature writers, like most of the rest of us, are also concerned with self-actualization and that they have found engagement with the natural world the means for achieving that lofty state. Maslow provides my framework, then, for exploring how nature satisfies human needs, each chapter focusing on one of the human needs identified by Maslow, working up from physiological needs to safety needs to the need for love and belonging to the need for esteem and then to self-actualization. My evidence comes from both personal experience and some works of nature writing, both prose and poetry, that I admire: Henry Thoreau's *Walden,* Homer's *Odyssey,* the poems of Pattiann Rogers, John Muir's mountaineering essays, and Walt Whitman's "Song of Myself"—important works by four classic writers (though Homer and Whitman are not always regarded as nature writers) and one contemporary (Rogers), literary Antaeans all, earth-touchers who also manage to touch us with their words.

On Maslow's Hierarchy, Mountains, and Me . . . On the ridgeline trail, sunlight spangles the snow. Overhead, three jet vapor trails gleam like pendants. At the flat, open area that I call Bald Spot, I place my gloves on a snow-dusted log and sit on them, pull a notebook out of my pack, jot down these words, take a swig from a water bottle.

When I say that Maslow's hierarchy provides the framework for my discussions, I mean that quite literally. My critical explorations are set on mountains, where the landscape takes on the pyramidal shape of Maslow's hierarchy. Each chapter, then, not only deals with a work of literature read in the light of one of Maslow's psychological needs, it is also about a mountain, or a range of mountains, and my experiences there. The usual mode of literary criticism, of course, is to remove the first person, to speak from some objective distance. For a variety of reasons I don't do that, preferring a more personal mode of critical discourse called "narrative scholarship." One reason for doing so is that I find a defense of the first person in the writers I choose to write about: "I should not talk so much about myself if there were any body else whom I knew as well," says Thoreau, who asked "of every writer, first or last, a simple and sincere account of his own life." But the idea is that what is true for oneself applies to others as well: "What I assume you shall assume," writes Whitman. "For every atom belonging to me as good belongs to you." The first person also seems to me more honest, for it reveals just where we are situated in relation to our subject (the preposition idea again). I feel personally and passionately connected to my subjects (both the literary works and the mountains), and it would seem false to speak of them in anything other than a personal and connected way. The first person also seems pertinent to ecocritical inquiry in general. John Elder writes that "It seems important to acknowledge that natural scenes engender and inform meditations on literature as well as the other way around," and so my meditations here on both literature and place are brought into conjunction with one another.[13]

Of course the first person is also relevant to a book that purports to study, among other needs, the idea of self-actualization. But it's time for some more deconstruction here. In Maslow's hierarchy of needs, the thing that looks like a mountain is the self. Are my experiences in nature and my readings of literature, then, simply paths by which I explore that mountain of the self? Well, sometimes. But just as often I see the literature as the primary concern, and theories of the self (drawn mainly from psychology) and my experiences in nature as ways of shedding light on the literature. And at times my main concern is with the mountain itself—as mountain, as part of the natural world—and literature and theory (psychological or otherwise) serve as the means of understanding the natural world and our connection to it. Which is the most important stuff of a mountain—the rock, plants, or animals? A mountain is made up of rock and soil, flower and tree, moss and fern, deer, grouse, hawk, snake, turtle. In other words, the mountain itself, the physical thing, is its inorganic form together with its flora and its fauna. Which is literature, which nature, which mind? Can we separate one out from the rest? Not if we still want a mountain. The layers of Maslow's hierarchy evoke Alexander von Humboldt's early nineteenth-century drawings of botanical life zones on Ecuador's Mount Chimborazo, but we feel no need to identify any of those life zones or their plant life as "the best." Isn't it grand that we have access to all of them in the wonderfully varied geography of a mountain.[14]

My impulse to deconstruct hierarchy applies as well to my uses of Maslow's ideas. Maslow claims that we seek to satisfy "lower" needs in order to move on to the good stuff higher up. But at other times he seems to be aware of the attunement of the self-actualized to all experience. Self-actualization can occur at all levels when we truly experience the satisfaction of each need, not simply by rising above them.

But I have to admit that there is something about a mountain that suggests hierarchy—that gives rise to the idea, so to speak. It is part of what makes mountains lend themselves so well to allegory. In *The Other Mexico: Critique of the Pyramid,* Octavio Paz speaks of the "metaphor of the world as a mountain," where the "summit represents the sacred space where the dance of the gods unfolds." At the same time he identifies the mountain/pyramid shape as an "image of the world [that] is a projection of human society," a "religious-political archetype" and social hierarchy that he wishes to deconstruct. Evolutionary biologist Richard Dawkins, in his book entitled *Climbing Mount Improbable,* bases his study of the often improbable course of natural selection and evolutionary adaptation on an allegory of the difficulty of ascent that we associate with mountains. Perhaps my allegorical uses of Mount Maslow are closest to René Daumal's in *Mount Analogue: A Novel of Symbolically Authentic Non-Euclidean Adventures in Mountain Climbing.* According to one critic, Daumal presents a "symbolic allegory of man's escape from the prison of his robotic, egoistic self," and the allegorical dimension is never far from the surface. Before setting out on the expedition to climb Mount Analogue, the narrator has written an article on "The Symbolic Significance of the Mountain," positing that "the Mountain is the bond between Earth and Sky," and "it is the way by which man can raise himself to the divine and by which the divine reveals itself to man." The climb, then, is a quest for spiritual enlightenment—which sounds a lot like Maslow's ascent of the hierarchy of needs, culminating in "peak experience." At the same time, though, the descriptions of Mount Analogue are based on Daumal's own climbing experiences in the Alps. The mountain, shrouded in clouds, makes itself visible only to certain believers, who must believe in its physical and material being.[15]

In Touch with My Shadow . . . Descending Bald Eagle, backlit by the still-rising sun, I stride toward a shadow of myself—a giant elongated shadow, thirty or forty feet high. Maybe "high" is not the right word, though, since none of it rises as much as a millimeter from where it is splayed on the snow. It has no vertical dimension. The stature of that shadow at first made me think of myself as Herculean (still pondering that TV show). Or, since every bit of it touches the earth, perhaps I am Antaean. But of course the shadow is not really me, just an emanation of my silhouette, connected to the corporeal me right where my boot sole meets the mountain. Before long, as I descend, I enter the mountain's shadow—and mine is overtaken.

I've still got Hercules on my mind. If the myths suggest that he actually contests against nature, why is he appearing on TV in the guise of some sort of Greco-Roman Natty Bumppo? Have we forgotten who he really is?

I'm also not quite sure whether the Greeks and Romans recognized the Herculean agenda in the original myths. If they worshipped gods who were so clearly associated with nature, why celebrate a hero, and imbue that hero with godlike status, if he were so frequently pitted *against* the forces of nature? It is possible that Hercules was a figure of wish fulfillment, embodying the desire to conquer nature at a time when people still felt themselves powerless in the throes of too much wilderness. It is possible, too, that Hercules was a transitional figure, one who appeared when the forces of civilization were sufficiently advanced that the Greeks and Romans could begin to conceive of themselves and their civilization as powerful enough to vanquish threats from the natural world—not knowing yet what would soon happen in the vicinity of Mount Vesuvius.

The power of Hercules as nature tamer has only grown in the last twenty centuries. Maybe his perverse equation with nature in his latest TV incarnation is the old story of the dominant culture, in this case a technology-worshiping culture, absorbing dissent. The terms of the contest long ago are now irrelevant. Nature is not a powerful enough foe these days to warrant the enmity of a Hercules. Upon further review, it is more apparent than ever that Antaeus is still defeated.

But maybe I shouldn't be too quick to celebrate Antaeus as nature's appointed gladiator. After all, those who lost their bouts with him also lost their lives, their skulls used to shingle the temple Antaeus was building in honor of his father. It's hard to claim much heroic status for someone who wants to use the skeletal remains of his foes for some sort of cut-rate roofing project. And why see the encounter between nature and culture as a contest or a battle in the first place? Only a culture that fears nature and seeks to dominate it would feel the need to devise a hero to contest against it. There are those among us who want to embrace nature—not defeat it.

But Antaeus is not the only alternative to Hercules offered by the myths of the Greeks and Romans. Consider Psyche—and if I'm going to play around with ideas from psychology, of course I should consider Psyche. She, like Hercules, was also assigned a series of seemingly impossible tasks, as told in *Cupid and Psyche* by the second-century Latin writer Apuleius.[16]

Psyche was so beautiful as to earn the jealousy—and enmity—of Venus (Aphrodite in the Greek). So Venus told her son Cupid (or Eros) to make Psyche fall in love with someone really ugly. But Cupid found Psyche irresistible and failed to obey his mother's command. As it happened, Psyche was admired by many, but only from afar. While her sisters married, she remained unwed. Her father consulted an oracle, who said that Psyche would marry a winged serpent and that she must go to a certain mountaintop to meet him. Up on the mountain, Zephyr, the gentlest of breezes, carried Psyche to a luxuriant palace in a nearby valley. The palace was full of treasures and fine furnishings and good food. Unseen hands dressed her, and her new husband came to her only in the dark. He was loving and kind, but told Psyche that she must never see his face.

When Psyche's sisters visited, they jealously convinced her that she must be married to a monster. So one night she peeked at him by lamplight. She was delighted to see that her husband was actually Cupid, the god of Love. As she sat admiring, she pricked her finger on one of his arrows. A drop of oil fell from her lamp, burning Cupid—and awakening him. Wounded and distressed by her faithlessness, Cupid went home to be cared for by his mother. When Venus found out that he had been consorting with Psyche, she vowed revenge.

Psyche was distraught at her own behavior and her loss of Cupid. She tried to drown herself, but the river's current carried her to shore. Knowing that the way to the god of love was through his mother, she sought out Venus. Venus had her slaves, Anxiety and Sadness, whip Psyche. And then, to punish her further and taint her beauty, she gave Psyche a series of tasks.

Psyche's tasks were daunting enough to be considered Herculean—but her means of accomplishing them differs sharply from the methods of Hercules. Rather than subdue antagonists by superior force, Psyche relies on aid provided by the natural world. An army of ants helps her sort different grains from a huge heap. A riverbank reed tells her how to gather the golden fleece of some fierce sheep—wait till night and collect the fleece from the brambles, it says. An eagle collects water from the headwaters of the Styx for her. Her final task is to bring back from Hades a box containing some of the beauty of Proserpine, the maiden of spring. It is intended for Venus, of course, but Psyche can't resist taking a peek, hoping to use some of the beauty to win Cupid back. She faints, then is rescued by her lover, waking with another prick from one of his arrows. Then Cupid asks Jupiter (Zeus) for help. Psyche has immortality bestowed upon her, and Venus has no objection to having a goddess for a daughter-in-law. Cupid and Psyche are married, and their daughter is called Pleasure.

Psyche, of course, means soul. Her story reminds us *why* we need to touch the earth. Quite simply, it is good for the soul.

1

PHYSIOLOGICAL NEEDS
The Laurel Highlands

It is quite true that man lives by bread alone—when there is no bread. But what happens to man's desires when there *is* plenty of bread and when his belly is chronically filled?

ABRAHAM MASLOW, *Motivation and Personality*

Food. Clothing. Shelter. How early it is that we learn these are our basic needs. Perhaps it is a sign of an advancement in human civilization that we need to spend so little time worrying about how to satisfy these needs. Their satisfaction we take for granted. To the extent that we do concern ourselves with food, clothing, and shelter, it is not out of concern for our survival. We are far more likely to use them to satisfy other needs—fondue by candlelight for love, a fur coat and a sprawling ranch that competes with the Jones's for esteem. Maslow suggests that this is a good thing—that we want to satisfy basic, lower needs and be done with them so that we can get on to things higher up the ladder. But I can't help but wonder if there's nothing lost as we take physiological needs for granted. Some knowledge, maybe, some awareness, some greater sense of what it is to be human—or to be alive.

Our most valuable literary treatise on how and why nature can be part of our lives, our most valuable consideration of what is essential to human life, is in my mind Henry Thoreau's *Walden*. Rereading *Walden* after brushing up on Maslow makes me conscious of the degree to which Thoreau takes physiological needs as his starting point. Those basic needs essentially constitute the topic of the first chapter, "Economy," making up about a third of the whole book. Thoreau says it would be worthwhile "to live a primitive and frontier life" in order to find out "what are the gross necessaries of life."[1] Thoreau, of course, tried to live that sort of life during his two-year stay in his cabin by Walden Pond. I don't have two years to devote to the question of necessities, but it's easy enough to load my backpack and head out for some hiking on the Laurel Highlands Trail in western Pennsylvania. I'll need to carry a week's worth of life's basic necessities.

Packing up, I heed Thoreau's classic advice: "Simplify, simplify" (91). It's the backpacker's credo. For the kitchen: water bottles and a filter, one pot with a lid, a cup, a knife and spoon, a cleanup sponge, a fuel bottle, a single-burner stove that attaches to the fuel bottle, lots of macaroni and cheese and cereal and powdered milk and granola bars and nuts and raisins and smoked cheese and sausage. For the bathroom: toilet paper and an overloaded first-aid kit, to handle everything from blisters to cuts to diarrhea to allergies to sewing emergencies. For the tool shop: nylon cord, duct tape, Super Glue, Swiss army knife. For the bedroom: ground cloth and sleeping bag and self-inflating inch-thick foam mattress. For the bedroom closet: (in addition to what I wear while walking—boots, socks, shorts, T-shirt, bandanna) two pairs of socks, a change of underwear, a change of T-shirt, one pair of lightweight pants, a long-sleeved shirt, fleece sweater, hat, rain jacket, gaiters. For the living room: candles, mini-flashlight, matches, a pennywhistle, notebook, trail guide, map, *Walden*. Total weight: about forty pounds. It isn't much. But it's all I'll need.

The Laurel Highlands Trail runs for seventy miles along Laurel Ridge, or Laurel Hill, from Youghiogheny Gorge, near Ohiopyle, to Conemaugh Gorge, near Johnstown. It's a different kind of trail than I'm used to in that there are restrictions about where you can camp—only at designated areas where four or five shelters are clustered, and where some niceties (or necessities), like a water pump and pit toilets, are provided. There's also a minimal fee charged for the upkeep of these shelter areas.

I park at the northern end, and some friends drop me off at the southern end. An hour or so into my hike, I come to Rock Spring Run, feeding the Youghiogheny. I think of dumping out my water from home and refilling my bottle with stream water. But I don't feel that I've really gotten to the woods yet, or at least I'm not yet properly immersed. When the water from home is gone down my throat, then I will have arrived. I hike just a few hours that afternoon, go six miles over a pair of six-hundred-foot humps. They're nameless on my map, but a hiker heading south refers to them collectively as "Dolly Parton." At the shelter, I spread out my ground cloth, prop my sleeping bag, still stuffed, against a wall for a backrest, lay out my foam pad mattress in front of the stuffed sleeping bag for a seat, hang food bags, get water. The pump water tastes rusty, so I get my water from nearby Camp Run, pumping it through a water filter. The pumping takes several minutes. Used to be, of course, that you could just dip your cup in streams and gulp it down, but these days you have to worry about a protozoan called giardia that will play havoc with your innards. So you have to filter. I don't mind it really. Thoreau says he went to the woods to live his life deliberately, and I love the deliberateness of the water-filtering process, the buildup of anticipation, the sense that I've earned the water by exerting some energy in order to get it. I also take satisfaction in the ritual of it all. I place the plastic intake bulb in the stream, where a hunk of foam rubber keeps it afloat. Attach an outlet tube to the top end of the filter, leading to my water bottle. Pumping draws the water up the first tube, through the filter, up into the second tube, and then into my bottle, one-liter capacity. When I've filled three bottles, I drink from the last one. A long drink—eight, ten ounces' worth. Release the obligatory gasping, satisfied "aahhh!" Top off the bottle.

This is one of the great joys of hiking. "If there is magic on this planet, it is contained in water," said Loren Eiseley.[2] It's not just the clean taste, or the cold on the tongue. Getting water from a stream is a treat for all the senses. Visually, you've got all kinds of special effects caused by the interplay of light and hydrologic motion, gravity having a heyday with the idea of fluidity. Around this rock, across these glistening stones, over this clump of decomposing leaves caught on a stick hung up on rock and streambank, the water jitterbugs downstream. Aside from the oral delights, there are the aural—the symphony of subtle sound, from a rivulet's flutelike trickling to the tympani of falls to the gush of water like a bow drawn across geologic gut. And overhead, woodwinds. All the senses engaged, except maybe smell, and I don't know, when I get near running water I swear I pick up the same delicious ions that make the air smell so good after a rain.

Back at the shelter I read, play my pennywhistle, listen to responding birdsong, check feet for signs of blisters. In the late afternoon, I begin the ritual of the stove—hook up fuel line from stove to fuel bottle, first sucking on the end to be inserted into the fuel-bottle valve top so as to lubricate, then twisting that end into the valve. Pump about thirty times. Turn the knob on the valve to open till liquid gas spills out of the stove nozzle and into the little cup below the burner. Shut the valve, light the spilled gas, let it burn down—about twenty seconds. This preheats the burner, so it will convert the liquid gas to gaseous gas as it exits the burner. Then turn on the valve again and stand back as the flame flares yellow-orange about a foot and a half. In a few moments it settles down to gently hissing blue flame.

Meanwhile I've got water ready—enough for a cup of tea or hot chocolate or cider plus whatever is needed to cook my noodles. When the water boils, I pour some into my cup, add noodles to what's left in the pot, return it to the stove. While dinner cooks I munch on some leftover gorp ("good old raisins and peanuts"—and M&M's, and peanut-butter chips, and dehydrated pineapple chunks). And I think about what nature can teach us about food, clothing, and shelter. I think of acceptance, awareness, appreciation, wildness, and connection. And I read *Walden.*

To some extent Thoreau anticipates Maslow's sense that we need to satisfy basic physiological needs—Thoreau identifies them as Food, Shelter, Clothing, and Fuel—so as to move on to bigger and better things. "Not till we have secured these are we prepared to entertain the true problems of life with freedom and a prospect of success," he says (12). But he sure does dwell on those necessities, taking a great deal of satisfaction in meeting them. He relishes the process of living at the lowest level of motivation. I can't say that Thoreau talks much about safety needs, or about love and belonging, or even about esteem—but in discovering how to live a life that in many ways seems preoccupied with the problems of our physiological needs, Thoreau has also written a treatise on self-actualization. The joy of living, he suggests, is not in dispensing with the necessities of life, but in savoring them. And paradoxically, the way to savor them is to minimize them. We don't need much, and the more we can minimize those needs, the more we can live more fully in other ways—but at the same time we should think deeply about how we go about meeting physiological needs.

So Thoreau eats his bread without yeast and doesn't miss it. He also does without salt, though he admits that it would make a good excuse for a trip to the seashore. He hoes his beans, an endeavor that he says gave him "strength like Antaeus" (155), munches his fill, and reduces his wants and needs. And he concludes that "to maintain one's self on this earth is not a hardship but a pastime, if we will live simply and wisely" (70). I'm gulping down my pasta now. Tonight's has a parmesan sauce. Tomorrow, it'll be flavored ramen with a can of tuna stirred in. Next day, stuffing and pepperoni. Then back to pasta. The law of backwoods cookery is "just add water." The secret ingredients are as follows: the seasoning of outside air, a good caloric deficit from lots of exercise, and enough fatigue to make anything taste good. But there is also the satisfaction of living within limits. I remember a conversation with a thru-hiker on the Appalachian Trail, a typical backpacker's conversation about what to pack. He sifted through supplies by applying the edibility test. "Extra socks? You can't eat socks. A candle? You can't eat candles." The flaw in his reasoning, of course, was that these things might contribute to other basic needs—for clothing and shelter, for instance. But I understood his thought process. A pack on your back necessarily limits you. It's like the old parlor game: If you were trapped on a desert island, what three things would you bring? Except on a hike, whether it's with a fully loaded pack good for a week's jaunt or a fanny pack readied for an afternoon picnic (as long as it's beyond the paved reach of a car), you've got to carry the desert island with you. And you've got to make some hard choices. I used to carry a miniature Scrabble game on my hikes, but the paucity of partners too often rendered those few ounces superfluous. Besides, you can't eat Scrabble. (Not even in Pennsylvania—that would be *scrapple*. Which is a whole different thing.)

This is enforced simplicity. Having a sense of limits requires that we pay attention to what we really need, that we focus on absolute essentials. And it means we cannot take anything for granted. There is a lesson here about living on the earth, an ecological lesson. There is not endless abundance. There is indeed only so much, and for me this week it's as much as I can fit in a pack—or more to the point, feel like carrying. Both the earth and I have our carrying capacity.

We generally live our lives so sated, with satisfiers of every gustatory whim so near—the stocked shelves of the corner convenience store, cupboards full of weeks' worth of food, even if we don't happen to have the exact brand of sweet gherkins we may crave at any given moment—that we don't, or can't, really, savor any of it. We rarely build up enough hunger, and we're rarely faced with any real sense or condition of limits. A good day of hiking, though, gets you good and hungry, and to fill your stomach you've got only what you're carrying on your back. But that limitation hardly creates fear or anxiety along the lines of "Oh my God, what if I run out of food?" Rather, it feels empowering to realize how little we really need.

Besides, the extras, says Thoreau, the luxuries, get in the way. These are "not only not indispensable, but positive hindrances to the elevation of mankind. With respect to luxuries and comforts, the wisest have ever lived a more simple and meager life than the poor" (14). Most of the time our luxuries are simply more of the same. "When a man is warmed . . . what does he want next? Surely not more warmth of the same kind, as more and richer food, larger and more splendid houses, finer and more abundant clothing, more numerous incessant and hotter fires, and the like. When he has obtained those things which are necessary to life, there is another alternative than to obtain the superfluities, and that is to adventure on life now" (15). In other words we try to satisfy higher needs with more of the same stuff that fulfilled lower needs—more food, clothing, and shelter. But these are satisfiers of lower needs—no wonder they don't make us feel very fulfilled spiritually.

But how do I go about beginning "to adventure on life now"? Time for hot chocolate. Ahhh. And, look, a scarlet tanager just swooped from tree to tree.

My Lobster Story: The cocoa is good, the pasta has hit the abdominal spot, and this is a delicious evening. But this pasta repast is hardly my best backpacking meal ever. That would have to be breakfast on Cape Breton Island in Nova Scotia about fifteen years ago. The interior of Cape Breton Island is a high plateau, about three thousand feet, with gorges cut in the cliffs where streams spill down to the Atlantic and the Gulf of Saint Lawrence. I had hiked down along a stream to Fishing Cove and camped in a meadow next to where the stream meets the cove. Rocky headlands wrapped around the sides of the cove.

In the morning, considering whether breakfast should be granola bars or cereal, I was taking down my tent when a boat chugged into the cove. I waved, watched a bit, started rolling up the tent. The guys on the boat pulled up some traps, basketlike webbing on a wood frame. "Hey," came the call, "y'want some lobster?"

I walked to water's edge, they pulled in a little closer and threw three small lobsters on the wet pebbles and stones of the littoral zone, then waved and headed back out into the gulf, aimed up the coast for the next cove.

Now what? Up to the meadow I carried the lobsters, fierce dainties, my thumb and fingers pinching their shells from above, holding them at arm's length where their claws snapped at air. Took two trips, since there were three lobsters and only two hands. Got out stove and pots. Back to the water to fill up a pot—salt water, of course. Got the stove going. Rounded up the lobsters, greenish with black mottling, where they were skittering about in the grass. Plunked them in my pot. It was not a big pot. Nor were they very large lobsters, but still the fit was tight. Their claws stuck out and I had to keep shoving them down into the water. I remembered what William Carlos Williams said about writing a sonnet—that it was like stuffing a crab into a box. If a crab in a box is a sonnet, what was this, three lobsters in a backpacker's pot? An even tighter fit—a villanelle, maybe. Watched the water rise to a boil, watched claws flail and shells redden. They did not go gentle on that good morning.

After a few minutes I turned off the stove, tilted the pot to empty the water, waited for the shells to cool a bit. Wished I had melted butter. Then decided it didn't matter. I sliced the thin hard membrane of the bellies with my Swiss army knife, did the rest of the cracking with my hands. Tucked my bandanna in at the neck for a bib. And I had lobster tails for breakfast. Couldn't eat everything, so I packed up the claws in a Zip-loc bag and ate them at noon, on another trail, sitting by a waterfall.

I tell that story a lot, and for different purposes. Sometimes it's when I'm out backpacking and the talk turns to food, and hunger, and the things we could eat if a restaurant should suddenly appear trailside. There I guess my purpose is to tease, to aggravate my companions' hunger. But at the same time I'm saying that the best meal—at least the best one of my life—is not available at any restaurant. Sometimes I tell the story to show what a joy it is to be outside, to illustrate what Nessmuck said: "We're not out here to rough it. We're here to smooth it. Things are rough enough in town." Or so the L. L. Bean catalog tells us.

But I'm also aware that for me what's contained in the lobster story is not just the delicious irony of having had an elegant meal in place of the dried, dehydrated fare we're usually able to pull out of a backpack. And it's not even just the purely sensual delight of that bright morning, where the sun's rays and the wind off the Gulf offset each other, and the water pattered gently on the stones, and I was refreshed by a good night's sleep after a good day's hike, and I had lobster tails for breakfast on top of all that. And it's not even the recollection of this gift out of nowhere, the act of generosity and sharing from a few moments of contact, the boat appearing, the call from the deck, the lobsters landing, then the boat gone again within a few minutes. I'm not even sure I said thanks. (It's only later that I realized the lobsters may have been below legal size for the lobstermen to keep.)

All of that is wrapped up in the lobster story. But there's also my curiosity as I watched the lobsters turn from creature to meat in that boiling pot, my satisfaction in having participated in so much of the process of taking them (or bringing them?) from sea to gullet, with no store and no profit intervening in the process. And my gut satisfaction at ripping open the shells and tearing the meat from inside, from this thing that just minutes earlier I had picked up alive from the shore. I savor in memory the mess of dripping juices and odorific greenish guts that covered my hands and face, that I then washed off in the cold stream water. I am not a sadist. I am not even very savage, not at the core or anywhere else. But I felt wild then, and that felt good, too.

The miles on the Laurel Highlands are marked by snacks. After a couple of miles and my biggest climb of the hike, a thousand feet up to the ridge, I stop at a rock outcrop with a view to the west and have granola bars. At five miles, by Little Glade Run, I pump more water and snack on handfuls of gorp. At seven miles I stop on the grassy verge of a clear pond—it's a bit too breezy even late in the morning to tempt me to swim—and eat smoked cheese and crackers. In the early afternoon it'll be some salami and a Tiger's Milk bar, high in protein and carob covered. Throughout the day, water, water, water. And at camp the rest of the day's allotment of gorp.

On this day I see three deer and one turkey hunter, sitting on a stump, resting, dressed in camouflage. The camouflage works—it takes me a while to notice him as I approach. Of course, he doesn't see me either, and I'm moving. He asks if I have seen any turkey, and I think he knows that I wouldn't tell him even if I had. I want the wild turkeys in the woods, not on his dinner table. But if I don't much appreciate the gun he's carrying, I'm aware of the irony and my inconsistency as I chew on turkey jerky a few hours later. And I absolutely appreciate the hunting license pinned to the hunter's cap. The money from hunting licenses buys up a lot of State Game Lands in Pennsylvania, and that is all habitat for wild things.

"I love the wild not less than the good," says Thoreau. He says that after talking about his own primal urges toward gustatory satisfaction, in the chapter of *Walden* called "Higher Laws." The chapter ends up being about ascetic virtue and chastity and morality and vegetarianism. In truth Thoreau sounds fastidious and prudish in that chapter. But the early part of the chapter, where Thoreau fantasizes about eating a woodchuck—that's the part we invariably quote from. He says he "felt a strange thrill of savage delight and was strongly tempted to seize and devour him raw, not that I was hungry then, except for that wildness which he represented" (210). He also indulges in an imaginary meal of fried rats, all of which makes it hard to believe that later in the chapter he says there is "something essentially unclean" about flesh (214). He's engaged in a dialogue for our benefit, of course, and having it both ways. It's a fine thing, he suggests, to be a carnivore, and to live off the fat and the juicy, bloody protein of the land. And of course it's also a fine thing to be a vegetarian, which makes sense both physically and spiritually. But somehow the stuff on purity, despite being placed at the end of the chapter, in the position where it might appear to refute what has gone before, just doesn't seem as convincing as the savory stuff on savagery. We read Thoreau for insight into the wild, not lessons on morality. It may seem ironic that the imaginary id-like indulgences of his appetite lead off a chapter called "Higher Laws"—but maybe that's Thoreau's point. It's not just the pursuit of the good that constitutes a higher calling. It is also a higher law to be in touch with our wild side—except it's not a side, it's deep *in*side, at our core. "I like sometimes to take rank hold on life and spend my day as animals do," he says (210). But to pursue the wild is not simply to hark *back* to our savage animal nature, it is to incorporate that wildness because it is part of our human nature.

Much of Thoreau's wild appetite seems to be satisfied by eating and drinking close to the source. About his beloved huckleberries, Thoreau says that "It is a vulgar error to suppose that you have tasted huckleberries who never plucked them. A huckleberry never reaches Boston" (173). Any hiker who has browsed off trailside berries knows what Thoreau is talking about here, and it's not just a matter of freshness. Again, it's the engagement of all the senses in the picking, the sense of where the berries have come from, the perception of all the sun and water and good air that have led to the flourishing of each plant so it can reach out and proffer each berry. It is the practiced tug of the fingers, firm enough to urge the berry off the bush yet gentle enough not to crush, and it is the sense of earning your belly's keep. Thoreau also speaks scathingly of the people of Concord trying to gain access to Walden's water without walking the mile and a half to the pond. He complains that "the villagers, who scarcely know where it lies, instead of going to the pond to bathe or drink, are thinking to bring its water, which should be as sacred as the Ganges at least, to the village in a pipe, to wash their dishes with!—to earn their Walden by the turning of a cock or the drawing of a plug!" (192). If a huckleberry has yet to reach Boston, neither has water ever made it through a faucet. Not the water of Walden Pond, nor the water of Bald Eagle Creek or Johns Brook or Potaywadjo Spring or Katahdin Stream, not Lick Run or Blue Hole Creek or Little Glade Run. Thoreau has more respect for those who have gone to great lengths to get their Walden water, if not by walking there, then by transporting its ice. He delights in the fact that Walden's ice gets shipped around the world, so that "the sweltering inhabitants of Charleston and New Orleans, of Madras and Bombay and Calcutta, drink at my well.... The pure Walden water is mingled with the sacred water of the Ganges" (297–98).

Part of my delight in those Cape Breton breakfast lobsters surely comes from the fact that they were fresh out of the Gulf, so recently wild. But Thoreau's satisfaction at the idea of sharing the beloved water of Walden with those who import its ice reminds me that eating and drinking close to the source is not the same thing as being self-sufficient. Without those lobstermen sharing their catch with me, I'm eating granola for breakfast. And I may carry my food in when I go backpacking, but I didn't catch it or hunt it or gather it—I didn't even make it. But that's OK. When I go hiking, I'm not in retreat from the civilized world. I'm not trying to escape from it, or from anything else. Rather, I'm trying to regain something, going *to* something, not away from anything, and I feel no obligation to renounce all ties to the civilized world. Just as Thoreau says in "Resistance to Civil Government" that he chooses not to be a good subject of an unjust state but he will nevertheless "make what use and get what advantage of her [he] can, as is usual in such cases"—so too will I.[3] And the best the civilized world offers the backpacker has got to be ... pasta. I didn't harvest the wheat, or process it into noodles, or package it, and I didn't dehydrate the powdered cheese and the powdered milk, but I am grateful to live in a culture that can provide such lightweight, compact food so well suited to backpacking. That, and Zip-loc bags.

The May night is more than cool, and by dawn I wish I'd put my knit hat on at bedtime. In the morning, much to my dismay, the Laurel Highlands have let me down. There is nary a breakfast lobster to be found. So it's raisin bran in my Sierra cup, milk made by the magic formula—a spoonful of powder and "just add water." An hour after waking, I'm packed up, have long pants and fleece sweater off, shorts on, and my Thoreau Sauntering Society T-shirt ("It is a great art to saunter," it says). I've also got a bandanna around my forehead (worn Aunt Jemima style in a hair-covering triangle in buggy conditions), socks, boots. And on this cool morning, the lightweight nylon wind shirt stays on, for the first hour or so at least, until the day warms up. I get an early start this morning, on the trail by seven. I pass a cemetery with stones over a century old, see a hummingbird by a ledge overlooking Laurel Run and a killdeer near the top of Seven Springs Mountain. She was pulling the old wounded-wing routine, trying to lure me away from her young.

The afternoon gets hot, but I beat most of the day's heat, helped out by a foot-soak in Blue Hole Creek and a nice cool hemlock stand a few miles from camp. I'm there by midafternoon. I put on lightweight long pants and the wind shirt, which is light enough to wear to keep bugs off even if it's a bit warm out. If it gets cold, and these nights have been getting cold, the fleece sweater goes on. At bedtime, the fleece goes in my sleeping bag's stuff sack for a pillow. And tonight I'll remember that hat.

That's about it for clothing on the trail, except for spare socks, spare bandanna, spare T-shirt (that one has a fluorescent constellation map on the front, inverted, so as to be visible to the wearer), gaiters, and a rain jacket.

Most of these items I reserve for hiking trips. They're too special to wear for everyday activities. Maybe the word is *sacred*. It's a pretty spare wardrobe, but every piece of it is carefully chosen. Each item makes me appreciate what it is for, how form should follow function. And it reinforces lessons about limits. We don't need much—but it has to be the right stuff. With what I've got in my pack or on my person, I can be comfortable in temperatures down into the thirties. Below that, I'd need another layer or two.

Of course all this seems obvious. The point, though, is to become newly aware of what clothing is for. It is to prepare our persons for external conditions. Placing ourselves amid those external conditions means that we must accept the need to accommodate ourselves to the world around us. Why do I need these particular clothes? Because the conditions—the climate in general, today's weather, the level of exposure to the elements inherent in this particular terrain, at this elevation—require them.

That should seem glaringly obvious as well, but in fact most of our clothing choices are motivated by something other than function. Thoreau says we are led more by "the love of novelty, and regard for the opinions of men . . . than by a true utility" (21). But it's not that he doesn't care what he's got on as long as it fends off the elements. Rather, he urges us to truly appreciate what we put on. We should "beware of all enterprises that require new clothes" not just because new clothes tempt us to forsake sense for fashion, but because we should relish the process of growing into our clothes, or allowing our clothes to become familiar on us (23). "Every day," says Thoreau, "our garments become more assimilated to ourselves, receiving the impress of the wearer's character" (21–22). If something works, we should not be in such haste to replace it. Remember the old Donovan song? "I love my shirt, I love my shirt, / My shirt is so comfortably lovely"? Just as a good pair of hiking boots requires some breaking in, so they can be shaped to the mold of your feet, so with all our clothes.

With a closet full of clothes to choose from, you are not likely to develop much of a close relationship with many of your shirts, or pants, or socks. But when you've got only a few things, as much as can fit in the bottom compartment of a pack, when you've had to select just one or two shirts because you can't carry more—then those few things take on special meaning. And they take on more meaning as they play some part in our personal history. My Thoreau Sauntering Society T-shirt has been with me from Maine to Georgia on the Appalachian Trail, atop both Springer Mountain and Mount Katahdin and dozens of high points in between, on many occasions serving as a conversation starter with fellow hikers. My star-chart T-shirt makes me useful around camp on clear nights. My bandannas have cooled me on July afternoons, kept sweat from my eyes, washed pots, and cleaned cuts. My boots, bought just a week before I left for the Laurel Highlands Trail when a cobbler said my old ones were beyond repair, have given rise to not a single blister, and as I write this a year later dust and dirt and dried mud from both the Alleghenies and the Rockies line their creases. I have come to cherish these things, even if they are just things, because of their associations with places where I have been happy, and because they have been part of me there. These few clothes have been markers identifying me to approaching hikers, as close to me as tattoos, but offering utility as well as decoration.

Again, this is not about self-sufficiency. I know that these Laurel Highlands are no desert island where I'm separated from the rest of the world, or from human civilization, and that's just fine. I have no desire to slaughter raccoons for their skins. Nor do I have the ability to do so—not to catch or kill them or skin them, and not to fashion a needle out of bone so as to sew them together. And even if I could do all that, I'd be allergic anyway. I am grateful for the invention of lightweight fleece, able to retain warmth even when wet and lighter than wool. These days they're even making polypropylene sweaters out of recycled plastic. Hurray for human ingenuity, especially when it helps me save a few ounces in my pack.

The need to select a few choice items reinforces the lessons of limitation and appreciation. You can't carry everything—hell, you can't carry much at all, and you're going to have to sacrifice variety. But that just makes the few things you have all the more valued. Fortunately for me, the outdoorsy look is de rigueur these days. It means that I can dress for the woods and not look like a total social outcast. I can take the best of what human culture has to offer (pasta, Zip-locs, fleece) without being a slave to some of its more absurd manifestations, like the world of fashion.

Sudden thought: Or is it that I hike because I like the look?

It could be—but these well-worn clothes become my "coloring" in the woods. They identify me. If I wear similar things around town, it is to retain some sense of connection to the woods and to display that connection. Much of the fashion world uses nature as decoration in a way that emphasizes our distance from nature, or our outright destruction of it. I'm thinking of things like fur coats, or the "bird hats" of the late nineteenth century, where American women—or rather, American hat manufacturers—went from decorating hats with exotic plumes to placing whole, stuffed exotic birds on top.[4] Fashions like these end up looking like symbols of conquest. My processed cotton T-shirts with literature and constellations emblazoned upon them, my synthetics, the polypropylene and the nylon, may not seem very "natural," but they are a tribute to the ingenuity of my species—and they are highly practical in the woods.

At the shelter I spend the late afternoon reading, writing, playing my pennywhistle. The whistle prompts exchanges with birds. I make occasional trips to the pump, and short exploratory journeys around the campground and to the woodpile. After eating dinner and cleaning up, I check out the next day's terrain on the map. More reading. Some boredom. Then it's time for a fire.

These shelters feature built-in fireplaces, placed right in front, where a lean-to is usually open all the way across. But there are still several feet of open air on either side of the rock chimney. The fireplace is raised a foot or so, level with the shelter floor. There's a gap of a couple of feet of hard ground between floor and fireplace. To the side of the chimney I stack wood. The first couple of nights I didn't bother with a fire, but then I figured that, hey, the woodpile is stocked, and the nights have been chilly, so why not. The fireplace faces in to the shelter, and the shelter is small, with a backward-slanting roof, so the fire warms the shelter very effectively. Tending the fire gives me something to do once the light gets too dim to read by. The flames occupy my mind, fending off loneliness as well as the cold. Thoreau says the fireplace is "the most vital part of the house" (241). Vital, from *vita,* life. I recall that Thoreau says all the necessities of life—food, clothing, shelter—are but means of helping "keep the vital heat in us." That's what it all boils down to. Food fuels us from within, fire heats us from the outside, clothing and shelter "serve only to retain the *heat* thus generated and absorbed" (13). Once a good bank of shimmering orange coals has built up, I heap a couple of thigh-sized logs on the fire and shimmy into my sleeping bag.

Comfortably ensconced here before the companionable light of the fire, I see reconfirmed the lessons of limitation, awareness, connection. The lean-to confirms that we don't need much in the way of shelter, and getting by with little makes us aware of our ability to make do with less and to appreciate it all the more. In regard to necessities, Thoreau asks, "Shall we always study to obtain more of these things, and not sometimes to be content with less?" (36). Of course, on the issue of shelter Thoreau sometimes went overboard (or should it be *under*board?). He claims that a large box would do. But a large box, while simple and economical, would sever us from the world as fully as a mansion. The ideal is to integrate the cultural artifact, the house, and its natural surroundings, to protect us from the elements without at the same time separating us from the world outside. In our culture, houses are mainly about keeping the elements out. They are boxes, and we're packaged inside, until we're delivered to a tighter box in the end and sealed underground. In Frank Lloyd Wright's words, "The crate now consecrate."[5]

Thoreau's overdoing it in saying we could live in a box in order to keep the weather out comes from his exasperation at the expense people go to in order to obtain and keep a house. In his concern for household economy, he establishes the formula that "the cost of a thing is the amount of what I will call life which is required to be exchanged for it" (31). Most of us, he says, spend too much of our lives trying to pay for the purchase (or rent) and upkeep of a dwelling. For much of that spent life, we are indebted to bank or landlord. In that regard, our civilization, claims Thoreau, is regressing. So-called primitive people at least own their own home, even if it's just wigwam or hut. And there are advantages to the Spartan life: "The very simplicity and nakedness of man's life in the primitive age imply this advantage at least, that they left him still but a sojourner in nature" (37). In fact, says Thoreau, for two-thirds of the year we really don't need any shelter at all. In contrast, we "civilized" folk think we need something more extravagant, and so we drive ourselves into debt, and our houses become a kind of debtor's prison— "such unwieldy property that we are often imprisoned rather than housed in them" (31). Outside the prison walls lies the freedom embodied by the natural world, the very thing we sought to keep out.

When we go camping, we still need protection from the elements, of course, but our shelters are so lightweight or primitive as to have the effect of not sealing us off from the world. I've always liked the kinds of shelters found on the Laurel Highlands Trail—Adirondack-style lean-tos that are common on eastern trails. To be sure, tents offer advantages, among them self-sufficiency and a kind of freedom. With a tent, you can follow Thoreau's recommendation that we roam all the day long, venture far, and let "the night overtake thee every where at home" (207). And at camp each night you can indulge the Thoreauvian pleasure of putting up your own shelter, on a small scale at least. Thoreau chastised our species for being like robber birds, like cuckoos or cowbirds, making our homes in the abandoned nests of others. "Shall we forever resign the pleasure of construction to the carpenter?" he asks (46). I may not have sewn the nylon or fashioned the aluminum alloy poles of my tent, I may not take much credit for the exquisite design that allows for the recurring magic trick of home for the night emerging from a stuff sack that can fit inside a pack—but I at least play my part in putting each night's roof over my head.

I suppose a tent can feel too enclosing, a lightweight version of Thoreau's railroad box. And I sure appreciate the roominess of a lean-to, with lots of nails on the walls for hanging food bags and wet clothes. But both the thin nylon of my tent and the open front of a lean-to allow the free exchange of sound between inside and out. In the lean-to, I play "Swallowtail Jig" on my whistle, and birds respond. They're making their own calls, of course, not really joining in my tune, but somehow the melodies mesh. Geographer R. Murray Schafer speaks of "acoustic space," where the boundaries of a territory are established by the range of a sound. He notes that in human culture sound is used as a means of asserting dominion over space, of establishing "territorial authority." The loudest sound wins, making its claim on our consciousness—the class bell, the blaring car radio with the cranked-up bass, the police siren, the factory claxon, the obnoxious TV commercial. In contrast, sounds in nature tend to share space, to overlap, creating a kind of dialogue or harmony.[6] I suppose it's possible that the birds answering my whistle are asserting a territorial claim, perceiving my whistling as the audacious heralding of some interloper. But recent studies in ornithology have shown that not all birdcalls are sparked by the practical concerns of mate finding or boundary marking. Surprise, surprise—it seems that birds sometimes sing for the fun of it. And why not—for any species, behavior that offers some evolutionary advantage becomes genetically encoded to be fun, so we do it more often and thus learn to do it better. On this night, neither the bird nor I gets the last word, or note. The wind and the leaves make "wishing" sounds through the night. Or maybe they're telling us to hush.

The point here is simply that with the lean-to open on one side, I still feel like I'm outside, even though I'm protected should it rain. But it's not just the open front that makes me feel connected to the outside world in a lean-to. These wooden shelters seem to belong where they are, as if they are imbued with something of the spirit of the place. I suppose the wood and rock they're made of are not necessarily native materials, but still they seem unobtrusive amid these woods—less so than the gaudily colored nylon of a tent. The shelters stay in place here, while tents come and go. All in all, the shelters achieve what should be the ideal of architecture—to offer shelter while at the same time allowing integration and connection with the surrounding environment.

I'm not suggesting that I'd like to live my life in a lean-to. I have something more like Fallingwater in mind. Just a couple of miles from the Laurel Highlands trailhead is Frank Lloyd Wright's architectural marvel, a place that epitomizes the integration of inside and out, connecting the human construct of a house, and the human life within it, to the surrounding environment. Organic architecture, Wright called it, where the house "aims to be a natural performance, one that is integral to site; integral to environment; integral to the life of the inhabitants."[7] He had Fallingwater built over a waterfall—not set off from it, separate from it, to be admired from afar, from outside the picture, but *in* the picture. Steps lead from the living room down to a platform by the stream. Leave the doors open and you've got air-conditioning. Also humidification and ionization. The living room is built around a boulder that was left in place, a boulder that can serve as table or chair or ornament. It extends through the wall to the outside of the house. The house is more horizontal than vertical, replicating the lay of the local geography. Walls of native sandstone echo the lines and contours of the exposed shelves of the waterfall, as if the house had grown from the rock. Outside almost every room, cantilevered concrete balconies hang out over the stream, seemingly supported by nothing more than moist air. About half the house's floor space remains outside. Windows open from room corners, so there is no supporting post or beam intervening between the leaner-out and the outside air. All the concrete is painted a beige meant to mimic the underside of a fallen rhododendron leaf, and of course rhododendrons surround the house. It's a remarkable place, and at Fallingwater Wright achieved in a permanent home the ideals of integration that we typically find only in temporary shelters along trails, the places we have to leave home to get to in order to renew contact with the natural world.

Fallingwater shows us why architecture is as much art as it is engineering. The art of Fallingwater is not just in the clever design or the technology of reinforcing steel that made possible innovations like the cantilevered concrete decks. It is in the constant flow between inside and outside. Typically, the more elaborate the construction of our buildings, houses included, the more disconnected from the outside world they are.

Thoreau's solution to the problem of shelter was, of course, to build his own cabin, ten feet by fifteen feet, with a loft, a front door, two windows, a bed, desk, and three chairs. His total cost, scrupulously and famously recorded, came to $28.12½. And all in all it was as basic as a lean-to. About the same size, but including a fourth wall with a door that Thoreau kept unlocked. His cabin was a wooden retort to the architectural ideas of the day, and perhaps our day as well, full of curlicues and gewgaws inside and out. Instead of ornamentation, he wanted a home with "a core of truth, a necessity, and hence a beauty." Again, as with clothing, it's the ideal of form following function. Thoreau says, "What of architectural beauty I now see, I know has gradually grown from within outward, out of the necessities and character of the indweller." That beauty, he claims, is most often found, "as the painter knows," in the "most unpretending, humble log huts and cottages of the poor" (46–47).

Well, you can't get any more humble than one of these log shelters—humbler even than my nylon tent, with its space-age fabric and high-tech aluminum poles. But if I see in the shelter some approximation of

Thoreau's architectural ideal, I also consider that even the ticky-tackiest architecture of the contemporary suburb may also, in fact, reflect the "character of the indweller." Unfortunately. Conformity is foremost, imposed not just by zoning laws that govern allowable lawn length, but also by peer pressure from the frowning Joneses that we're trying to keep up with. And just as we mark property lines very clearly with fences and hedges, we also put down a firmly demarcated line between inside and out. We live in enclosures so extensive and airtight that from within we no longer retain much of a sense of what they are sheltering us from. Our houses and workplaces have become worlds unto themselves, and the effect is that we forget too much of the world outside. The fact that the natural world has become synonymous with the word "outside" shows how much we have separated ourselves from that world. Aside from our decks and porches, modern houses fail to integrate us with the world, at least as measured by the test of shared acoustic space. I keep hearing the line from Keats's "La Belle Dame sans Merci," "And no birds sing."[8] Keats is describing a landscape turned barren by loss. These days, there may yet be birds singing by withered sedge, but we can't hear them through our insulated walls.

When biologists speak of the basic needs of a species, they focus on food and water, shelter, and space. That last physiological need is the one we tend to ignore. Space—the first frontier. The space of, say, a trail winding through highlands filled with laurel and granite, or the woods surrounding a pond. If Thoreau in "Economy" deals primarily with food, water, shelter, and clothing—that fabric shelter we wrap tightly around us—then the rest of the book deals with space. His account of his experiment in living begins by telling us how to get the other necessities at least expense, so that we can develop the mind-set and have the time to appreciate space—earthspace, not outer space, nor inner space either, the psyche, but the world around us. *Walden*'s chapter titles offer some suggestion of Thoreau's space explorations. Whither did he wander? To "The Village," "The Ponds," "Baker Farm." The guy gets around. When he says he has traveled widely in Concord, he's not just being metaphorical.

It is in "Solitude," though, that he most directly addresses the question of how much space a person might need. And he finds that there is plenty around us, if we care to seek it out. Actually, we don't even need to seek much. We only need to notice it. "There is commonly sufficient space about us," says Thoreau. "Our horizon is never quite at our elbows" (130). Even in Pennsylvania, where they say you are never more than five miles from a road, I can find plenty of space and solitude. Even in late twentieth-century America. These are beautiful May days out here in the Laurel Highlands, with the mornings blissfully cool, the afternoons sunny and warm, wildflowers beginning to dress and primp for the spring prom, and I've seen only a handful of people. Like Thoreau, I can feel out here that "I have, as it were, my own sun and moon and stars, and a little world all to myself" (130). Thoreau reminds us to take note and appreciate what we are still able to see. "Sometimes," he says, "when I compare myself with other men, it seems as if I were more favored by the gods than they, beyond any deserts that I am conscious of" (131). Let me count my blessings, the favors I've been granted on this hike—incredibly nice weather, the house-high boulders along the trail, where you wind through tunnels a yard or so wide, the streams with plentiful cold and good water—Little Glade Run, Blue Hole Creek, Spruce Run. My legs carrying me well, feeling good.

And yet, when I hike alone, I experience pangs of loneliness. Hiking alone has its advantages in terms of my being able to set my own pace, set my own itinerary, do things my way. But for the most part, going in solitude is something I choose only when I can't find a good companion to go with.

But even that loneliness has a positive effect. Not only am I always thrilled to get home again, I delight in meeting strangers on the trail. I become effusive, I stop and chat for several minutes. We have all heard about the experiments with rats, when scientists have crammed them into a cage and noticed, hey, when there are too many, they start to become surly and then apparently psychotic. They turn on one another. And we have all followed the analogy to human cities. We may not all be in attack mode when we encounter one another strolling down Broadway, but we seem able to cope only by pretending that the human beings before our eyes are not really there. Or we glower and scowl to ensure that nobody invades the invisible boundary lines of our personal space.

Or as Thoreau puts it: "Society is commonly too cheap. We meet at very short intervals, not having had time to acquire any new value for each other. We meet at meals three times a day, and give each other a new taste of that old musty cheese that we are. We have had to agree on a certain set of rules, called etiquette and politeness, to make this frequent meeting tolerable. . . . we live thick and are in each other's way, and stumble over one another, and I think that we thus lose some respect for one another" (136). Out on the trail, I get as excited at running into another person as I do at seeing a bear, a deer, a wild turkey. Quite simply, we appreciate each other more when we are not in each other's way, or in each other's faces, all the time. I meet a guy from Ohio at the campsite water pump—he's heading south and I'm heading north. We trade trail info, he tells me a ranger told him there's been bear activity here. He offers the use of his shower bag—a water bag that you fill up with heated water, hang from a branch, and stand under. What, and ruin this reek I've got going? That's what's keeping the bugs away. We never actually exchange names, but we talk for five minutes and help each other pump while the other fills water bottles. It's enough to get me through to the next day. That, and looking at pictures of my kids.

Thoreau evidently did not struggle with loneliness, asking, "Why should I feel lonely? is not our planet in the Milky Way?" (133). He seems to have found companionship within himself, but also with his surroundings, with his "Brute Neighbors," "Winter Animals," even "Former Inhabitants," the people who once lived by Walden Pond. It's a populated world, with much to occupy us when we crave contact. Perhaps we need to learn again the art of connecting not just with other people but with all the other inhabitants and elements of our space. "Shall I not have intelligence with the earth?" asks Thoreau. "Am I not partly leaves and vegetable mould myself?" (138).

And me, on this day. Can I not be boulder and clear, slow stream and open forest with ferned floor and laurel thicket and ridge walking? I feel within me now a grouse's drumming, quickening and fading, the emergence of a deciduous leaf, the cradle of darkness, and a point of starlight finding its way through.

My last full day on the trail is a long one, over eighteen miles. Turns out that the miles go well—the trail at the northern end is less rugged and rocky than it is to the south. In my head the words *rugged* and *rocky* switch to *ruggy* and *rocked* as I hike, and soon my steps are following the rhythm of the old tongue twister, "Round and round the rugged rock the ragged rascal ran." The miles float by—the usual boulders and ferns and hardwoods. Of course the pack is light now, little food left, and my legs are feeling stronger.

Most of my thoughts on those miles have to do my body. I mean, all our concern for physiological needs comes down to taking care of, or at least taking note of, our bodies. To be conscious of ourselves as physical beings—to live life a little closer to the bone, if only for a little while—that is part of the appeal of the woods. I feel good covering these eighteen miles, not just in the bones and muscles but in the psyche. Athletes must have this sort of consciousness of their bodies. The so-called "runner's high," we know, is a physiological response to extended exercise, made possible by a body capable of performing that exercise long enough to get to the point where endorphins are released.

In truth, even as I'm feeling strong, and feeling good and proud of what my body is doing for me, I'm also aware that much of the time my thoughts are about assorted aches and pains. How's that hot spot on the right pinky toe? How's that shooting pain on my left foot—the one that jolts from the ball of the foot behind the second toe and on up? (I find out later it's an enlargement of nerves called a neuroma. And it's progressive. All my future hiking will be accompanied by that pain, or worse.) How's the pimple covered with moleskin on the right upper thigh? How's the abrasion-raised rash on the left upper thigh? On other trips, my anxieties have focused on tendonitis in the heel, a sore knee, sore bones where the pack's hip belt presses in, sore neck muscles, and various rashes in the crotch area. When I rest, I check out these ailments and apply first aid. And here's the thing—even the aches and pains are good. It's all part of the revivified awareness of the body. That's the glorious point. You have to pay close attention to what's going on, you have to monitor your body because out here you have to rely so much on your body. At home I'm generally oblivious to how my body is doing. I'm not even sure exactly what time of year various allergies kick up.

I recall again Maslow's idea that once our physiological needs are taken care of we ought to move on to higher and better things. I can't help but feel that intense awareness of our bodies is something we feel at a very high level of well-being. Perhaps at our highest level of psychological satisfaction, one of the things that is going on is that we feel very good physically. We tend to think of meeting "higher" needs as something that takes place inside us. We are too quick to leave the world of the senses, too quick to retreat inward from our bodies, to the place where we think the soul is. But in truth it's right here, on the bottom of my feet where they touch the earth, and here, where I feel a breeze touch my face, and on the spot behind my ear that has just been gnat-bitten, and where the sweat on my T-shirt makes it cling to my chest, and in the breathing in and breathing out, and the strain in my calf as I step up an incline, and the tender spot on my hip where the pack belt chafes, and the ache in the back of my neck where it meets shoulders, and my God it's a gorgeous day.

The soul is here all over our bodies and not just contained within, here where we are in direct contact with the world around us. And if we seek to connect ourselves to that world, we do so via the part of ourselves that is in contact with it. I don't and can't know what goes on in the mind of another creature—with the possible exception of the occasional articulate human. But I do know that we share bodily experiences with all kinds of creatures. On the trail today I saw a box turtle with a large growth on the side of his head. At first I thought he was a two-headed turtle. Then I saw his shell was cracked and broken behind that growth. Either something broke his shell by attacking him and the growth is the result of the trauma, or he had some sort of disease that caused the growth and it broke the shell. Either way, the result is that he couldn't retreat back into his shell. The protrusion was too large, and in fact there was no shell right there anyway. Very bad development for the turtle.

What occurs to me now is that putting ourselves in position to have to attend to physiological needs—to savor our attention to them, to live deliberately—is not just to rediscover some part of what it is to be human. It is to become reacquainted with that part of ourselves that has something in common with other living things, sharing concerns for basic biological needs, which are the concerns of the body. That turtle having trouble with his shelter—he reminded me that it is wise to keep track of my various rashes and sore spots and muscle strains before they develop into something more threatening. That awareness, that being in touch with our body and its needs, is the source of the renewal we feel out in the woods. Sometimes I think it is something deep in the core of our being that is reawakened, something like the reptilian core of the brain, a part of the human animal that we keep caged deep in our inner being, and it's the part that reminds us of our connection to and kinship with all other creatures. But that's not really it, because the things we share with other creatures are right there on the surface of our being, on the outside, where our senses feast themselves upon the banquet of the world. If there is a cage here, it is one we have built around ourselves, around our inner being, to keep the world out. And in doing so we have also locked out the part of ourselves that is in touch with that world.

I get to camp by midafternoon. A stream gurgles just below the shelter. I soak sore feet and consider the disadvantage of the pump as water source at most of the Laurel Highlands campsites—no stream for foot-soaking and general hanging out. But there is one here, and I take advantage. I wash armpits and crotch and begin to feel human again. Listen to chickadees. Hang wet clothes to dry on sun-dappled, breeze-stirred bushes. Munch on gorp and write. The life. That's what this is. I read Thoreau, come to the closing lines: "Only that day dawns to which we are awake. There is more day to dawn. The sun is but a morning star" (333). The theme of awakening crops up throughout the book, and of course Thoreau is referring to something more than mere consciousness. Awareness, we call it. Of the world around us, of the physical senses with which we come into contact with that world.

In the evening I sense rain in the air. Must be the shifts in the wind, the darker tinge to the air even below the canopy of oak leaves, though I can't quite make out whether the sky is cloudy or dusky. Maybe I smell something different. In the night the rain comes, a delight to hear in recitation on the roof. In the morning I hike out the last six miles of the trail in drizzle and mist. No views of the Conemaugh Gorge. I do encounter a deer, about fifty feet away. He dashes off a few yards on first seeing me, then stops to watch me, as I watch him. I recall Frost's poem "Two Look at Two," where a human couple see a couple of deer across a crumbling stone wall in a forest. In a brief moment of contact, people and deer check each other out, Frost's title giving equal billing to both sets of viewers, the nonhuman and the human.[9] Here on the northern end of the Laurel Highlands Trail, one looks at one. After a half-minute or so, I look away. The deer does too, right at the same moment. We both seem aware of the odd synchronicity in our movements, and we jerk eyes back to each other at the same time. When I shuffle on a few feet, he does too. Our body language rhymes. We seem to share the same attention span before our muscles seek thawing from our frozen positions. We look at each other again, around at the woods again, relax a bit, look back at each other. Still in perfect time. After several minutes I am no longer surprised at our slow dance. Here we are, two mammals, sharing space and time, this sunlit patch of the Allegheny Highlands in spring, right here and now—of course our feeling is mutual. We seem to get enough of the meeting at about the same time, and walk away, unhurried. I don't know about the deer, but I am grinning.

2

SAFETY NEEDS

On the Colorado Trail

The healthy and fortunate adult in our culture is largely satisfied in his safety needs. The peaceful, smoothly running, stable, good society ordinarily makes its members feel safe enough from wild animals, extremes of temperature, criminal assault, murder, chaos, tyranny, and so on. Therefore, in a very real sense, he no longer has any safety needs as active motivators.

ABRAHAM MASLOW, *Motivation and Personality*

"We need to rethink things"—these are the first words out of Julie's mouth when she meets me at the airport in Durango. Our plan had been to hike the southernmost seventy-five miles of the Colorado Trail, starting at the trailhead outside Durango, climbing from about six thousand feet to over ten thousand in the first day or two, so I could acclimate before reaching the eleven- and twelve-thousand-foot elevations. Then we'd make our way north to Molas Pass, near Silverton. Two years ago, Julie had hiked the rest of the trail from Denver down to Molas, over four hundred miles, but was turned back there by an unrelenting series of thunderstorms. The problem now is that the trail is closed just seven miles in, on the way up Kennebec Pass. Though it is the end of June, several feet of snow fell a few weeks ago, and then the warm weather softened it. In that kind of soft, rotten snow, each step would be an ordeal—sinking in, lifting out, getting wet.

We drive to the southern terminus of the trail and lay out maps on a picnic table. Ultimately we decide to drive up to Molas Pass and walk south as far as we can, realizing we'll have to backtrack if we run into impassable snowfields. And if we can't get far, we'll just do short trips around Molas Pass—lots of good hiking there, says Julie.

We feel better about Plan B when we get near Molas Pass and run into a couple who had snowshoed up from Durango. They'd gotten through, but it was a struggle. When we say the trail is closed now, they say it should be. We set up camp near Little Molas Lake, then take an exploratory walk to the north. We're at about eleven thousand feet, but I don't seem to suffer too much. The mountaintops—Vestal Peak, the Needles, Turkshead, Snowden, Rolling Mountain, Engineer, Twin Sisters—are neck-crickingly high, hanging on to winter on their upper slopes. In the dry, clear air, it seems as though sky and cloud, tundra, granite, and snow are painted on the surface of Little Molas Lake. It's as if I've just put on glasses with the right prescription. Everything seems sharper. And bigger. I have a feeling I'm not in Pennsylvania any more.

If these Rockies seem alien to me, that is part of the point of my being here. I want to feel at least a bit unsettled. It may be true, as Maslow says, that we are no longer motivated by safety concerns these days, but that may not be such a good thing. He claims that "the average adult in our society generally prefers a safe, orderly, predictable, lawful, organized world, which he can count on and in which unexpected, unmanageable, chaotic or other dangerous things do not happen." In our search for "safety and stability," we exhibit a "preference for familiar rather than unfamiliar things . . . for the known rather than the unknown."[1] But then, why do we go skydiving, or bungee jumping, or whitewater rafting, or mountain climbing? Isn't it precisely to experience the unknown, to put aside safety, orderliness, and predictability? If there are those among us who prefer to live vicariously, there are also those who prefer to live precariously. For them, order and routine, rather than being a necessary precondition for our rise to higher concerns, may well be barriers hemming us in, preventing our active pursuit of happiness, which requires us to seek and explore and discover.

I'm reminded of the narrator of Melville's "Bartleby the Scrivener," an "eminently *safe* man" who deems his "first grand point to be prudence" and whose life needs some shaking up (and gets it in the person of Bartleby, he of the staunch negative preferences).[2] Prudence can be overrated. In fact, by suggesting that we need order and routine, Maslow seems inconsistent. When he describes self-actualized people, he stresses their ability to accept the unknown and the unfamiliar: "Our healthy subjects are generally unthreatened and unfrightened by the unknown, being therein quite different from average men. They accept it, are comfortable with it, and often are even *more* attracted by it than by the known."[3]

Their comfort with the unfamiliar and their ability to explore it without fear suggest that self-actualized people are more mature, according to Maslow. He points out that children are afraid of many things, but that "knowledge and familiarity . . . make these dangers less and less dangerous and more and more manageable." In fact, says Maslow, "one of the main conative functions of education is this neutralizing of apparent dangers through knowledge, e.g., I am not afraid of thunder because I know something about it."[4] To enter the wild, then, is to gain knowledge of the world. We may go fearfully at first, until we gain knowledge and it becomes familiar and we can see it as "predictable, lawful, ordered." Without that entrance into the wild, all we do is shut it out, and our fears remain. Maybe many in our culture despise wilderness and seek to eradicate it out of fear of the unfamiliar.

It strikes me that literature functions, as often as not, to introduce us to the unfamiliar, geographical or otherwise, in order to prepare us to cope with the unknown. This may sound like the opposite of Russian literary theorist Viktor Shklovsky's claim that literature relies on a process of "defamiliarization."[5] But maybe not. The pattern of a story or poem is to take us into unfamiliar territory, finding it in even an apparently familiar setting—our world, our culture, our bedroom—and showing us what we hadn't previously recognized or recorded in our mental maps of experience. That's the defamiliarization. But eventually the story leads us into an exploration of that new territory, thereby, as we say, "expanding our horizons."

My reading material for this trip is *The Odyssey,* the archetypal story of such journeying into the unfamiliar, of facing and overcoming a series of obstacles and finding one's way through the rocks and hard places of a dangerous world. Not that I'll be walking in the footsteps of Odysseus in the Colorado Rockies, but like him I'll be traveling in strange lands. No pissed-off Poseidon to deal with, but we will be above tree line, exposed to thunderstorms and encountering high water in streams fed by snowmelt. And there is historical precedent for safety concerns in these mountains. We are in the San Juans, and a bit to the east of here, in the La Garita Range, John Fremont's fourth expedition became trapped in the winter of 1848–49. Caught in deep snow and extreme cold, the party lost all their mules, over a hundred of them, to freezing and starvation, and ten of the thirty-three men. Some of the survivors resorted to cannibalism.

Of course any trepidation I may have about unknowns on this trip is tempered by confidence in Julie's knowledge of these mountains. Besides having hiked most of the Colorado Trail, she lives in the Rockies, at about nine thousand feet. She's also a professional musician and storyteller. If it's true what she says, that stories are "repositories of know-how," we are well equipped to face some of the hard places of the Rockies.

We go about ten miles the first day, a little more than we had planned, given the altitude (consistently over eleven thousand feet), but I managed to lead us on an unintended off-trail detour that added a couple of miles. I'd been too busy looking around at the views to notice when our trail branched off. The trails loop over open tundra much of the time, and I'm not used to such luxurious sight lines. Slabbing sharply angled slopes creased by thin cascades of glittering, hissing snowmelt, we're headed for Rolling Mountain, and it's a gorgeous sunny day—too beautiful for us to feel much concern about safety needs. Even losing the trail, which could be a major problem in the forested east, turns out to be no big deal here—not when you can see landmarks all around in order to place yourself on the map. At every step you can see where you are supposed to be and can plot your own course from here to there.

In the morning I see a bluebird. Just great, I think. I'm out here considering the natural world as a place to court danger, and I see the bluebird of happiness.

Unless that was his evil counterpart, the Bluebird of Death.

I shouldn't kid myself, though. This beautiful place should not be underestimated. If bad weather were to roll in, it would be a different story up here. Above tree line, lightning will seek out the highest objects—us. Getting wet up here if the weather turns cold could also set us up for hypothermia. And the thin air, too, is a concern, potentially leading to altitude sickness. That could take the relatively benign form of a persistent headache and mild nausea, or lead to full-fledged pulmonary or cerebral edema, where oxygen deprivation and low air pressure cause the capillaries to leak fluids into the lungs or brain. The extremes are highly unlikely, but I'm being careful. When I cannot get a good breath, I slow down till it can catch up. Amid one of those pauses to inhale some oxygen, I see part of the appeal of danger. It is awareness. When you are in a place or a situation that poses a threat, whether it's a jaunt above tree line on the Colorado Trail or in the Death Zone of Everest, you need to be very aware, hyper-aware, not just of all that is around you (like a turn in the trail crisscrossing your path), but of your own self in that place. You get up high enough, and you can't even take breathing for granted.

A story told by Joseph Bruchac seems apt here. It's an Abenaki story about a trickster figure named Gluscabi, who received from Grandmother Woodchuck the gift of a magic game bag that could hold all the animals in the world. Gluscabi announced to all the animals that the sky would soon be falling (shades of Chicken Little!), but that they would be safe in his magic bag. Once they were all snug inside, he cinched the top and crowed about his feat, proclaiming that he would never have to hunt again. But Grandmother Woodchuck said, "Oh, Gluscabi, no. It is right that we should have to hunt the animals. It makes us better, and it makes them better."[6]

What she meant by that, I imagine, is that hunting makes us sharper of sight, quicker of limb, and steadier in aim. And probably a whole lot smarter, too. If we had only to reach into our game bags (or run to the market) for dinner, we would lose some of our best qualities, the very traits that make us most human and alive.

Gluscabi saw the wisdom of Grandmother Woodchuck's words and let the animals go. I see in the story not just a defense of hunting, but a reason for seeking out danger in places where we cannot exert absolute control over ourselves and all the life around us.

And I vow to keep better watch for turns in the trail.

As with Gluscabi, so too Odysseus. Think of the wiliness of Odysseus—and Homer says "wily Odysseus" as often as he says "wine-dark sea." Think of the Trojan Horse gambit, or my favorite part, the blinding of Polyphemous, the Cyclops. When Polyphemous imprisons Odysseus and his men in a cave, Odysseus tells him his name is "Nobody." In the cave, they fashion a huge spear, hardening the tip in the fire, which they jab in the Cyclops's one eye when he comes looking for a few good men at dinnertime. Polyphemous then calls out to all the other Cyclopses for assistance, "Help! Help! Nobody is killing me!" To which they reply, in essence, "So if nobody's killing you, what's all the fuss about? Shut up already!" And Odysseus gets away.[7]

My point is not only that his intelligence allows Odysseus to escape from one dire situation after another, but that the encounters with repeated dangers have helped *create* his intelligence. When he first told Polyphemous his name is Nobody, he didn't know yet that Polyphemous posed a threat—Odysseus was being crafty and careful, just in case, because he had learned from experience. When we climb a big mountain, or try to cross the Atlantic solo in a rowboat, or do any of the other things that make many people scratch their heads and wonder why, we exercise our senses and intelligence and take advantage of the recorded experience of the human race in order to overcome obstacles. And we do it—well, at least some small proportion of our species does—because we sense that it makes us better. And maybe it makes the world better too—or it seems so to us. When Maslow says, then, that safety needs are no longer "active motivators" for us moderns, he ignores the extent to which some people seek out the wild, the edge of existence where a misstep, miscalculation, or mistake can bring disaster or at least a taste of real danger. And he ignores the satisfaction we take in finding and walking that wild edge.

We take naps in the late afternoon, make dinner (pasta—what else?), clean up, and hang our food. A flat boulder at the edge of our campsite makes a good perch for taking advantage of the last of the daylight. Marmots whistle alarms to each other until I get comfortably settled with *The Odyssey*. The Twin Sisters above are the Sirens, the syrupy endof-the-day sunshine a visual representation of their song, a hearkening beauty. Tomorrow we'll strap ourselves to the mast of our backpacks and make our way closer to the source of the ethereal sounds and sights that beckon.

It is that image of Odysseus bound to the mast that I take to be of special relevance to us these days. As *The Odyssey* begins, Odysseus is living a life of ease and comfort on the island of the goddess Calypso. Ostensibly the story is about his impulse to get back home to Ithaca, where Penelope waits, fending off suitors who covet Odysseus's kingdom. Odysseus is away twenty years, half of that time engaged at the Battle of Troy, the rest of the time facing obstacle after obstacle on his return home. But in truth, he does not spend all ten years on the high, roiling sea or fending off the depredations of sea monsters or one-eyed giants. For seven years he has been the beloved of Calypso—trapped with a beautiful woman, a goddess no less, in a palace on a lovely island with all the food and drink he could ask for. Despite his protestations of homesickness, no wonder it has taken him seven years to get homeward re-bound. The cad.

The Calypso idyll is typical of the temptations faced by Odysseus. He has spent a year with the sorceress Circe, again as her beloved, living high off the hog, until his men convince him to resume the journey. Of course, his men have succumbed too, lingering in the land of the Lotus Eaters, tempted by opium as opposed to dalliance with a beautiful woman, Odysseus's narcotic of choice. The recurring theme is the need to resist the temptation to stay in a place of comfort and security, where you have all you seem to need, when duty, or home, or the journey beckons.

It seems to me that we live these days on the Isle of Calypso, or in the Land of the Lotus Eaters, bewitched by the sorceress Television and ensconced on a comfy sofa, residing on a cul-de-sac called Easy Street, where the name on every mailbox reads "Reilly." Our every physiological need is apparently satisfied, and we are free of threats to our physical well-being. And yet ease shades into malaise, and most of us sense that something is missing.

For Odysseus, too, the good life is not enough. Eventually—although admittedly at times it takes him a while—he forsakes safety and security and resumes the journey. Of course, even amid the journey he is less than single-minded about returning to Ithaca. In passing the Sirens, the prudent thing would have been for Odysseus to do as he commands his men to do—stop up their ears with wax so they cannot hear the Sirens' alluring songs. But no, he has himself bound to the mast so that he cannot steer the ship into disaster, while at the same time he gets to hear their song.

And that, I say, is what we need to do—strap on our backpacks and go a-journeying. Most of us suspect that there is something out there—maybe it's home—but we are unwilling to set out from the place of comfort and security, the safe place. We need to hear the siren songs of the mountains, and get as close as we can.

First thing in the morning we cross a good-sized stream, which confuses us since we think it may be Upper Lime Creek, which we thought we had passed yesterday. Or it could be that this stream is just an unmapped seasonal rill gushing with snowmelt. It is the first of many confusions on this day. We hike uphill, under the Twin Sisters, past several trailside tarns, then up into snowfields. The first few we go around, then they get large enough that there is no going around, so we go over, following sun-cupped traces of old footprints. The snow is softening, and we fall in knee-deep in places, then crotch-high, and we become more and more careful trying to determine where the firmest snow might be. We're headed for Rolling Mountain Pass, elevation about 12,400 feet. The northern slope we must ascend stays snow covered into August, and the snowfields are deep and extensive with the recent snowfall.

Our main concern is that the warm days are melting the snow and ice, creating rushing streams that eat away tunnels and caves under the snowfields. If we fall in, we could get caught in a strong and cold current under several feet of snow, sucked under, and buried. Even if we managed to clamber out, it would only be by wiggling out of our packs, and then we would have no warm clothes to put on. The whole situation is an invitation to hypothermia.

At times we see a pole marking the trail up ahead in a snowfield, only about half a foot of it sticking above the snow. From there we extrapolate where the trail must go, and we try to move from hummock crest to hummock crest, keeping the apparent path in sight. Invariably there are times when we must descend and cross a snowfield. We learn to watch where the snow is slightly sunken and mottled along a stream line, and we look at the lay of the land surrounding the snowfields to see where the water would likely run. We try to think like gravity. Where we see a trouble spot, we find another route, and it is often a long way around.

When the top of the pass is in sight, we can see the tips of trail signposts at the far end of an expanse of snow the size of several football fields. We can see water pouring off the rocks in a series of cascades, and we can see the lines of sunken snow where the runoff must be flowing below. After talking it over, we map an alternate route up scree fields and across steeply sloping snowfields and patches of exposed rock, then up to a tundra hummock. It is a complicated set of zigs and zags requiring many tentative steps across loose rock and softening snow, with some sinking in, some slipping, but no disasters. Then there's just one more snowfield, firmer than the ones below, to the top of the pass.

The climb is no more than five hundred feet up, but it takes us almost three hours, and neither one of us would have tried it by ourselves. I'm not sure we gave each other courage, exactly—maybe we just figured that if trouble hit, help was close by.

I have found my taste of danger, and have met it with something less than undaunted courage. More like craven timidity. "Healthy fear" is the nicest way I can put it. But maybe that is the appropriate response to danger. If we were fearless, we would have gone directly across the snowfield, right over the running water underneath, assuming that the snow would hold. But we were fear*ful,* or at least careful, and we had to read the landscape and use our ingenuity to find a safe way across. The satisfaction is a product of our heightened awareness, our sensitivity to the landscape. Julie is generous enough to suggest that my getting us lost on the first few miles of our hike was helpful, serving as a warning to keep close watch on our surroundings. She says those warnings often come to her in dreams before a hike, where she sees herself caught on an exposed ridge in a lightning storm, slipping and breaking a leg, or stalked by something unseen. Julie interprets those visions to mean, in essence, be careful, pay attention. But she didn't have any of those dreams before this trip.

We camp by a pond below Rolling Mountain, tent set up under nicely spaced-apart pines. As I stroll around the site, the pond's ability to display all the surrounding mountains seems like a magic trick. The art of reflection is not to be taken for granted. I'd swear those mountains are contained in that water, and the pond's a bowl of fresh landscape, evergreens etched on the brim. A breeze ripples the images, and now the pond is an Impressionist painting.

Odyssey in hand, I reflect on our experiences at Rolling Mountain Pass. I think about the word "Pass," considering it not just in the nominative, as the gap between mountains, but in the verb form, to pass beyond or to pass a test. It was a challenge getting through the pass, as much mental as physical. Picking our way through the snowfields required interpretation. We had to read the land to find our way through. You can probably see where I'm going with this. The skills required to climb a mountain are akin to those involved in reading a book. On the page or across a snowfield, we try to make sense of ambiguous signs and plot turns. Where did the magic trick of writing come from? According to David Abram in *The Spell of the Sensuous,* the earth around us "is shot through with suggestive scrawls and traces, from the sinuous calligraphy of rivers" to "the swooping flights of birds . . . a kind of cursive script written on the wind." On the page, "the scratches and scrawls you now focus upon, trailing across the white surface, are barely different from the footprints of prey left in the snow. We read these traces with organs honed over millennia by our tribal ancestors."[8] There's an obvious survival skill in this ability to read tracks or to read landscapes, to know where the woolly mammoth is headed or where the underground stream runs. In our ancestral past, those who possessed that skill had a better chance of living longer and passing on more genes, until the ability to read and make sense of signs became an established part of our species identity. In turn, the ability to create signs, in the form of a map or a message, would have conferred some survival advantage as well. And imbued with those skills, would we not take satisfaction in exercising them even in contexts beyond the hunt? In evolution the general rule for any adaptive advantage is "use it or lose it."

I have no doubt that the ability to land-gauge had something to do with the development of written language, both having to do with the reading and interpretation of signs. But I'm not saying that we read stories and poems these days in order to hone our hunting and gathering skills. It is simply that interpretive skill has become part of who we are and that exercising that skill in any context brings us pleasure. In evolutionary terms, pleasure is a means of reinforcing behaviors that provide an adaptive advantage. We are genetically prepared, then, to take pleasure and satisfaction in interpreting signs, both as individual marks scrawled on snow or dirt or cave walls or bark or papyrus and as a sequence of such morphemes that together make a story.

I am suggesting, then, that literature arose in part from the exercise of our interpretive faculties, faculties required for making our way in the world. At its core, literature is really a means to an end—the end, for us as for all other living things, being survival. Or so I tell my students, ever since the recent semester when a student challenged me to explain what literature is good for. Two colleagues and I had put together a block of courses integrating field trips as part of our overlapping course work in creative writing, environmental science, and the literature of nature. On our first weekend trip, we and our students went white-water rafting, visited Fallingwater, and backpacked for a couple of days on the Laurel Highlands Trail. We held classes around campfires and on rock outcrops overlooking the Alleghenies. Afterwards, students wrote brief evaluations of the trip, telling us what worked well, what could be better. As you can imagine, given the fact that they were getting credit for going white-water rafting, the students' responses were, all in all, very positive. Except for a couple of jarring notes. One was a painful reference to my pennywhistle as "that nasty fluty thingy"—but I guess that's what I get for using "Swallowtail Jig" as an eight A.M. wake-up call. The other was a comment from an engineering major who said that he especially liked the environmental science course work, as opposed to the creative writing and literature, because there we could get, and I quote, "useful knowledge."

Well, that prompted, in our next class, the standard spiel about the purposes and value of study in the humanities, with the usual emphasis on the development of analytical skills and the need for cultural self-awareness. Literature is "equipment for living," I told them, quoting critic Kenneth Burke. It is "the best that has been thought and said" in our culture, I said, quoting Matthew Arnold, and it is part of being an educated person to have some acquaintance with your culture's literary heritage, quoting every English teacher in the country. My students bought it, for the time being at least, but that skeptical student got me thinking about how we measure the usefulness of literature. Typically, we think of literature benefiting us as individuals, helping us work through moral choices, for instance. Or we think of it as a reflection or production of a culture, representative of its time and place—and so we have English professors who are "medievalists" or "Americanists." But besides using literature to help us better understand ourselves as individuals or better understand our own or some other culture, we can also consider its usefulness to us as a species, by considering the adaptive advantages it provides, or reinforces, in evolutionary terms.

That, in fact, is the agenda of "bioaesthetics" or "biopoetics," which I first became acquainted with in *Consilience*, biologist E. O. Wilson's call for a meeting of the minds from disparate academic disciplines. Wilson devotes a chapter of *Consilience* to a discussion of the biological basis for art. The presumption is that we can find in art, in its prominent themes and character types and plot movements, certain "epigenetic rules" that offer some adaptive advantage. A bioaesthetic study might ask how this work, a poem or story, say, offers some evolutionary advantage to the culture acquainted with it. In the evolution of our peculiar species, wielder of language and symbol and narrative, natural selection has emphasized certain traits. Some of those, like interpretive skill, may have given rise to the creation of art and literature in general. Others, like valor and virtue, perhaps, may well be expressed in the art and literature we create and admire. It's a provocative idea that suggests many possibilities for considering how evolutionary theory might contribute to an understanding of art.[9]

Consider, for example, the recurrent patterns of fairy tales, myths, and legends—the quest motif, the movement out into the world and back home again, the presence of a guide who bestows upon the hero the information he needs to complete the quest. These patterns are so familiar that the Russian structuralist critic Vladimir Propp identified thirty-three "functions" that make up the movement of all Russian fairy tales. These functions are essentially plot moves, or actions, and in truth, they recur in some form in most stories, realistic fiction as well as fairy tale and myth.[10] Jung's archetypes constitute another attempt to identify the literary motifs and character types that reverberate with special meaning in our stories—reverberate, perhaps, because we are genetically prepared to respond to them, as they offer some adaptive advantage to those who are equipped for life with that particular set of narrative tools. Wilson identifies several prominent archetypes that seem so basic to narrative as to suggest the influence of epigenetic rules in human nature. In terms of plot development, narrative moves from "in the beginning," the tribe's creation as "special beings at the center of the world," to emigration to a promised land, meeting evil in a "battle for survival" and triumphing; the hero descends to hell or exile to a wilderness, then returns "in an odyssey against all odds past fearsome obstacles along the way," perhaps discovering "a source of great power"; the world ends "in apocalypse" and is "restored by a band of heroic survivors." Recurrent character types are the nurturing woman, the seer, the virgin, the trickster who "disturbs established order and liberates passion," and the monster who "threatens humanity."[11]

Sounds a lot like *The Odyssey,* and not just in the part where Wilson speaks of "an odyssey against all odds." But Wilson is not the first to consider *The Odyssey* as central to the human storytelling tradition. How might the values celebrated in Homer's epic improve the survival chances of the members of a culture or species who have come to know this story? In the person of Odysseus, the man "of many devices," the story tells us, among other things, to rely on brains more than brawn, to treat strangers with generous hospitality, and to honor the pair bond of marriage. In the incident of Scylla and Charybdis, where Odysseus steers his ship away from the whirlpool that threatens to destroy the whole ship and chooses instead to take it close to the monster that he knows will take six (but only six) of his men, we learn that sometimes individual sacrifices must be made for the good of the community, and that a true leader will unflinchingly make those costly and difficult decisions.

The Odyssey also suggests that it is good to have a home to yearn for and return to, but that at the same time we should resist succumbing to a life of ease, for it is also good to venture out away from home. If the ending of The Odyssey implies a reinstatement of harmony upon Odysseus's return home, Tennyson's poetic coda to The Odyssey, his blank verse poem "Ulysses," asks us to consider how long that harmonious note is likely to last. In Tennyson's version, the aging Ulysses (the Roman name for Odysseus), years after his return to Ithaca, yearns for new adventure. His kingdom is back in order (though he calls his people a "savage race"), things with Penelope are presumably peachy (though he calls her an "aged wife"), and he's as miserable as Homer depicts him after his seven years with Calypso. But now it's not homesickness that pains him. He feels the urge to wander again: "'Tis not too late to seek a newer world," he says. The famous last line of the poem expresses the appeal of a determined exercise of will required by a hard journey: "To strive, to seek, to find, and not to yield."[12]

So The Odyssey tells us that both home and the road have their place in our hearts and lives, which makes perfect sense in terms of behavior that may have provided advantages to our tribal ancestors. A home place offered love and community and the benefits of mutual cooperation, and to know a home place well offered the advantage of learning where the best hunting could be found, where the edible plants are, and when they are ready to be picked. Being able to identify local rocks and plants made possible a learning curve where everything could be put to use. But nomadism offered advantages, too, when the herds had moved on and the supply of local plants had been exhausted. The appeal of both home and the road is bred in our bones.

The catch in trying to read literature as a rhetoric of evolutionary adaptive strategies is that we can't really tell whether any particular theme or character type or stylistic choice is a product of genetic encoding or a response to culture. It's a new twist on the old nature/nurture argument. Wilson points out that genetics and culture can and do influence one another, in a process he calls "gene-culture coevolution." But how do we know when that process is taking place in any particular piece of literature?

Critics of sociobiology and evolutionary psychology argue that their adherents try to read all human behavior and attributes as somehow adaptive, and that they underestimate the influence of culture on human behavior.[13] I would not want to reduce literary criticism to a branch of sociobiology and claim that it is the one true critical methodology, but it does seem to me that literary critics have said a great deal, especially in the last thirty years, about literature as a product of culture and almost nothing about any possible genetic basis or adaptive value for literature. Surely both culture and human nature have their say in the stories we tell. My theory is that the work we recognize as great literature—the stuff that tells us something we know in our bones and feel in our hearts—often arises from the genes in response to the circumstances of our culture. That is, great literature addresses the culture in a corrective way, reminding us of appropriate adaptive strategies (this kind of heroism, that brand of virtue) for coping with conditions arising in our culture. And if our sense of what constitutes "greatness" changes with time, as it most certainly does, it does so in response to new cultural conditions. But keep in mind that shifts in human culture arise from the range of possibilities prescribed by human nature and human behavior, which arise from our genetic heritage. Or as Wilson puts it, our "genes hold culture on a leash."[14]

Part of what I'm interpreting as a genetic response to cultural circumstances is the pendulum swing between classic and romantic sensibilities. As one rises into prominence, there's a reaction calling us back the other way. For at our core we are creatures of both heart and mind, reason and emotion, senses and intellect, perceiving both order and disorder, randomness and chaos as well as plan and design. We are complicated creatures with the capacity, on the one hand, for single-minded willfulness and determination and a propensity for the exercise of brute power, and, on the other hand, for compassion, caring, and gentleness—for our own kind and for other living things. Both sets of values, or rather a wide range of differing values, traits, and ways of being provide advantages in coping with a variety of circumstances—circumstances that may be culturally constructed. How do we know if a work is simply mouthing the pieties of its culture or arising from our genetic core? Perhaps it is a matter of knowing how well a particular adaptation happens to work. Does the organism succeed? Perhaps we judge success through the old "test of time" method. If a work continues to speak to us, to show us how to be in the world, then we will continue to read it. So literature, too, may go through a process of "natural selection."[15]

The Odyssey, presumed to have been composed just after *The Iliad* in the mid-ninth century B.C. (and written down three centuries later), has certainly passed the test of time. Clearly, something in the flow of that narrative still matters to us a great deal.

Now that Julie and I have been out a couple of days, we have a better sense of what the streams are like, and we realize that we're not going to be able to get any further. A mile and a half down the trail is Cascade Creek, and there's no way we'll be able to cross that with the high waters we've been seeing. We could hike down to the creek just to see, but we decide that we ought to make our way back over the pass in the morning, before the snow softens in the sun. Just below the top, we try a big snowfield that would cut off some of our zigging and zagging, but within the first few steps we fall in hip deep. My walking stick slips far into the snow, up to my knuckles. So we retrace our intricate route from the day before, crossing snowfields and ascending slopes to link rock outcrops and humps of tundra, then down a final talus slope. At the edge of a steep snowfield, I slip on dirt-covered ice and slide several feet before grabbing a fist-sized point of rock jutting out of the ice. My knee and shin are cut and bleeding, my elbow and hand banged up, my breath momentarily punched out of me by panic, but I'm fine. I remember what I've read about ascents of Everest—that more fatalities occur on the way back than on the ascent. Not that I was risking death—at most a broken bone or two, or more likely just scrapes and bruises—but our path through the snowfields seems like a tamer version of Everest's Khumbu icefall—not the high point of Everest but often the trickiest part, a maze winding over and around crevasses and under shifting seracs.

We make our way across the rest of the snowfields below the pass and reach a trail junction below Jura Knob by late morning. While Julie rests and bandages blisters, I make my way up the snow-free slopes of Jura. It's just a little higher than Rolling Mountain Pass, still not quite a thirteener. At first I intend to go up just to a saddle—there are some dark clouds moving in and we want to get below tree line before any early afternoon storms hit. But up at the saddle, I look to the southwest and see that the nasty-looking cloud overhead is the last one for a while. I push hard, feeling good, scramble up, and yell to Julie from the top, waving my walking stick, assuming she can see and hear me, though I can't really see her, just the blue of her pack amid the bushes. I revel in the sight lines for a few minutes, my eye on the grassy approach to the next mountain to the northwest, an unnamed peak also between twelve and thirteen thousand feet. Everything's relative, I think. Put that mountain in the middle of Pennsylvania and it would be the number one tourist attraction in the state—and it would certainly earn the honor of some sort of appellation.

The return trip off Jura takes no time at all—the downslope makes the walk effortless, simply a matter of setting each foot down where gravity leads it. I am water flowing.

We walk just a couple more hours, down past the tarns and below tree line, setting up camp under ponderosa pines. After dinner, Julie teaches me some whistle tunes—"Road to Lisdoonvarna," "Fanny Power," "Merrily Kiss the Quaker." Then it's story time. I read aloud Odysseus's encounter with the Sirens and tell Julie my ideas about literature offering adaptive advantages to us as a species. She points out that for oral cultures stories are a means of packaging information in a memorable way. Earlier we had traded stories of bears getting into hikers' tents and food bags—a reminder to ourselves to hang our food. She also mentions the close associations of oral tales with landscape, whereby a certain mountain or tree or bend in a stream serves as a mnemonic device to trigger a story about that place, a story that tells us something about how to be in the world. The land literally serves as sacred text.

I mention my thoughts on Rolling Mountain Pass, how the land required interpretation, and Julie points out the prominent place of riddles in oral tales. Typically when the hero needs essential information, it is presented in riddle form—which also calls for interpretation. In essence, any literary work is a kind of riddle. Students sometimes go overboard in their ingenuity to find the "hidden meaning" of a poem or story, but their search gets to the heart of the experience of literature. We seek to interpret, to make sense of a story. According to the aptly named critic Robert Storey, all narrative is "both concrete and emblematic." That is, it is *about* something specific, and at the same time it *represents* something, thereby inviting interpretation and explanation. Paradoxically, notes Storey, narrative also "resists explanation"—because it is inherently ambiguous.[16] Storey sees the ambiguity as a means for narrative to legitimize opposing interests. Just as a savvy politician, all too often, speaks so as to avoid being pinned down to a definitive position, so too does narrative. That is how a story survives, perhaps, serving different purposes from generation to generation, or serving the purposes of different readers within a generation.

The key ambiguity of *The Odyssey* is that mixed message about the value of adventure versus home. Storey might say that the ambiguity serves the interests of both those who encourage staying put and those who celebrate wanderlust. I made the case earlier that both arguments could be seen as reinforcement for behaviors that offer an adaptive advantage—different behaviors for different circumstances. And it is true, too, that—as neurobiologist William Calvin suggests—stories help prepare us for life's contingencies through the exercise of "scenario-spinning"—laying out the possibilities of existence for us and thereby preparing us for them.[17] This is essentially A. E. Housman's defense of poetry in "Terence, this is stupid stuff"—a defense he relates by way of a story about a king who dosed himself with a little poison every day in order to inoculate himself against assassination attempts. "I tell the tale that I heard told," says Housman's narrator, "Mithridates, he died old."[18]

But surely, too, we delight in the ambiguity of stories and their meaning simply because we like to make sense of things. We take pleasure in interpretation because it is one of the skills we have had to develop as a species, whether for tracking prey or finding our way. We make use of the same talent in other situations fraught with ambiguity as well, as in charting our course through, as Thoreau puts it, "the terrible rapid and whirlpool called a dinner."[19] We are the creature with the "meaning-making mind," says Storey.[20] And literature gives us a place to exercise our highest faculties—faculties of meaning-making that were honed because they were useful to us, because our very lives depended on them.

The next day we walk just five miles and camp near the saddle between Lime Creek and Bear Creek drainages, right below tree line and not far from West Turkshead Peak. Our plan had been to climb Turkshead in the afternoon, but by midday thunderheads have started to move in. At noon Julie takes stock of our overhead and predicts that lightning will arrive in an hour and a half. She's accurate within five minutes. First we hear far rumbling even while we're still in sunshine. Then clouds like horses' heads race in, edging out the sun. The rain starts slowly. Then lightning leaps over the ridge of the Twin Sisters. I'm counting Mississippis to measure how far away it is—one, two, boom—less than half a mile. Then the hail starts. It thumps hard and loud on the thin nylon of the tent.

I'm glad I'm here with someone who knows these weather patterns, and I'm glad we didn't try to go up Twin Sisters today, one of the options we had considered. The lightning moves even closer—no Mississippis at all away—and inside the tent we squat on our boot soles, the only insulation we can muster. Thirty feet from our tent a pine stands lightning-seared and split. Contrary to idiom, we know, lightning does like to strike twice in the same place.

The hail is BB-sized, lying in patches like snow. Later in the afternoon there's a bigger hailstorm, with pea-sized pellets. Between hailstorms there is rain, with thunder rolling through the mountains, each echo engaging in heated discussion with the next approaching rumble.

When we're not squatting in our boots, Julie and I talk, write, read, and tell stories. I ask Julie for a story about danger. She tells me a Russian story, where the hero, Ivan, needed to warn his people about approaching Mongol hordes. Told to get a magic horse from Baba Yaga, the witch, Ivan wandered in the woods for three days looking for her house—which had legs so it could move around. (Sort of a folkloric predecessor to a Winnebago—the wheeled kind, that is.) Famished, Ivan climbed a tree and found some eagle eggs. But the mother eagle asked him to please put the eggs back, reminding him that those were her babies. Despite his hunger, he said OK.

Later that day, Ivan found Baba Yaga's house. She said if he could watch her horses for three days and get them back in the corral by sundown, she would give him one of the horses. If he failed, then she would eat him.

Each day the horses ran off into the forest but came dashing back right at sundown. Baba Yaga kept her word and gave one to Ivan. But she asked the horses, why didn't you run off like I told you to?

They said a pack of eagles had chased them back.

I ask Julie, so what's the riddle at the heart of that one? She says that heroes at risk in oral tales typically survive by cleverness (like Odysseus) and that frequently the cleverness takes the form of altering one's thinking, of learning to see things in a new way, often from the perspective of other living things. It is a process of honoring or respecting or connecting with nature. In her Baba Yaga story, of course, Ivan had to adopt a new way of seeing eagle eggs, as something other than breakfast for a hungry hero. Often, says Julie, the protagonist must enter a cave or climb a mountain in order to receive a certain kind of knowledge, and that knowledge usually involves a fresh perspective.

She offers another example, the story—a true story, and a recent one—behind an instrumental song of hers called "The Lion Didn't Eat Us."[21] To protect the children involved, who helped her write the song, Julie wouldn't tell me where this happened. To the same end, I won't hazard guesses, except to say that I don't think it happened in the United States. Apparently in some places drug dealers keep dangerous and exotic animals for protection—cobras in a suitcase, for example. Then, when the police come knocking on the door, the dealers open up the suitcase and duck out the back. The police enter, and they have a more immediate problem staring them lidless in the face than the pursuit of drug dealers. Well, one couple kept an African lion in a cage in a spare bedroom. The knock came at the door, they told their two kids to stay in their room, then they let the lion out and slipped out the back. Except that it wasn't the police at the door, just an insurance salesman or something, who left when there was no response. So there was no one to let the kids out—or the lion. The kids stayed in their room for three days, listening to the lion pad back and forth out in the hallway, until hunger and thirst forced them to take action. Of course, there was also a very hungry lion outside their door. Let's pretend to be invisible, they said, so the lion can't see us. They walked down the hallway and across the living room, as calmly as they could, not looking at the lion. And the lion didn't eat them. Probably, says Julie, because they didn't act like prey. Their room was their cave, their underworld, and the knowledge they emerged with was something about appropriately managing fear of the wild, about avoiding becoming prey by not acting like prey.

I think of Moses on Mount Sinai, coming back from the mountain with new knowledge written in stone. And I wonder if any of this mythic motif about the acquisition of new knowledge applies to Odysseus. Certainly—there's his visit to the underworld, where Circe has told him to seek the prophet Teiresias for instructions on the route home. Teiresias warns Odysseus not to eat the golden cattle on the island of the sun god Helios. Of course his men do, and they all die, only Odysseus, who abstained, surviving. I doubt if Homer is recommending that the Greeks turn vegan, but he is saying something about restraint in claiming for our own every morsel of beefsteak or eagle egg we come across. As Robert Pack says of Odysseus's sailors, "Their disregard for nature, their violation of nature's sanctity, brings about their ruin."[22] Most of Odysseus's encounters involve solving a riddle and emerging with some new knowledge. In his approach to the rocks of the Sirens, for instance, he must figure out how to hear their glorious song while escaping with his life—and the song is especially alluring because the Sirens sing of knowledge. And there's his imprisonment in the cave of Polyphemous, where he solves the riddle of how to escape from the giant. But is the knowledge he receives the result of any sort of closeness with or connection to nature? For the most part, nature seems pure antagonist in *The Odyssey*. The seas, at the command of Poseidon, actively thwart Odysseus in his quest to return home, and the difficulties of the voyage are personified as various sorts of foes—from monsters like Polyphemous and Scylla to temptresses like Calypso and Circe, even the Sirens. Doesn't Odysseus need to *defeat* natural forces, to actively *avoid* becoming one with them?

At four A.M., the wind's hiss through the pines takes on a nasty edge, enough to rattle the tent walls. A stab of fear passes through the tent fabric, where neither hard rain nor hail had managed to pass through and find me. For the first time on this trip I feel as though things are out of my control, or at least my fate is. Even when the lightning had come close, I could take some sort of action to cope—the squatting on heels. But what kind of action can we take against a big wind and a falling pine?

I can understand the Greeks' praying to Aeolus. If I'd known the name of the god of the ponderosa pine, I would have started praying to him as well (or her, as the divine case may be). Or the god of this mountain. Mixed with the fear is the recognition of something larger than the self—and sudden humility. This wind, this situation, is more than I can handle, and if I make it through, it is not really my doing. This is a humility we don't often feel in civilization, where we tell ourselves that we can control everything. And we believe it. We don't feel much humility, either as individuals or as a species. We don't feel ourselves much at the mercy of any of the gods associated with natural forces.

In a monotheistic belief system, of course, the process has been simplified, the power and authority over the elements centralized in one omnipotent God. Arrogance can ensue when you become convinced that you are one of those privy to the Truth enjoying the favor of that one God, confident in His blessing. There is a danger of losing the humility you might feel before many gods, knowing you cannot be the favorite of all of them. Odysseus may be beloved of Athena, even Zeus is pretty much on his side, but Poseidon (father of Polyphemous) has it in for him, and so Odysseus spends those ten years battling storms and contrary winds on Poseidon's aqueous turf.

So what is the nature of the secret knowledge that Odysseus returns home with? Maybe this is the key lesson of *The Odyssey,* the idea that most provides an adaptive advantage: To respect the gods, who are of course associated with natural forces—Zeus of the thunder and lightning, Poseidon of the Sea, and so on. And to make our way through the natural world with respect and humility as well as determination.

On the morning of the Fourth of July we linger in camp, waiting for some dry to get to the tent. When the clouds look like they might be breaking up, I set off for Turkshead. The way up leads through tangles of willow, up a sloping meadow, behind a big triangular rock slab. On a ledge under another boulder, behind an ornately eroded column called a "hoodoo," I pause to regard the clouds. They are low and darkish, but I'm not sure if they are thunder bearing. I decide to check again at the top of the next scree slope. The rock is very loose, the slope steep enough to make me nervous about looking down. At the top, pitched more on the vertical than the horizontal, I inch over to the beginning of the steeply inclined grassy meadow that leads to the summit ridge. Looking out I see thick, irregular-shaped clouds rolling in, and I imagine I see anvils taking shape. The summit is socked in, and the arriving clouds look uncertain.

I turn back, skidding down the scree slope. Thunder and lightning never do arrive, and I am left to wonder if it was just my touch of acrophobia that turned me back. That's the sort of thing a hero ought to overcome. Or was it warranted and prudent caution? There is the fine line we walk—balancing the courage to overcome our fears with the wisdom to recognize that which is beyond our control. Looking up at the mountain, I see I could have made it to the summit ridge in another half hour, up a slope not as steep as the one I had come up.

We get to Little Molas Lake by noon, the lake now surrounded by holiday campers. I swim in the lake, which is very cold, and thereby earn the respect and good-natured applause of picnickers and fishermen on shore. We take another walk to the north in the afternoon, headed for Big Molas Lake, but the customary afternoon storms turn us back before we get there.

The next morning is sunny, gorgeous. Why couldn't we have had this weather yesterday, I wonder. And I answer: Because the gods did not arrange it so. I'm catching the spirit of Homer now, thinking of how, in the past week, the gods of snow and hail, rain, thunder and lightning, and clouds—the scary anvil-shaped ones with dark undersides—have dictated delays and forced us to alter our plans. Of course I've had only a week of it, not a decade. But from an envelope tucked in my journal I lift out pictures of my kids and long for home.

Odysseus, of course, has not undertaken his journey for the sake of the journey. He wants to get it over with ASAP and get home. But the yearning for home is part of every trip. There it is, waiting for us at the end. While we're away we write letters home, we record our observations in journals or on film so we can report once we get back.

To venture out and return—that is the shape of the journey. According to Joseph Campbell it is also the plot line of myth and the path of the hero—one who goes on a journey, meets and overcomes obstacles, and returns home with a boon or gift. *The Odyssey* is the oldest story we know of in that tradition, but the story recurs in all cultures, appearing in ours in the spate of contemporary wilderness adventure stories, recent books about dangerous encounters with nature like Jon Krakauer's *Into the Wild* and *Into Thin Air,* or the polar variants like Andrea Barrett's *Voyage of the Narwhal,* or the whole cottage industry of books about Ernest Shackleton's 1914 expedition to the South Pole.[23] There's no telling if these works will pass the test of time, but if there is validity to bioaesthetics as a mode of literary criticism, it should allow us to look at any work of literature, without waiting a couple of millennia or so, to consider how it might serve as a guide to evolutionary success or an encapsulation of useful knowledge for the species.

In all these recent wilderness odysseys, an interesting tension surfaces. On the one hand, they seem to tell us that the wild is scary and we should stay the hell away, stay home and sit back and take our doses of danger only from the comfortable confines of an armchair. It is not a pastoral or romantic world out there. It is not Mother Nature out there. It is not even nature as femme fatale—there is little personification at all. In a word, the wild is alien, or at least not human, territory. On the other hand, the wild in these stories also entices and allures. Which is to say that these are ambiguous narratives calling for interpretation, asking us to consider the paradoxical nature of the natural world. They suggest that the appropriate attitude to maintain in relation to it is appreciative respect. We must be careful and attentive, both to the world outside us and to our physical well-being, and we must not take anything for granted when we are out there. Krakauer raises the possibility, in both *Into the Wild* and *Into Thin Air*, as does Sebastian Junger in *The Perfect Storm*, that even when we are attentive, and careful, and capable, and fit, we may still run into trouble.[24] And die. It's not that the world is out to punish us if we make a mistake—it's not willful punishment. It's not even that we bring punishment upon ourselves. On a big mountain, or out in the wild, you cannot possibly predict all that could go wrong.

But if the world out there is powerful and potentially deadly, its extreme conditions seem to bring out the best of humanity—our questing spirit, our courage and strength, our ability to take deep, gut satisfaction in the simple glorious fact of life and to give expression to that satisfaction. It is impossible to read accounts of the Shackleton expedition like Caroline Alexander's *Endurance* and not be astonished at the skill and determination of Shackleton and his crew. They endure a winter trapped in ice off the coast of Antarctica, watch their ship get crushed in that ice, drift on ice floes for hundreds of miles, then, armed with only a handheld sextant, make an incredible crossing of more hundreds of miles across open sea in a rowboat, through a hurricane—and they hit the exact island they're aiming for. Then they must cross uncharted territory across a ten-thousand-foot range of mountains, return for their mates left on another island—and they never lose a man.[25]

Why these stories now, at this particular cultural moment? They serve, I think, as a reminder that there is a world beyond our nicely self-contained civilization, one that deserves respect and cannot be taken for granted. It is a world that calls forth the best of us, our highest capacities, physical, intellectual, and spiritual. These lessons, of course, echo the themes of *The Odyssey.* It's the same old story—but it's a great story, one that we need to keep telling ourselves. Maybe because it increases our chance of survival.

I consider that very useful knowledge.

Next morning we drive into Silverton and hunt for trinkets for my kids—a wooden frog percussion instrument and a dinosaur T-shirt. Not much of a boon for a hero to return home with, but at least these souvenirs may serve as instigators of a story or two. That's usually the most meaningful gift we return with anyway.

After our trip to the gift shops of Silverton, Julie and I head down to Kennebec Pass, accessible via a pitted dirt road, set up camp, then hike the last few miles through Cumberland Basin, past an old mine site up to a notch cut out of the rock at the pass. We can see where the Colorado Trail comes in from the north, along Indian Ridge and past Taylor Lake. Further in the distance, we can see where we've been the past week—the Needles, Twin Sisters, Jura Knob, Engineer. Back at camp, we wash in the stream and play more whistle tunes. In the night more thunder and a light rain arrive, and we hear coyotes howl.

We still have a day to kill before my flight home, so we pack up the car again and head for Mesa Verde National Park to see the Anasazi cliff dwellings. These are extensive stone apartments, plazas, and circular underground kivas perched in alcoves of the cliffs, built with sophisticated mortar work and impressive architectural design—impressive enough to last eight centuries. The dwelling now called Balcony House is perched particularly high in the cliffs, with a low protective wall at the edge of the cliff and a tunnel where the Anasazis entered the assemblage of apartments. The way down from the Mesa involved a steep and exposed climb, with shallow toeholds worn in the rock. Clearly the Anasazis managed to overcome their fear of heights.

Part of what is so impressive here is a sense of accommodation to the land, the Anasazis' acceptance of the land, with all the dangers of life on the cliffs. They did not shy away from those dangers—they went right to the edge, where life tastes sweetest and we can see farthest. But it is not likely that they were driven here by some sense of danger. I had always heard that the Anasazis, ancestors of the Pueblos, set up house high in the cliffs for defensive purposes. But the heat of the day convinces me otherwise. It is scorching and dry up on the mesa, where the "Ancient Ones" grew their crops. Down in the shade of the cliffs, though, it is cool. And that's where the water is. The notches in the cliffs are formed by water seeping through the upper layer of porous sandstone till it hits a layer of hard shale. There the water flows out to the canyon wall, washing out loose sandstone. In the winter, moisture works its way into cracks and crevices in the sandstone and wedges out chunks once it freezes. Thus the seeps eat into the sandstone, leaving an indentation like a gaping mouth in the profile of the cliff face. Often the seeping water collects in small pools at the back of the caves. Forget defense—the Anasazis set up camp in the cliffs for the shade and the water.

The "mystery" of why the Anasazis disappeared from here seems obvious as well. They lived here and built these dwellings for about seventy-five years, beginning around 1200. Not coincidentally, a twenty-four-year drought began in 1276, and the Anasazis were gone by the turn of the century. Do the math. They had probably created a wood shortage by that time as well.

So they left when their physiological needs were no longer being satisfied in this place. But a bit of a puzzle remains. When the Anasazis departed, they left behind valuable pots and food on the shelves of their dwellings. Perhaps they headed down to the rivers in the first years of the drought, then returned in the winters until they adjusted to life off the mesa year-round. Maybe they left pots and food because they figured they'd be back. But the lack of return haunts us. It violates our expectations of how a story ought to go. The shape of the narrative is disrupted. They embarked on a journey and never returned home.

After our tour of the cave dwellings, I hike out to Pictograph Point. The trail winds through cactus and yucca and beige sandstone sculpted by wind and water; shafts of trail a foot or so wide slice between cliff and columns and leaning boulders. About a mile down the trail I round a corner of a canyon and see a deep cleft in the rock. Now if I were an Anasazi, I think, that would seem a likely spot for a dwelling. The trail passes under the overhang, then rises to the level of the alcove floor, and sure enough, along the ledge are some ruins, maybe four or five rooms, just about a foot or so of the walls left standing. The alcove is nearly ten feet high in front, four in back, the ceiling smudged black from old smoke. Sitting on a few feet of ledge in front of the foremost walls, I look around at the rock and out at the canyon. It is delicious in the shade under the lip of the cliff above, a cool relief from the heat of the trail. I gulp water, look, look, hear feet scuffing on rock and voices approaching. Rounding a cliff corner are a couple from Florida whom I had passed earlier on the trail. I call out a greeting so they won't be startled, invite them up to share what I'm now thinking of as my space.

I spend a satisfying hour inhabiting this well-settled space. I won't claim to have come to understand the Anasazis, but I know why they'd chosen this spot. A body can be comfortable here, as well as safe.

A few minutes further down the trail I come to the drawings. Pictograph Point is actually misnamed, being full of petroglyphs—designs etched into the rock rather than painted on. Much of the drawing is easily recognizable. Several imprints of hands—artists' signatures? A man and child, holding hands. A stylized elongated human figure, Giacometti-like, knees bent as if he is squatting to hold up a great weight, elbows bent and arms raised as if the great weight is the sky. There are actually quite a few of these figures, some apparently with tails. Humans or gods, I'm not sure. A six-legged creature, more monster than insect. A snake. A bighorn sheep and several birds and assorted other creatures. That doglike figure—is that a wolf or coyote? Of course, the rock etchings do not reveal any facial details, so there are no expressions to read. I'm not sure if the animals pose a threat, as predators, or if the pictures are a kind of account ledger or history, recording memorable kills. The pictures could be invocations to animal spirits—to insure success in the hunt of those animals, or to incorporate some of the energy of the creatures. In general, the poses of the animals do not seem threatening. No teeth or claws show, and they do not seem to be attacking or devouring. If these creatures have brought danger, the artists have not held it against them, no more than we blame the sky for thunderstorms.

The prominence of animals in these pictures contrasts with my own small wanderings in the past week, where encounters with creatures have been few and undramatic. Most people, of course, equate wild creatures with danger in the natural world—as if hikers spend most of their day evading charging bears and striking snakes. The truth is, hikers are more concerned, most of the time, with the weather and the terrain and the condition of our soles—the ones on the bottom of our feet, not in the region of the gut—and encounters with animals, especially dangerous ones, are not that common. In all my years of hiking, I have seen exactly six poisonous snakes, only one of which took any notice of my presence. Perhaps our species has reduced the numbers of animals that pose any threat to us—most dramatically the populations of wolf and bear and mountain lion—but I imagine that encounters with animals loom large in our mythologies not because those encounters ever made up a significant portion of our daily activity, but because every such encounter is memorable. The sensation is part fear, for we see how those creatures are equipped for survival in this world, in a way that makes us on occasion mutual antagonists—but it is also part kinship awareness, for we see how we and, say, the snake are adapted to the same world, often in ways that instruct us.[26]

I am reminded again how fluid are the dividing lines between fear and respect and appreciation. We fear the snake for good reason—and that fear gets genetically imprinted as instinctive response, or even phobia. Those who react with instant fear upon sight of a snake have a better chance of surviving and passing on their genes. But that hyperawareness is also a kind of fascination, so the snake winds its way into our stories. As Wilson points out, that's how genetics leads to culture and culture reinforces genetics: "Close attention to [snakes], enhanced by dream serpents and the symbols of culture, undoubtedly reinforces the chances of survival."[27] We may even come to appreciate the snake for its beauty, or learn from it something about how to be, something about patience and the quick strike and the shedding of old portions of ourselves. The fact that these fascinations can persist in our psyches is testimony to the power of evolution. Fear of lightning, heights, snakes—these are holdovers from our ancestral past when they were more common and legitimate threats than they are today. If our fears were guided only by logic or if evolution moved more quickly, notes Wilson, we would have an imprinted fear of things like guns and automobiles. We are creatures adapted to a different way of life than most of us currently experience, and so it feels good—and it feels right—to return to the landscapes of our origin, where our senses and our instincts and our highest faculties become activated. Or as Wilson puts it, "The human body and mind are precisely adapted to this world, notwithstanding its trials and dangers, and that is why we think it is beautiful. In this respect *Homo sapiens* conforms to a basic principle of organic evolution that all species prefer and gravitate to the environment in which their genes were assembled."[28]

Wilson echoes a common theme in ecopsychology, that humans evolved to live in wilderness, and so the very fiber of our being responds to it. It is not too much to say that in wilderness we are most fully human. Paul Shepard points out in *Coming Home to the Pleistocene* that we belong in the "wild landscapes to which our DNA remains tuned." We evolved as human creatures over the course of three million years, says Shepard, and our experiences during those three million years created our genome. The agricultural revolution, beginning a mere ten thousand years ago, has changed the way we live, but that has not changed our genetic heritage.[29]

So by venturing out into the unfamiliar, we find ourselves returning home.

The rest of the petroglyphs consist of a series of swirls and whirls chipped out of the stone. In one section, a line connects several pictures, suggesting a sequence of events, so that the picture becomes a combination map and time line.

I look at the narrative line here long and long. I'm not able to solve all the riddles of these drawings, but I recognize elements of the story. Reading right to left and up to down, from east to west as I regard the rock, the path could be one of descent from the mountains, into the valleys, then over the mesa into the cliff dwellings—essentially the path Julie and I have followed in the last few days. Up high, there are eagles and a bighorn sheep, lower down other birds, maybe ravens. A doglike figure, wolf or coyote, stands off the western slope of the mesa. These could be reminders of specific hunts or just a general picture of the life-forms encountered in different terrain. There are rises and falls on what I'm thinking of as the time line or the plotline—these could be topographical indicators, a record of terrain experienced. At the lower left the line makes a sharp turn and rises up to a table land, doubles back parallel to and above the lower line, then spirals into an overhang. Inside what looks like a cave are two figures, one recognizably human with one arm raised, the other with arms meeting overhead to form a circle, like a halo. A sort of stump descends between the legs, not particularly phallic looking, making the whole figure seem part tree, part man.

I'm seeing all this as more picture than map, depicting cave walls and mountain slopes rather than cross-country routes. There are no directional arrows, of course, and there is a spiraling in (or out) at either end, so the story could be read in reverse, as a movement from the cliffs and across the mesa up to the mountains. But either way, I see an account of a journey.

As it turns out, my reading is not far off from what some Anasazi descendants see in the drawings. According to a National Park Service trail guide, some twentieth-century Hopis interpreted the sequence as a history of the Pueblo people, beginning with their emergence from the earth and the separation of several of the clans. A "lizard spirit" led the Horned Toad clan "into a period of wandering without direction," until "whipping kachinas . . . straightened out" the people. Their migration ended at Mesa Verde. An animal spirit (a mountain lion—which I had taken for a coyote or wolf) watches over the path of these wanderings.[30] It is a story encapsulating many of the basic archetypes of narrative.

This high desert landscape is far removed, geographically and culturally, from Homer's Mediterranean Sea. And yet here, too, we find traces of an odyssey. There is a journey, linking encounters with places and other living things. There are monsters and helper spirits, and there are hardships encountered along the way, all of them celebrated because they brought us to where we are. Those spirals of swirling lines at either end of the path, either widening gyre or zeroing in—what are they? The voyage outbound, direction at first uncertain? Or the return home? I see a coiled snake, the suck of Charybdis, and the double helix of our DNA.

3

LANDSCAPES OF LOVE AND BELONGING

The Montérégie, Adirondacks, and Catskills

... this unsatisfied hunger for contact, for intimacy, for belongingness,
... the need to overcome the widespread feelings of alienation, aloneness, strangeness, and loneliness ...

ABRAHAM MASLOW, *Motivation and Personality*

We cross the border, welcomed with "*Bonjour*-Hello," the undeclared
purpose of our visit to see if it's true that you can't go home again. And
at first it seems Thomas Wolfe was on to something. We stop at an information booth, a two-centuries-old British blockhouse, and the
woman and I plead mutual ignorance of each other's language ("Only
a bit"—"*Seulement un petit peu*"). "Mont St. Hilaire?" I ask. "*Ah, oui, le
Montérégie*," and she pulls out a map.

It turns out her English is much better than my French, but she seems
to appreciate my limited efforts, and I get directions and information
about campgrounds. I grew up here in Québec, a couple of miles from
Mont St. Hilaire, but I don't remember exactly how to get there, and I'm
acutely aware of the language barrier, which reminds me that my childhood was long ago and far away—literally in a foreign country.

My son Jacy, nine years old, is with me, and we head up the south
shore of the Richelieu River. Road signs begin to refresh my memory of
the French I'd learned long ago. In truth, when I was a boy, it was quite
possible to be almost exclusively English speaking in Québec. But things
have changed, and properly so, given the discriminations of the past.
French is the dominant language now, and towns are less segregated

along language lines. My smattering of French starts to come back to me, but I am a long way from bilingual, and I feel embarrassed by my ignorance. The best excuse I can offer is to proclaim my American citizenship. Which is to reinforce my estrangement from this, my native land.

Alienation. Aloneness. Strangeness. Loneliness. Sounds like a diagnosis of our cultural ills. Or so the literature of the past century has had it. These are the recurring literary themes of our times. We are alienated from each other, our society, our culture, our past, and our land, and clearly we are unsatisfied, even as we pile up stuff intended to satiate our needs. And clearly we are hungry for contact, intimacy, and belonging—with each other, our society, our culture, our past, our land. Yet we know what to prescribe ourselves. To quote sappy greeting cards and pop songs ad nauseam, love is the answer. But love comes in such a variety of forms, from eros to agape, and it can seem so elusive much of the time. Where do we find love? The want ads? The workplace? The Internet? Fern bars?

More song lyrics come to me—"Looking for love in all the wrong places." I want to consider the forms of love we are most familiar with—familial love, romantic love, and love of country—and consider how nature figures in our appreciation of each of these. My strategy is to revisit the geographies of past love, mountain landscapes suffused with some of the varieties of love, places where its seeds were planted in me, or where it blossomed, where maybe it still grows.

I must have been younger than Jacy when I first climbed Mont St. Hilaire, on a family trip. Our house was a couple of miles away, angled so as to have a direct view of the mountain. A sleeping giant we said it looked like, with the summit knob, the Pain de Sucre (Sugar Loaf), the giant's protruding belly button. Up on top, we'd look for our house, easy to find because it was on that slant right next to a triangular park. My father's recurrent joke on top was to say, "Look at that guy down there— the one with the dried egg on his shirt." Of course the distance was really too great to make out a human figure.

A few years later my brother dated the daughter of the caretaker on the mountain, and he dislocated his shoulder riding a horse on the mountain's lower slopes. (Well, actually, it wasn't the riding that dislocated the shoulder, but the falling off. Or not the falling off but the landing.) After the family trips became less frequent, my friend Beezers and I would walk up to the quarry on the western side of the mountain, catching frogs, newts, and garter snakes, then hauling them home to keep in pails and cardboard boxes. The snakes usually escaped, of course, to be discovered by my mother in her garden, encounters which she handled with good grace. When we had caught our fill, Beezers and I would climb up the steep slope from the quarry to the Pain de Sucre, and sometimes head down to Lac Hertel on the southeastern slope.

On Mont St. Hilaire the seeds of my fascination with mountains were sown. Driving up now along the Richelieu, I expect to be disappointed when I see it again, from the Thomas Wolfe effect, where the reality turns out to be infinitely less remarkable than memory has it. But no—if anything, after all my years and all the mountains I have climbed, Mont St. Hilaire looks even more impressively vertical than I had remembered. It's only about thirteen hundred feet high—heck, I live about that high in the Pennsylvania Ridge and Valley country. But it rises distinctly from the plains like a Shasta or Katahdin. The cliffs on the north side are sheer, and the whole thing is a sprawling massif.

Driving into Otterburn, where I grew up, I see that the town has established a park right next to the river. My old elementary school is still there, though quite a bit the worse for wear. Just a brick block surrounded by cracking asphalt and a cyclone fence. Not much to speak of, but the bricks are mortared solid with memories. We drive up my old street, surprisingly narrow, now pitted, more like a country road than a suburban street. The houses are small but neat, built with lots of stone and brick. We stop at my old house. The maple out front is gone, but large pines line the front and side yards. Two of our four apple trees are still there, but our favorite—the best for climbing in and lounging under—is gone, just the stump of it left, ankle high, now home to fungi as it rots.

The trees in the park and the surrounding yards have grown high enough to block out the view of the mountain. Roaming the park, I point out to Jacy my old friends' houses—Timmy Sim's, Jimmy Sproule's, Ponko Pete's, Beezers'. Driving up through town, more loss—they call it "development," but it's really replacement, isn't it? The little pink store at the top of Prince Edward Avenue is gone, and now there are gas stations and convenience stores and new houses along the highway that I knew as Montée de Trente but is now called Rue Ozias Leduc.

We turn up Rue de la Montagne to the mountain, now the Mont St. Hilaire Nature Conservation Center, run by McGill University. My relief at the mountain's preservation makes me almost grateful for the admission fee. Jacy and I hike up to an information center, and he is delighted to see a signboard talking about peregrine falcons nesting on the mountain. I translate a few lines before I realize that he's way ahead of me, reading the English translation at the bottom of the sign. Apparently the cliffs on the north side of the mountain provide the only peregrine nesting site in the Montérégie, the mountain region of southern Québec. The falcons have been here since the 1960s, back when I still lived here, and when they were nearly wiped out by DDT, which made the shells of their eggs too thin to be viable. Now, though, they are thriving again.

We make our way up an easy trail to the Pain de Sucre. On the way up a woman resting at trailside greets me with "AO." "AO?" I ask, smiling blankly. A few steps later I catch on: "*Est haut*," as in "*Il est haut*," it is high, or, I guess, it's steep. I decide that "AO" will become part of my hiking vocabulary—there's something upbeat about those syllables, an acceptance of ascent, like a cheery version of "high-ho" but requiring less aspirated panting.

We clamber up the rocky knob of the Pain de Sucre. This requires finding hand- and footholds, which is something that has always made me think of this little mountain as a "real" mountain. These last few feet make the climb more than just a walk-up. In my mind, I've always associated the "St. Hilaire" with Edmund Hillary, climber of Everest. *En haut*, it is very windy, clouds thick and gray cantering past, but the view is incredible—the Richelieu dominating, winding through the scene, towns spread around the plain, more mountains of the Montérégie, even Mount Royal and Montreal clear and large. The city is only thirty-five kilometers away, near enough to see individual buildings. Closer to the mountain, I look for my old house, but there's so much green down there now that neither the house nor the triangular park is distinguishable. I look, too, for the guy with the dried egg on his shirt, but he's gone.

When I first planned this trip, I had thought of distributing my father's ashes from this spot. The ashes have been sitting in a box at my mother's house for four years. I brought up the idea one Christmas, but some of the family had other ideas, and some were uncomfortable with the whole discussion and left the room. So Dad's ashes stay in a box, maybe for four more years.

The wind up here is really ripping, and releasing the ashes would have taken mere seconds. Like lint blown out of the belly button of the Giant. And to what end? I guess we bring ashes to places the deceased cared about because we figure whatever particle of the loved one remains attached to the remnants of the corporeal self would be happy to return here, to this place. Maybe, too, we recognize the reciprocity principle of love at work. Here is a chance to give something back to the cherished place. The scattering of ashes constitutes a physical manifestation of the spiritual desire to get back to nature. My sense is that Mont St. Hilaire is a place my father would like to give part of himself back to, his ashes a small contribution to the making of more mountain, something to help preserve what is here before any more erodes away under the boot soles of the next generation of visitors, or maybe to provide a little something to be caught in the crevices of the next hiker's lug sole in order to journey somewhere further. Or to be brought back home.

Etymological tidbit: The word *human* comes from the Latin *humus,* the earth, like the humus we use to enrich our gardens.

Amid the summit rocks, lots of puddles and pools testify to recent rain and the impermeability of granite. The drop-off to the west is sheer and dramatic. Made cautious by the wind and the verticality, Jacy hunches low as he makes his way around the summit, keeping one hand in touch with the rocks.

We decide we do not have time today to make our way to the next projecting point, above the Dieppe cliffs, but agree to come back to-morrow. On the way down, I share my thoughts with Jacy. Here is the place that I cherished above all others as a kid. I had feared that I would come back as an adult and see my childhood ruined by development. But I find instead homes in my old town built to last, and it all still looks darn quaint. And my mountain—not only has it been protected, but its special nature has been granted official recognition, by the United Nations no less, as the Mont St. Hilaire Biosphere Reserve, the first Canadian reserve in an international network of preserved lands. People come from all over the Montreal area—and some from much further—to appreciate this mountain. It is as if the special value of my favorite childhood place has been granted official recognition by the whole world. All our passions should receive such acknowledgment. And wonder of wonders, I have yet to see a piece of trash on the trails.

Jacy and I drive to the park along the Richelieu to cook on our back-packing stove, then find a cheap motel near the mountain. The rooms are actually cabins, and after we have settled in I put the last few minutes of daylight to use, for reading on the porch. To illuminate my thinking about love on this trip, I have brought along *Firekeeper,* a book of poems by the contemporary poet Pattiann Rogers. Her two great themes seem to be love and nature—or maybe it is one great theme, sung with endless improvisations. I settle on "Suppose Your Father Was a Redbird," one of her many poems of "supposition." The baby cardinal, she imagines, must attune itself to glimpses of red, because it would care about the comings and goings of its father. It would be able to discern "a single red bloom / Five miles away across an open field." It would dream in red, and she concludes:

> If your father was a redbird,
> Then you would be obligated to try to understand
> What it is you recognize in the sun
> As you study it again this evening
> Pulling itself and the sky in dark red
> Over the edge of the earth.[1]

The evening sky cooperates in its timing, and amid dwindling and re-treating crimson streaks I am left to wonder just what it is that I might be attuned to, since my father was not a redbird. Mountains? Loss? Deliciously bad puns? And what is it that my son is becoming attuned to?

∿

The next day we hike up to Dieppe, Jacy chattering away about the successful bedtime story last night. Our stories feature "Charlie and his Friends," time-traveling dinosaurs. Jacy's alter ego in the stories is Charlie Compsognathus; Glasses Brontosaurus is a thinly disguised version of me. Last night's story was based on a board game that we play sometimes, called "Survival or Extinction: The Dinosaur Game." Each player selects a card that designates him as a certain dinosaur species, with an assigned habitat and specified strengths and weaknesses. A T-Rex, for example, lives in the forest and has above-average size, weapons, defenses, and speed; average intelligence and senses; and a below-average rate of reproduction and ability to adapt. The object of the game is to gather food tokens and get to the finish line first. Food tokens are won or lost by attacking other dinosaurs, meeting various challenges, encountering natural disasters, or entering your habitat, at which point you announce, for example, "I'm a T-Rex, and I live in the forest, and I want my food token!" If you run out of food tokens, you go extinct and you're out of the game. In our bedtime story, Charlie invented "Survival or Extinction: The Human Game," featuring such lines as "I'm an accountant, and I live in the suburbs, and I want my paycheck!"

On our walk, Jacy and I fill in the details of the "The Human Game," imagining "Unnatural Disasters," like "Economic Downturn: Are you sufficiently diversified in the market?" Instead of speed, size, and weapons, the attribute categories include insurance coverage, salary, investments, level of education, make of car. We giggle our way up the mountain, struck by the absurdity of human lives in our time, fearful of economic recessions and interest-rate hikes rather than volcanic eruptions and climate changes. Funny—we think of business, politics, and law as the "real world." Acquaintances chide me for working in academia, far removed from the "real world," that realm which I and my academic ilk are clearly incapable of understanding. But both Jacy and I sense that Charlie and his Friends live in something closer to the real world than we do.

At Dieppe, we walk out to the edge of the cliffs, snack on a rocky overlook, admire more views. I hadn't remembered Montreal being so clearly visible. We can even see some of the buildings from Expo '67, the Montreal World's Fair, held the year my family moved away.

Jacy suggests returning to the Pain de Sucre, and on the way I tell him about my father at his best. I tell him about our family trips up here and Dad's jokes about seeing the guy with egg on his shirt. I tell him about the time Dad seeded our neighbors' lawn with his initials, TAM, ten feet high, using special grass seed, while they were away on vacation. Weeks after they came back, they noticed the patch of darker-hued grass and realized what their lawn said. I tell about the time he and his friends attached all the hoses in the neighborhood so a neighbor's sprinkler ended up six yards away. The time they put another neighbor's prize watermelon up in an apple tree. The weekly bonfires in our backyard. The time he and his friends got wood for the bonfire from the scrap lumber pile where a new house was going up. When the nosy lady next door asked, "Does Mr. Charbonneau [the builder] know you're taking that wood?" they hollered back, "Hell, no, lady—we're stealing it!" The annual, all-night lobster broil, when even the kids were allowed to stay up past midnight.

Jacy thinks it is all very funny, and I like remembering my father that way. He lost some of that impish spirit when we moved to New Jersey, and he never seemed to have such close friends again. I think he associated the fun he had back then with the drinking that accompanied it, so he tried to recreate the joy with just the drink. But it became less and less fun—it was just alcohol after all, and no longer part of cele-bratory goodwill among friends.

Isn't it odd that those memories come back as "time" memories— as in "the time that . . ."? Clearly it is place that has brought all that back. The time is gone, but the place remains, as if it is a container for time. But that is why we revisit old haunts, isn't it? To time travel. That's why it is so often disappointing to return to childhood places and see them altered. It is not just the physical dimensions of the place that are thus affected, but the experiences that have become part of that place. To see the land only as it is physically is to see it as little more than a map, which does not contain memory. In *Sight and Sensibility: The Ecopsychology of*

Perception, a book on seeing in nature, Laura Sewall says that to see a landscape with proper depth perception is a matter of perceiving time, the fourth dimension. She calls space and time "permutations on the same theme. Place is a space with experience added in." And depth, says Sewall, is the result of "our experiences in both time and space, lived and made meaningful by the further deepening of events into experiences."[2] That depth is what I am sensing on Mont St. Hilaire. A small mountain, maybe—but deep.

I note the incongruity of the image. A mountain is high, not deep, right? Sewall's metaphor for depth perception is the Grand Canyon, fittingly deep, with the geologic past visibly layered on the canyon walls. And then I flash on another appropriate image of depth, elaborated upon in E. B. White's "Once More to the Lake." My journey up Mont St. Hilaire has been in essence a rerun of the situation described in White's classic essay. As a grown man, he returns to the lake in Maine where his family had summered when he was a child, only now he is with his own son. White notes what has changed at the lake (some details, like paved roads in place of dirt, loud outboard motors instead of quiet inboards) and what has stayed the same (the essence of the place), and he experiences a series of identity shifts. He sees the lake through the eyes of a child, his own and his son's, and he sees the lake through the eyes of the father, his own and his father's. He is his father with his son, he is the son with his father. And though he never says so, we sense that his father is gone. And though he never says so, we sense that White is becoming aware of his own aging. What makes the essay so poignant is that White blends this dark undertone with a celebration of the continuing power and beauty of the lake, and of childhood, and the eternal, joyful, deep connection between the two.[3]

In an essay called "Going Truant: The Initiation of Young Naturalists," Gary Paul Nabhan reports on a poll that revealed that while only 8 percent of adults consider quality of the environment a major issue, over 90 percent of children do. What happens in the interim, suggests Nabhan, is the process of education, which in our culture operates by bringing children indoors and telling them that the important things they need to know about our world and our culture can be taught within these four walls. What lies out there beyond the walls, we are told, is distraction.[4]

But if education is what makes many of us *lose* our interest in the natural world, what is it that accounts for children's intense interest in it to begin with? In her book *In the First Country of Places: Nature, Poetry, and Childhood Memory,* Louise Chawla reports on research that shows that people remember more events from their childhood and youth than from their adult lives.[5] Could there be a link to children's sense of the importance of place? Whatever it is that makes nature fascinating to children also makes it stick in our memories.

Chawla notes that psychologists have not much explored the connection between childhood and nature, but Freud is one of the exceptions. That makes sense, of course, since Freud traced much of our adult thought, and all our neuroses, back to their sources in childhood. And in constructing his symbology of dreams in *The Interpretation of Dreams,* he paid a great deal of attention to our preoccupation with natural landscapes. Woods, water, gardens, flowers, and of course caves represent the female, or more precisely female genitalia. Mountains, hills, knolls are female breasts. Upright things like trees and things that penetrate (a bee in a flower) are phallic. According to Chawla's summary of Freud's ideas, we dream in landscape symbols "as a strategy for neutralizing public threats" and because nature is a "safe symbol," disguising the true objects of our desires or fears. But nature is also, notes Chawla, "one of the great protagonists in Freud's thought. He considered the basic motive behind civilization to be to raise defenses against nature, to extract wealth from it, to dominate and control it. The great tragedy of human existence, he believed, is that however much civilization may alter our relations with nature, it cannot free us from ultimate subjection to it." Of course, there's an Oedipal twist to all this. Humanity's relation to the natural world is precisely that of the child's relationship to the parent. Noting that we generally conceive of nature as female, Freud says that feelings of oneness with the universe evoke memories of being nursed in the mother's arms.[6] So when we go to nature seeking peace or imagining that we feel connected to the world around us, we may in fact be sublimating our desire for our mothers.

Especially those of us who have a thing for mountains, I guess. And all this time I thought I liked the fresh air.

As always, Freud's ideas are provocative and interesting. But the usual objections can be raised here: He takes male experience to be the norm (all this as Oedipal, not Electral), and he overstates the role sex plays in our lives—which is hard to do, considering the very large part sex unquestionably plays in our lives. The question is whether sex is at the heart of *all* our pleasures. Or fears. Occasionally some of us do think of other things. Besides, wouldn't children be less likely to sublimate desires for the mother with the neutral images of nature? I can see why adults, thoroughly indoctrinated in the mores and taboos of our culture, would need a safe outlet for desires deemed inadmissible by our conscious minds—but wouldn't children be less apt to have developed the coping mechanism of using nature as a screen to cover unacceptable desires? And wouldn't children thus feel less attraction to things in nature, having less of a need to repress other desires through those "safe" images? And if our repression of inadmissible desires only grows stronger in adulthood, why would we lose some of our attraction to the safe images from nature?

So I am not buying all of Freud's ideas about childhood and nature. But I do think he's onto something in focusing on connectedness as key to our desires in nature. Here's how I see it: In infancy, we are bundles of egotism, concerned about our own needs and expecting those around us to attend to them—feed me, hold me, clean me, warm me up, calm me down. In childhood, we begin to feel love and affection for those around us, and not just out of gratitude for all the feeding and holding and so on. The loving is an innate capacity, and it is directed at the important people in the child's environment—and maybe the important nonhuman elements of that environment as well. We come to love a place just as we come to love our parents. It's the same process, taking place at the same time in our development, a movement of affection beyond the self. And the two, love of family and love of place, impress themselves upon our psyches at the same time, linking the two ever after.

It may be, too, that children actually perceive place as part of family, or don't see the two as clearly distinguished. Developmental psychologists point out that children tend to have an animistic worldview, seeing all things, even the inanimate, as possessing thought and feeling, seeing all the world imbued with life—or soul. In our culture, of course, at least since Descartes's *Discourse on Method* was published in 1637, we see ourselves as clearly set apart from the rest of the world by virtue of consciousness, which Descartes equates with soul. The rest of the world, that part without soul, is akin to machine, that which we are capable of understanding through the power of abstract thought. Notice that other living things are not presumed to have soul.

It is worth reminding ourselves that most other cultures do not take such a restricted view. So-called "primitive" cultures universally see the world as animated by spirit, a concept familiar even in the pre-Cartesian days of Western civilization. Chawla notes that the word "animated" derives from the Greek idea of *anima mundi,* the "world soul," "believed to be immaterial but inseparable from matter."[7] In reference to both other cultures and children, we equate faith in animism with a lack of intellectual sophistication. But let us consider another possibility. Could it be that our culture makes a concerted effort to replace innate beliefs self-evident even to a child with a quirky set of learned values that serves to justify our sense of moral superiority to other cultures?

Is it possible that when children are coming to love something other than themselves, they extend the love outward not indiscriminately, but towards all things possessed of spirit?

Jacy and I near the Pain de Sucre, the Giant's belly button, the outie omphalos of Mont St. Hilaire. On the way up, Jacy makes his first attempt at French, a tentative *bonjour* to some men on their way down. He does well enough that we get a response I can't follow, so I ask for it again, *lentement, s'il vous plait.* It's a joke about a McDonald's *en haut.* More views of Montreal and the Richelieu, a quick intake of handfuls of gorp and gulps of water, then we head down the mountain. I'm thinking about people, places, and things. Things to do, places to go, people to see, as they say. As *we* say, usually in a jaunty way, as a way of saying "so long, gotta run." But ultimately isn't that exactly what life is all about?

The things to do—that's experience. The people—the ones we love, the ones we share our experiences with. And places seem to me inextricably woven with the things and people that matter to us. My enjoyment today has come not just from reminiscences set in old haunts. Jacy, wanting to see peregrine falcons, brought me on a new trail, to Dieppe, where I hadn't been before because when I was a kid that trail wasn't there. It was not a relived experience but a new one, and for that part of the trip I was neither my father nor my son; I was me, with my son, here and now.

We pause by a small algae-slicked tarn, attracted by the water-plops of frogs made skittish by our approach. We can smell the ooze of muck ringing the pond, and I am gratified to realize that for a moment I have come to my senses—I remember Thoreau complaining in "Walking" that sometimes he enters the woods with his mind preoccupied with other things, and so he is "out of [his] senses" on those occasions and not really in the woods at all. "In my walks," he says, "I would fain return to my senses."[8] I remember, too, a Pattiann Rogers poem that I glanced at the night before, "On the Existence of the Soul." She doesn't quite argue for some sort of Oversoul that all things of the world share in, but she does suggest that the human soul feeds on sensory information absorbed from the natural world. The appetite we have for such information is her argument for the existence of the soul. Solicitous of soul, we nurture it "on the sight / Of the petrel motionless over the sea," and such garden variety delights as "the chartreuse stripe / And the fimbriated antenna, the bulbed thorax / And the multiple eye." If not for the soul, she asks, "why would I go / Out into the night alone and stare deliberately / Straight up into 15 billion years ago and more?" (142). Or why would I come back to Mont St. Hilaire? Why do we go to the woods at all?

Though psychologists other than Freud have had little to say on the subject of childhood memory of nature, poets have said plenty—Wordsworth being the classic example—and their thoughts, like their language, turn to the senses. Affected by Lockean ideas about the mind developing through experience garnered via the senses (the blank slate scribbled upon by life), Wordsworth saw childhood as a time of reveling in pure sensation. Why are those early sensations and impressions directed to nature? Chawla points out that children simply have closer and more direct contact with nature than most grown-ups do. "For most of us," says Chawla, "it is the only time when we get down into mud puddles and up into trees." The tragedy of adulthood is that many of us, taught that mature intelligence consists primarily of "logico-mathematical" thinking that removes us from the evidence of our senses, lose much of that passionate, sensuous response to the world. But not poets. Poets capture the fresh response of the child to the world by working with words that appeal to the senses. Poetry is born not just from "emotion recollected in tranquillity," as Wordsworth's famous dictum has it, but from *sensation* recollected in tranquillity, since emotion is born of sensation.[9]

Pattiann Rogers has said that her children, though not often addressed overtly as they are in "Suppose Your Father Was a Redbird," have influenced her work by encouraging her "participation in their first discovery and meeting with the world," whereby she could "see life with their eyes."[10] A poem like "Till My Teeth Rattle" suggests just what it is that her children have taught her, what children always teach poets, and what it is about childhood that poets remain attuned to. The poem presents a series of everyday (and everynight) images from nature—a "metal-sharp / disc of moon," "weasels humping cattywampus across / the gravel road," "popped / yucca pods" and their "confetti-spilling deluge of seeds." These images lead Rogers to articulate what could be the credo of any poet: "Whoever said *the ordinary, the mundane, / the commonplace?* Show them to me." Show them to her because as a poet she simply does not see anything ordinary, mundane, and commonplace about everyday life, and she is curious to see what she has never seen before. But show them to her, too, because in the ordinary, the mundane, and the commonplace she discovers the stuff of poetry. She has a "body / just made from the beginning to be shocked, / constantly surprised, perpetually stunned" (379).

Poets are those who continue to respond to the world as apprehended through the senses and are able to connect those perceptions to ideas. Or, conversely, they are able to take ideas and demonstrate them sensibly—that is, by illustrating them with examples that appeal to the senses. Perhaps as adults we work deductively, demonstrating general ideas with reference to particulars, so the particulars of the world are of interest as proof. But children (and poets) work inductively, beginning with particulars and moving to newly discovered general ideas, so that the things of the world are freshly gathered raw data emerging from their experiments with life, leading to general principles about things.

Maybe poetry is not so far removed from science after all. Later in life, our curiosity becomes blunted when we start thinking we know all the answers. When it snows, we say, ah, yes—snow falling, we're familiar with that principle. But to children, that information being collected by the senses is still exciting data, and they watch closely to see the effects of each new snow. It is not all generalized under the principle of "snow falling"—it is snow that melts on the ground but sticks on the limbs of conifers, or snow good for snowballs, or snow on top of crust that is perfect for sledding. Every snow seems as unique and fresh as every snowflake, and as worthy of attention. In short, maybe childhood places mean so much to us, even years later, because we truly noticed them, with all our senses, in ways that we may never reproduce ever after.

Jacy and I stop at Lac Hertel, and I show him the spot where Beezers and I used to see turtles and try to catch huge bullfrogs. More often we caught tadpoles—polliwogs, we called them—some of them the size of the catfish we can see now just a few feet offshore. Across the lake is an area of the mountain without trails, reserved for research in undisturbed forest. It has its allure, but I accept that I will likely never wander over there. On the beach by the caretaker's house, Jacy throws a few rocks to hear them plunk. Each plunk is the shutter sound of mind-camera, catching Jacy at the end of his follow-through, his attention directed toward the small water-statue rising and falling in the moment before the ripple rings spread and dissolve back into the lake. Out further a light wind lifts the lake surface into ridges, but we are in the lee of the breeze, and the water here is calm enough to let the ripples run their concentric course. Jacy throws more, marveling at each stone penetrating the surface, leaving its momentary mark in the mirror that can never crack.

I retreat to a picnic table, pull *Firekeeper* from my pack, find the poem I'm after, "The Family Is All There Is," a litany of behaviors and anatomical features held in common by living things. First on Rogers's list is the "old enduring connections / found in all flesh," threads, veins, ligaments, filaments. Then there's "the open / mouth" found "in catfish, moonfish, forest lily," in "barker" (human and canine, I imagine) and "yodeler." As the poem goes on, Rogers more consistently includes human versions of the noted behavior in her list. The sumo wrestler is right there with "warthog, walrus, male moose" among the snorters. The "familiar / whinny and shimmer [is] found in river birches, / bay mares and bullfrog tadpoles, / in children playing at shoulder tag / on a summer lawn." The "family" she speaks of includes:

> . . . weavers, ranchers, winders
> and connivers, pumpers, runners, air
> and bubble riders, rock-sitters, wave-gliders,
> wire-wobblers, soothers, flagellators—all
> brothers, sisters, all there is. (308–9)

Perhaps that is what children sense in their early awareness and expression of love. It's not just that they consider place as the setting for their first sensations of love of family, but that the love and conception of family includes their place and other living things within it. I am reminded that the third level of Maslow's hierarchy is not simply the need for love, but the need for love and belonging. In their sense of belonging to a family, children include place (which is not the same as domicile—I remember the slopes of Mont St. Hilaire better than I remember the layout of our old house), and they include the other living things that share their place. I grew up with my brother and sister, Beezers, Tim Sim, and Jimmy Sproule, and Garter Snake, Polliwog, Red Eft, Sugar Maple, and Apple.

Among the common propensities of living things, Rogers lists the "pervasive clasping" of everything from lichen to mating crane flies, and to "fingers around fingers"—and "the grasp / of the self on place" (308–9). Jacy clutches another water-smoothed stone. The throw arcs from the shore, hangs in air for several decades till gravity draws it down. Stone. Lake. A sound like "now."

Then my son and I walk down the trail past the visitor center, holding hands.

We eat a quick lunch by the car then head back to the States. By midafternoon we're in the Adirondacks, and by dinnertime we've hiked a couple of miles in to Marcy Dam. Our plan for the morrow is to head up Avalanche Pass, then along Avalanche Lake and Lake Colden up to the Opalescent River, then maybe from there head up Mount Marcy, highest point in New York State. This is Jacy's first backpacking trip with a full (though lightly loaded) pack. He has gone on overnighters with me before carrying just his clothes in a day pack. Now he's also carrying his own sleeping bag, water bottle, book, and a small stuffed moose to sleep with.

As it happens, this is also the site of my first backpacking trip, as part of a high-school outing club. It was an active club, to say the least. We were led on a series of hiking, camping, and biking adventures by the indomitable Mr. Weiss, a physics teacher. One of our trips was a one-day, one-hundred-mile bike ride, which after about forty miles or so became pelvic torture. But just when we'd be flagging, having moved from muttering our misery to ourselves to out-loud proclamations of rebellion ("This sucks! I can't believe he's doing this to us!"), along would come Mr. Weiss, nearing sixty (in age, that is, not m.p.h.) but having the time of his life, pedaling comfortably along, greeting us in his cheery, high-pitched voice, "Oh, what a glorious day! Isn't this wonderful!"

We went on the backpacking trips over Memorial Day weekend, and in the Adirondacks that means there is still some snow, and where the snow is melted, there is mud. After some thigh-deep post-holing steps in soft snow, then ankle-deep squishing through hungry mud, a slip or two, abraded knees from snow crust and mud drying on palms and shins, we'd start again—"This sucks!" The first year we arrived at camp in a fury, and there was Mr. Weiss handing out hot chocolate, beaming, "Now wasn't that a lovely hike!" The next day my friend Pesch would lead me and Ropes and Neiwirth on an ambitious hike to some local feature, a rock slide on the far side of Avalanche Lake, or Lake Tear of the Clouds, from which we'd return late but happy, telling all our classmates what a "wonderful hike" we'd had.

Eventually we started organizing our own trips, many of them in the Adirondacks, and after college Pesch and I and another friend spent ten weeks hiking from New Jersey to Maine on the Appalachian Trail. And to this day, on a bad day on the trail, whenever I find myself mumbling with displeasure, I remind myself in a high-pitched voice, "Oh, what a wonderful day!"

At Marcy Dam, Jacy's throwing stones again. Ripples on a pond—that is the way of our affections. From immediate family outward to friends, then to others who touch our lives.

There are several lean-tos around Marcy Dam, but Jacy prefers to camp in our tent. Which is probably wise, since the wet spring has made black-fly season last especially long this summer. We set up the tent, filter water from the dam, eat Jacy's favorite meal—pasta and tuna. Nightfall has crept close by the time we hang our food bags on a line strung over the dam's outlet stream. It has been a long day and we turn in early. I read a bedtime story to Jace, tell him a "Charlie and his Friends" story (more visits to the "time of the people"), then tuck him in. I take out *Firekeeper* and a flashlight, but leave the book unopened and the light off. Instead I listen to woods sounds, close my eyes, and think, oh, it's been a glorious day.

In the morning we make blueberry pancakes, revisit the dam, then head up Avalanche Pass. At the top we wind through a recent blowdown that looks as if it has been bulldozed, with trees uprooted by windrush and mudslide. After a rest, we start on the rugged trail along Avalanche Lake, first along a boardwalk bolted to the cliffs leaning out over the water, then through bouldered terrain, hopping and jumping from rock to rock and occasionally climbing ladders up and down the boulders. Those sections make Jacy nervous, and in some spots I have to carry his backpack. But he does incredibly well, showing some good balance, great fortitude, and a terrific attitude. Not one whimper or complaint through some challenging spots where he had to jump down off rocks and grunt with the effort to step up. Through it all, he continues to notice that the cliff-bordered lake is beautiful.

Along Lake Colden there is more rugged terrain and some tricky footing on steep slopes just above the lake. By early afternoon we arrive at the Opalescent River, which was going to be our lunch spot. We sit on moss atop the stream bank, just below the swinging bridge we crossed on, and watch the water glimmer and gush. I tell Jacy he has done great, and if we go no further we've already had a fine trip. So if he wants to stop now, that's OK. I'm really hoping we can go on another mile and a half up the slope of Marcy, to put us in position to get to the top tomorrow. Jacy says he's game, but once our packs are back on he says it makes him sad to leave this beautiful spot, and he wants to stay.

We set up camp in a clearing not far from the stream and discuss options for the next day. We're thinking we can climb Marcy or Algonquin Peak, then either return here or head back to Marcy Dam. If I were by myself, I know I'd be headed up a mountain—or probably both Marcy and Algonquin. But I'm not out here to make Jacy prove anything to me or to himself—and if I were, he has already proved it. If I had remembered how rugged the trails around the lakes are, I would have gone elsewhere. But he did it, and in good spirits.

Tent up, Jacy and I perch on boulders in the river. I filter water, soak my feet, read and write, while Jacy prowls the geography of water and stone. Here by the river the bugs aren't bad. Water upstream makes a sound somewhere between hissing and thundering—like a distant train maybe. Jacy announces that the distance around the world is twenty-four thousand miles.

"The circumference," I say.

"What?"

"The distance around—that's the circumference."

I study the map and plan possibilities for the next day, and I think about love's circumference—or its circumferences. I'm seeing ripples on a pond, topographic lines emanating from a summit called self.

We check on our packs and find that a red squirrel is busily chewing through the fabric of the top flap of my new pack, right where the gorp is. I grumble about the squirrel's depredations, and Jacy objects that the squirrel is just doing what is natural for it—scavenging. I accuse him of being sympathetic because he too would like to pilfer the M&M's from our gorp. He's feeling a sense of community with the squirrel. I'm feeling a couple of hundred dollars' worth of pack under attack.

After I hang our food we retreat to the tent, and I immediately embark on a search-and-destroy mission against the black flies that made it inside. Jacy suggests that I try to shoo them away, but they don't shoo very readily. Besides, I say, the little bastards don't deserve to live. Jacy gets upset, and I say I'm just kidding—maybe they deserve to live, but not necessarily in this tent.

We have one more encounter with wildlife in the afternoon. Jacy is out of the tent, peeing upslope, when I hear a commotion from a group of campers downstream. I poke my head out the tent and here comes a bear, a big one, heading right up the trail. I stand, find where Jacy is, turn back to the bear. The bear runs up to about ten yards of the tent, sees us, and veers off to the stream. We watch him splash across, less hurried now, and then he clambers up the bank into the woods on the other side. It is my second closest encounter with a bear—and the first was a year ago when I first took Jacy backpacking. My son is a wildlife magnet. Or maybe the bear is his totem.

Obviously, given my lack of sympathy for the black flies, my capacity to feel love and belonging with other living things has deteriorated since childhood. For children, once the boundaries of our capacity to love begin to expand, the circumference of our affections seems vast, maybe endless—from family and home to all living things and the whole living world. Not that there is no qualitative or quantitative difference in Jacy's feelings for me versus the black flies. But the ripples of his love travel far, even if they diminish further out from the center. Somehow in adulthood we start to restrict the scope of our love—we love more selectively, we feel ourselves belonging to less and less. Part of what we ought to feel that we belong to—and obviously Jacy is capable of this— is the biotic community, our neighbors in a town called Ecosystem. Aldo Leopold says that it is the mark of a fool to object to any part of the ecosystem (nylon-chewing red squirrels, flesh-eating black flies) just because we cannot see what they are good for: "If the land mechanism as a whole is good, then every part is good, whether we understand it or not," because all the parts are necessary. And I remember David Quammen's defense of mosquitoes in his essay "Sympathy for the Devil: A More Generous View of the World's Most Despised Animal." Mosquitoes, he says, are among "the great ecological heroes of planet Earth," because they protect forests (especially rain forests) from their greatest threat—humans.[11]

One more point in favor of black flies: As opposed to both mosquitoes and humans, they don't whine.

It may or may not be soul that constitutes the common bond of living things—maybe it is life itself. Or maybe life itself *is* soul. Or maybe soul is not something contained within us, but is something that reaches from us, like invisible threads, phantom umbilical cords, that connect us to earth—and to each other. "All life," says Pattiann Rogers, "beautiful or reprehensible, dangerous or benign—takes sustenance from the earth. . . . And all forms of life are one in their tenacity, in their determined grip on existence." Rogers's most memorable version of that life lesson is delivered in her poem "Justification of the Horned Lizard," written in rebuttal, she says, "to the whining and complaining I was encountering from so many of my human contemporaries, as if they felt life weren't worth the effort, their lives so relatively comfortable and safe."[12] The poem begins with the statement, "I don't know why the horned lizard wants to live." It is unattractive, with an "Embarrassing tail" and "warty hide," it lives in a grim environment of dust and heat, "grit, thorns and stickery insects," it "will never know / A lush thing in its life," and "The only drink it will ever know / Is in the body of a bug." And yet, "threatened, it burrows frantically into the sand / With a surprisingly determined fury," and shoots blood out of its eyes, as if "the propulsion of the blood itself, / Were justification enough and the only reason needed" (187–88).

I admire this poem for what it tells me of nature's creativity. How delightfully bizarre a defense mechanism! What will this world think of next? But of course, for all its unusual way of coping, for all the unfamiliarity of its way of life, the horned lizard at heart is just like us—living on earth, being in the world, trying to make do. That is what Jacy admires, perhaps—or maybe it is just that he is still capable of perceiving or recognizing it—even in the black flies and that darn squirrel.

I join him in trying to shoo the black flies out of the tent. He captures one in his palms, I unzip the tent, and Jacy flings him to freedom.

E. O. Wilson has dubbed our innate affection for other living things "biophilia," and it is clearly evident in young children, delighting as they do not just in the antics of cats and dogs but of spiders and beetles and worms as well.[13] And yet at some point the love of life—of other species' lives at least—gets acculturated out of us. Jacy is not the most social kid in the world, and a benefit of that is that his affection for things like black flies has lasted long; he has been uncorrupted by the usual cultural practices of wanton boys, killing flies for their sport. (Preparation for the worlds of business and politics? Or as Shakespeare has it, for the ways of the gods?)[14] I imagine, too, that the influences of a father who is acquainted with the concept of biocentrism (in theory at least) and a mother who takes her children on evening excursions to a local park to howl at full moons have also had their effect on Jacy's respect for living things. But how about the rest of us, who have moved away from our sense of belonging to a community of life that extends beyond the human realm? It would be beneficial for the alienated adult population of our culture to get back in touch—and I mean that literally—with the earth, to get our hands reacquainted with bugs and dirt, and to marvel at the strange and wonderful ways of other living things. As parents often discover, children can serve as guides in that process. We also have a series of relevant maps for exploring the territory out there, where we can survey the boundary lines between us and other living things, or cross those lines to connect with those other lives. Those maps we call nature writing. One function of literature has always been to take us out of ourselves, to allow us to try on other lives, to move us into the consciousness of Others. And so a twentieth-century middle-class white male reading, say, Toni Morrison's *Beloved* may come to understand something of the life of a nineteenth-century African American woman; we may even find ourselves understanding (and partially excusing?) an act of infanticide, something we previously would have found unthinkable. Nature writing follows the ripple effect of literature all the way out to the ways of life, and sometimes even the consciousness, of other species.

Most of us, I am aware, when we think of love and belonging, think not just of family, friends, and community, but of romantic love and marriage. Before the ripples of our love spread to the far shore of consciousness, that of other species, we hope to enter or engage the consciousness of one lover. The beloved, in sickness and in health and all that. Maybe that is the next circle, after family and friends, in the concentric rings of love that we encounter in our lives. And the question on my mind is this: What's nature got to do with it? Or, more specifically, why is it that when we try to convey in words the essence of romantic love, we do so invariably with images from nature? If it is true, as Richard Wilbur says, that "Love Calls Us to the Things of This World," most of the time it is the things of the natural world we are called to. Shakespeare compares his lover to a summer's day, Robert Burns's love is like a red, red rose, Emily Dickinson wants to moor herself in the harbor of her loved one, John Donne wishes he were a bloody flea, T. S. Eliot's Prufrock yearns to be a passionate lobster.[15]

And Pattiann Rogers is ravished by a hummingbird, in the most erotic nature poem that I know of, "The Hummingbird: A Seduction." This is another of her poems of supposition, this time with the poet imagining that she's a female hummingbird watching her mate's dance of hoverings and plummetings, a "sweeping and sucking / Performance of swirling egg and semen in the air." Part of the poem's passion comes from its breathlessness—it is four stanzas and twenty-nine lines long, but all one sentence, full of enjambment. Twenty-three of the lines end without any punctuation, and the last six lines contain nary a comma. Part of the passion, too, is a function of word choice; the descriptions suggest not just the mating display of hummingbirds but the sexual practices of humans. All that talk of sucking and semen, of "Most perfect desire" and "soaring rump," builds to a climax in the final stanza:

> Then when you came down to me, I would call you
> My own spinning bloom of ruby sage, my funnelling
> Storm of sunlit sperm and pollen, my only breathless
> Piece of scarlet sky, and I would bless the base
> Of each of your feathers and touch the tine
> Of string muscles binding your wings and taste
> The odor of your glistening oils and hunt
> The honey in your crimson flare
> And I would take you and take you and take you
> Deep into any kind of nest you ever wanted. (170–71)

When I read that to my classes, I pause a moment at the end of the heated recitation and ask someone to "hose me down." For all the ostensible focus on hummingbirds, the language here evokes human sexuality. Evokes, hell—it's darn near pornographic. It is worth recalling that the poem begins with "If I were a female hummingbird . . ." The whole poem is about what she would do *if* she were a hummingbird, but she never really detaches herself as human lover from the description that follows.

So clearly the seduction taking place is as much human as hummingbirdian, with the seducer being as much the female poet as the male hummingbird. But why does Rogers bother with the birds to begin with? Why not just write a poem directly to her lover without imagining that they are hummingbirds, a "here is what I'd like to do to you tonight" poem? Let us count the reasons. Or at least try to think of some.

In *A Natural History of Love,* Diane Ackerman identifies six key themes of love poetry, from the earliest times to the present. Among them is "Idealizing the beloved in images drawn from nature." Also on her list is "Redoubling of the senses."[16] Perhaps there is a connection here. In general, our senses have more free play outdoors than in—the touch of rough bark and gentle breeze, the sound of an unseen woodpecker and your own feet on leaf duff, the sight of a far horizon or a bug or a bud on a bush you have just brushed by, the smells of pinesap and advanced log-rot, the taste of cold water and tart ripening berries. There are simply a greater range and variety of sensuous activity for us to experience and exercise our senses upon out there. Indoors, our senses are generally constrained by the walls that contain them. Jerry Mander suggests that the insides of our houses are "sensory-deprivation environments." The object of most of our sensory attention indoors—television— makes its limited appeal to only two senses, sight and sound, and as both Mander and Bill McKibben point out, even in those two areas television's range is small. Visually, TV specializes in close-ups and tightly focused shots, rarely offering vistas or any sort of image collage and, of course, doing away with peripheral vision. Aurally, TV presents only one sound at a time and eliminates faint sounds; even "background" music, says McKibben, is pretty much foregrounded. The effect of all this is to give us, in our indoor lives, "the sense of living in a muffled, shrunken world."[17]

Except when we make love. Then we are sensitive to the slightest sounds (from heavy breathing to tiny whimpers), and our other senses become similarly alert. We luxuriate in a whole variety of caressing and touching, we get close enough to really smell and taste someone (her shampoo, her sweat, her . . . well, you get the idea). Perhaps, then, we write about love via nature imagery as a way of awakening and evoking sensuousness. Think of how readily we conflate and confuse the sensuous and the sensual. (As I recall the distinction, it's S for senses, the L for lust. Or is it an S for sex and . . . no, I've got it right the first time. I think.)

Perhaps, too, nature is the figurative language of love because it is so openly sexual. Why does the cactus bloom? Why is the honeysuckle fragrant? Why does *Pyrus malus* wrap its seeds in apples? Why does the snake dance, the cat yowl, the peacock preen, the ox musk, the poet write? Why does the tree leave? Why does the chicken cross the road? For sex, that's what—the means of reproduction. "Urge and urge and urge / Always the procreant urge of the world"—so observes Walt Whitman in "Song of Myself," but it's really the song of every living thing.[18] Most of what is going on out there is about procreation, and it is all happening right out there in the open, no closed doors or discreetly drawn shades. So nature reminds us of our sexuality—or more likely it is the other way around. Perfume, borrowing the essence of the aromatic come-ons of both flora and fauna, their fragrances and musks, makes the reminder explicit.

Ackerman notes that we frequently link our sexuality with the idea—and the language—of the wild. To some extent, we seem to fear that connection. We speak of male "sexual carnivores" as "beasts"—though Ackerman also notes that prior to the twentieth century it was women who were considered the wildly sexual ones, temptresses in the tradition of Eve, and like Eve, blameworthy for their sexuality. The association of women with agriculture, "fields to be sown and reaped," suggests a desire to tame their wild sexuality. At the same time, though, we seem to yearn for the wildness we see in nature, in our love lives at least. Witness our high regard for "animal attraction" and our willingness to give all for love. "Love is anarchic," says Ackerman, capable of diverting us from our orderly plans for the future. (Though perhaps not from our "best-laid plans.") (Sorry.) In this context Ackerman's comments on the sensuality of hair seem relevant. We find long hair sexy, she suggests, because "it echoes the sheer disarray of nature. . . . like ourselves, and like our feelings of love, despite our constant efforts, it will always be just a little bit out of control"—a loss of control devoutly to be wished.[19]

But perhaps nature offers us images of something we yearn for in our love lives even more than a walk on the wild side—"the powerful desire to become one with the beloved," as Ackerman puts it, the wish of all lovers "to lose themselves, to merge, to become one entity." It is the old Platonic idea that somewhere out there is our better half, our one and only that can make us whole. When we find it—him—her—we become worshipers at the shrine of love. These, of course, are familiar ideas—love as a search for wholeness and holiness. Why does this quest evoke nature? In nature we see an image of all things melded into a whole, a whole that we call creation and consider the sacred work of a creator. It is whole, a unit, an idea of oneness such that we encompass it linguistically with a singular noun, nature. And sacred? Ackerman points out that the concepts of wholeness and holiness, not surprisingly, are related. Tracing the word "holy" back to its Indo-European linguistic roots, she finds that "it meant the healthy interconnectedness of all living things, a sense of connection to the whole."[20] By that definition, ecology is the study of the holy.

We think of nature when we think of love or feel love, then, because it is the realm of the senses, of the wild, of oneness, and of the holy—and these are the ends of love approached by the means of the natural world.

I recall a trip to Niagara Falls, when I was doing a presentation at a nearby college. I stayed in a hotel right next to the river, just upstream from the falls. Most of the hotel's business, of course, was from honeymooners, so there was a small bottle of champagne in the refrigerator, which I had to myself, listening to the rapids rush by outside. I savored the irony, sitting by myself sipping champagne alone in this haven of honeymooners. I remembered the wonderful Gregory Corso poem "Marriage," where he talks about going to Niagara Falls to "deny honeymoon," to stay up all night talking with the desk clerk (instead of in bed with a bride) just to disrupt everyone's expectations. He also imagines being a "scourge of divorce," trying to wreck everyone else's honeymoon.[21]

But despite relishing Corso's cynicism, I also felt how impressive the falls are—more so than I'd imagined. So much water, so much power. So many variations on the theme of water falling.

Mark Twain once said, sure it's impressive seeing all that water tumbling down the falls. But "it would be a deal more wonderful to see it tumble *up* there."[22] My thought was that it would be a deal more impressive to be there with a romantic partner, which got me wondering just what it is about the falls that makes it a hot spot for honeymooners. The falls are impressive—but why erotic or romantic?

Maybe confronted with all that power, the power of Nature, we cling to each other all the more, feeling small in the face of it all. Maybe the river is like passion, a moving onward, onward, a mad rush, an earnestness that is full of playfulness, playfulness with earnestness, yin of water meeting yang of rock, cavorting with rock, moving rock, arriving at the climax of the falls, a constant climax, always, always coming.

Maybe that is the hope of honeymoon. It is a climax of love, the rapids of passion leading up to it, and the hope is that like the falls that climax can last forever—or as good as forever as we can measure it in human lifetimes.

Freud would say that the use of nature imagery to express sexual passion is a kind of sublimation—a polite way of releasing subconscious desires. Our culture doesn't allow us to openly express sexual desires, so we couch them in safer images of nature. But on a honeymoon don't we have, literally, license to be naughty? Of all times that is when we would least need to be sublimating sexual desire. It seems to me that the falls remind us of the sensual and the wild, or speak them for us. They trigger or evoke passion rather than take the place of it.

The Opalescent River makes its sounds—chuckles, laughs, chatters, bellows, sings, gets symphonic, tells us to hush and listen. Topographic map still out, I show Jacy how to read the contour lines. He sees the clustering of the lines on the steep slopes of Mount Marcy. I explain what that would mean for our possible ascent tomorrow. The map is a representation of space, of course, but suddenly it is the setting for a kind of fluidity in time. I'm talking to Jacy about our route for tomorrow's hike, and in my mind I'm travelling backwards—not exactly down Memory Lane, more like up the Path of the Past.

Our trip here to the Adirondacks is a planned visit to the terrain of romantic love—hence my selection of Pattiann Rogers for reading material. Upstream is Lake Tear of the Clouds, right around tree line, and above that is the summit of Marcy, where maybe Jacy and I will head tomorrow, and where eleven years ago I asked Jacy's mom if she wanted to get married.

Our relationship had been grounded in the natural world—day hikes along the Chesapeake Bay and the Jersey Shore, up to Little Flat Fire Tower and Mount Nittany and Wopsononock—berry-picking jaunts to local fields—walks around the neighborhood—and once to Mont St. Hilaire. But she had never backpacked before we climbed Mount Marcy.

We hiked up the other side of the mountain, along John's Brook, then up, and yes, I guess I was asking her to prove something to me—that she had a feeling for mountains and that she had the commitment to get up the mountain. Publicly, though, after she said yes, I told our friends that I had asked on the summit so I could push her off if she said no.

I guess, too, that I was thinking of that trip as allegory—the climb symbolizing the tough haul of a life's journey together. She made it up, but complained enough about the heat and the bugs and fatigue that I got annoyed, which I tried not to show but did anyway. Not a good sign. At the end of the day she said, "That's the hardest thing I've ever done."

Marcy as Mount Metaphor. The hike lasted all day, the marriage seven years. It was the hardest thing I've ever done.

So here I am with our first child, of two (Jacy's younger sister not quite ready to carry a pack), thinking about peaks and valleys. You cannot stay long at the peak, can you, no matter how exhilarating it feels. Most of life flourishes in the valleys, and you have to pay attention to the small stuff in order to catch its beauty. I flash on Judy's current flower garden, full of bee balm, moonbeam coreopsis, black-eyed Susan, tiger lilies, balloon flowers, pink loosestrife, sunflowers—names as resonant as the rocky appellations I am so fond of.

Suddenly it strikes me as funny that Judy and I went up Marcy from the other side.

The Opalescent River chuckles too.

There is more to the story (and, to be sure, another side to the story as well). The day after Judy and I got engaged on the summit of Marcy, we met my brother and his son walking in to meet us along John's Brook. Judy was hurting, so she hiked all the way out to stay at a bed-and-breakfast in town. My brother and nephew and I stayed in a shelter, and at about ten P.M. a group of about a dozen teens came in, in the dark, wet and discouraged. They had been out rock climbing in an all-day drizzle. They wandered around trying to get tents set up and dinner going, and we were puzzled by their disorganization—puzzled until we found out that their leader, a young woman, had passed out behind the shelter. She had been on belay much of the day, exposed to the cold and wet, and she was hypothermic. My brother got his stove going for soup and hot chocolate. I stripped her wet clothes off and put her in my down sleeping bag and got in with her to warm her with my body heat—standard treatment for hypothermia. Within an hour or two she revived and was fine.

Next morning we hiked out with the group and then picked up Judy. We were bubbling to tell the story of how we'd saved somebody with hypothermia. But her reaction was not what I expected: "You slept with someone else the day after we got engaged?"

Not a good sign.

The Opalescent River giggles. Laughs uproariously. Guffaws. Reminds me that in the disintegration of our marriage I deserve a full share of blame.

The next day quickly turns drizzly, so we pass up both Marcy and Algonquin, knowing they would be cloudy and windy above tree line. Rather than try to impose my will on the conditions, or to put my will to some sort of test, I am pleased to allow the conditions of the time and place to shape our experience, and pleased to accommodate the needs of my filial companion.

Along the rough trail by Avalanche Lake, I lash Jacy's pack to mine. Without his pack, he clambers up and down the angled boulders and ladders without needing a hand. He feels more confident about his ability to master awkward footing, and more trusting in the traction his boot soles give him. I, however, labor mightily with the extra weight. Still, I'm hoping we run into someone who would see me with two packs on, so I can say, "This way I'm having twice as much fun!" No luck.

In the light, scattered drizzle, the gray sky matches the cliffs above Avalanche.

Carrying Jacy's pack, I'm still thinking allegorically, wondering if I made my marriage fit the allegorical pattern of our Marcy climb, chiding myself for not always being willing to carry Judy's burdens as well as my own. Or is it typical for us to go that far only for our children and not for each other?

It occurs to me that much of my camping experience has been used to test others—a good companion does chores when asked, or better yet pitches in without needing to be asked. And hikes at my pace. Some meet my tests . . . but I also end up hiking alone a lot.

But today, for this whole trip really, I have readily accommodated to Jacy out of a sense of responsibility to him, his welfare, and his state of mind. And because I wanted to be with him and do things his way. So I gave up my own ways of being in the woods to accommodate his. That's how you build a family, or a marriage, or a community, maybe even a country, or an ecosystem. You give up something of yourself and your desires for others, make accommodations for the needs of others. Ultimately, and ideally, maybe that accommodation even extends to other species.

The drizzle turns to all-out rain as we approach Marcy Dam. I'm hoping to reach a shelter there for lunch before we get soaked. My tendency in rain is to walk faster, as if I can beat it to my destination, or as if I'll get less wet if I move fast. Neither of which is true, of course, and Jacy's pace requires me to slow down. Can't beat the rain, so I join it, or it joins me, running down my socks and the back of my neck. I'm irked at first, but I come around to appreciating it, or at least accepting it. Jacy, of course, doesn't mind the rain a bit, stomping through puddles, seeking them out on the trail just as he does on a suburban street at home. By the time we get to the trail's end, I have given up trying to dodge between drops, allowing myself to simply be in the rain, even tilting my head up to let drips off the trees splat on my upturned face.

Jacy and I drive south and camp at the North Lake campground in the Catskills. Though it is late afternoon, we get in a walk to the site of the Catskill Mountain House, just uphill from the lake, at the edge of the dramatic escarpment facing east to the Hudson. This is the next topo line in my expanding geography of love. I have been following a path through landscapes that have nurtured, or provided an outlet for, a variety of loves—of family, friends, lover, biotic community. But there's another contour line in there that I've overlooked—love of country. Hence our stop in the Catskills, not so much this time for any personal associations but because it was here, less than two centuries ago, that Americans first came to express, artistically, their love of country—here that American art and literature staked their claim to their distinctiveness. Both the visual and verbal art of the time were grounded in landscape, finding there—here—the basis not just for national pride, but for national identity.

Our view from the scarp is the same as one admired by the first great hero of American fiction, James Fenimore Cooper's Natty Bumppo of the Leatherstocking Tales. In the 1823 novel *The Pioneers*, set mainly in the Lake Otsego area, Natty gives a digressive but ecstatic account of this scene, overlooking "rivers looking like ribands" and far mountains like "haystacks of green grass," and encompassing, it seemed, all of "creation." As if this were Eden, which was one way American writers distinguished the American landscape from Europe's. Theirs was a fallen landscape, altered by human habitation. Ours was wilderness, "virgin land" in the eyes of Americans, straight from the hand of the Creator.[23]

Our view is also that of the opening of Washington Irving's 1819 story "Rip Van Winkle"—though in reverse, as we look from the top of the mountain down on the river instead of from the river looking up. Ironically, Irving had not yet been in the Catskills when he wrote the story, having seen them only in passing from a ship on the Hudson. The story is actually based on a German tale, that of Peter Klaus the goatherd. Why, then, is this story considered a landmark in the development of an indigenous American literature? American critics of the early nineteenth century, most notably Ralph Waldo Emerson in his 1837 Phi Beta Kappa Address "The American Scholar," repeatedly called for a native literature, most claiming that American nature, wilder than Europe's, could be both the inspiration for a national literature and the source of its uniqueness.[24] The only thing Europe's landscape had that ours lacked was "associations"—that is, stories and legends associated with particular landscapes, and that's where the writers' work lay. Irving's opening description of the Catskills—or rather the description offered by his narrator, Diedrich Knickerbocker—makes the implicit claim that our mountain landscapes are the equal of any in Europe. He describes the mountains "swelling up to a noble height, and lording it over the surrounding country," mountains of "magical hues and shapes" that serve "as perfect barometers," for "when the weather is fair and settled, they are clothed in blue and purple, and print their bold outlines on the clear evening sky; but, sometimes, when the rest of the landscape is cloudless, they will gather a hood of gray vapors about their summits, which in the last rays of the setting sun, will glow and light up like a crown of glory."[25]

Obviously, this is an appreciative description in the sublime mode, indistinguishable perhaps from word paintings of the Alps, but preceded by the pointed assertion that this is a view of the "Kaatskill mountains." In the rest of the story, Irving moves beyond singing the praises of the landscape and begins "storying" it, in the process weaving myth into the fabric of American history. Rip's long sleep—reputed to be in a vale just below here, along the path of the old Mountain House road—takes place during the American Revolution. To him, the United States of America has come into being literally overnight, and when he wakes up the portrait of King George hanging outside the Doolittle Hotel is now labeled George Washington. (Perhaps a wry comment there on the theme, "the more things change, the more they stay the same.") The strange bowlers who have intoxicated Rip with their mysterious liquor, and who are presumably responsible for thunder in the mountains, are associated with figures of more distant American history, the lost crew of Henry Hudson—namesake, of course, of the great river of the Catskills.

I am reminded of something I heard about marriage in Ghana—that a couple is not ready to commit to a life together until they share a hundred stories. Maybe the same applies to a people as well—we are not really a nation until we share a hundred stories or so. Surely "Rip Van Winkle" is one of the stories that we all know. I make a mental note to make "Rip" one of Jacy's bedtime stories, and to prepare for it with a "Charlie and his Friends" story about "Rip Van Velociraptor," who sleeps through the extinction event of sixty-five million years ago and awakes to find mammals ruling the earth.

Among American artists, the preeminent visitor to the escarpment was the progenitor of the Hudson River School, Thomas Cole. He spent much of his adult life in the town of Catskill at the foot of the mountains and made frequent trips to the Mountain House area. In part because of its fame as the source of American art, the Catskill Mountain House became the first famous American tourist destination, busy with visitors from New York and New England during its heyday from the mid-1820s through the 1840s. It hung on as a going concern well into the twentieth century, until it closed during World War II and was torn down in 1963.

At the Mountain House site, I take lots of photos, hoping to catch some of the same spots featured in Hudson River School paintings and to see if I can demonstrate how things have changed—or stayed the same. I take one of a "lake with dead tree"—title of a Cole painting set on the shore of South Lake. My dead tree, though, has initials scratched in it.

We discover that graffiti is not a twentieth-century invention. We find hundreds of sets of initials carved in the sandstone around the Mountain House site, some of them dating back to the 1840s. People took much greater care with their graffiti back then, it seems. The letters are elegantly and deeply carved—no hasty spray-paint jobs.

After a quick swim at the lake, we drive a couple of miles to the trail-head to Kaaterskill Falls. The half-mile trail to the falls is rugged, rocky, and wet along the cascading creek. We see the lower falls and go wow. Then we see the thin silver line of the upper falls. Double wow. Combined, the falls are the highest in New York, which is of course home to Niagara. We hike up the steep, loose slope to the upper falls, and Jacy finds the last piece of the cliff-edge trail pretty scary. But the trail behind the falls is amazing, the most astounding piece of landscape I've ever seen. A path follows a recess cut under the overhang behind the upper falls, arcing in a horseshoe. The water crashes in a pool below, gathering itself for the leap down the lower falls. I recognize the perspective of another of Cole's five paintings of the falls, his 1826 *Kaaterskill Falls,* which includes a bit of the overhang as a framing device—occasion for another photo.

Cole himself described the falls as "a singular, a wonderful scene, whether viewed from above, where the stream leaps into the tremendous gulf scooped into the very heart of the huge mountain, or as seen from below the second fall—the impending crags—the shadowy depth of the cavern, across which darts the cataract, that, broken into fleecy forms, is tossed and swayed, hither and thither, by the wayward wind—the sound of the water now falling upon the ear in a loud roar, and now in fitful, lower tones—the lonely voice—the solitary song of the valley." The upper falls he saw as "like a gush of living light from Heaven," and the cavern under the overhang he called "the most remarkable feature of the scene."

I am reading all this in Louis Legrand Noble's *The Life and Works of Thomas Cole,* an early biography that includes some of Cole's essays and poems and letters, reprinted recently with a cover photo of another 1826 painting of the scene, *The Falls of the Kaaterskill.*[26] The painting, I see, accords with Cole's visual description. The central focal point of the picture is the rock ledge between the falls. A tiny Native American figure stands on a rock above the pool, above the white plunge of the lower falls. Red-leaved trees reach above the ledge to the left. To the right is a twisted, bleached, skeletal tree. The cascades are white and bright leading into the left center foreground, but to either side the foreground is dark. To the right of the lower falls a few more vermilion-tipped trees ascend the cliff. Above them the upper falls drops. Only about a seventh of the painting is devoted to sky, most of it filled with dark, glowering thundercloud, but with a bright opening in the top right corner. The light pours from there to the falls and autumn leaves, so that both light and water seem to flow from heaven, visible evidence of God's presence. It is typical of Cole's work in the diagonal flow of light, the suggestions of power in the storm and moving water, and the vivid coloring of the leaves. And amid all this, human figures are dwarfed. This is the landscape sublime—vast and powerful and awe inspiring—rendered American by being placed in a recognizable American setting, with recognizable American characters (the lone Indian) and our distinctively vivid autumn foliage. In place of the ruins often found in European landscape paintings, Cole substitutes the blasted tree. The whole scene is presented from an elevated viewpoint. It seems to be based on the view from nearby Prospect Rock, but there is no foreground detail to place us, so the effect is that we seem to see the falls from a vantage point suspended in midair.

It is a beautiful picture, one that long ago made me a fan of Hudson River School art and that has now led me to check out the scene in person. But it is a guilty pleasure I feel. Paul Shepard has critiqued the whole genre of landscape painting, claiming that it tends to distance us from nature because of its use of perspective. Perspective, says Shepard, presupposes our removal from the scene to some objective distance where we can look from the outside; tracing the development of perspective to the Renaissance, Shepherd observes that "the price of stepping back from the world to see it objectively was separation." In essence, we are removed from nature as soon as we start to view it as picture. Geographer Denis Cosgrove, exploring these ideas further in a book-length study of the idea of landscape, contends that perspective is an attempt to impose "the control of space" and "the illusion of order" on the land.[27]

Some art critics have also pointed out that an artist's selection of the elevated prospect is hardly an innocent choice. Like perspective (and Cosgrove points out that the words *prospect* and *perspective* share etymological roots), the prospect implies removal from the landscape. We speak of a prospect offering a "commanding" view, implying an attitude of domination.[28] This is more insidious than just being separated from the scene; it is to assert dominion and control, to take possession. If this were a marriage, we would fear abuse.

In light of these viewpoints, Cole's selection of a Native American for the lone human figure in the painting becomes suspect. Cosgrove points out that the insider's view of the land, the experience of those most closely involved with the land, is "implicitly denied" in a prospect. Rather, the view is "the property of the artist and the viewer—those who control the landscape—not those who belong to it."[29] The tiny Native American figure is, perhaps, one more item in the landscape subject to the controlling gaze of the painter.

Is Cole's art, then, implicated in distancing us from the American landscape he was trying to glorify? Is his art one of the cultural forces that has led us to abuse the land? Is it an assertion of dominion over the land and its original inhabitants?

My own subjective impression is that Cole is innocent of these charges. Despite the elevated prospect, for instance, *The Falls of the Kaaterskill* seems to defy limitation to a single perspective. I have read criticisms of Cole charging that in his early paintings he recorded too much detail, all of it in focus, so that the painting does not seem like a true perspective, like a real scene caught in a single glance. A Cole painting is not like a photo with one focal length—it is like a view where you adjust your eyes to each item in the landscape as you watch. Cole's *Falls of the Kaaterskill* looks realistic, but I can almost see the painting as a collage of perspectives put together, which seems to be the sort of entry into the scene that Shepard believes is more involving. I find other details similarly involving in Cole's paintings, mainly the energy and motion. The flowing water and light so typical of Hudson River School painting make the scene far from static. Often, too, shapes in the sky echo elements of the landscape, like the dark cloud and the dark cavern behind the upper falls in *The Falls of the Kaaterskill.* The suggestion, given the transcendentalist bent of much American art and literature of the day, is that matter, the matter of mountain and falls and trees, reflects spirit, the spirit of sky and cloud and light. I wonder, too, if the so-called excess of detail is not the sort of admirable lavishing of attention that we devote to something we love. I sense passion in the vivid colors of the foliage, a perception of glory in the streaming light effects, something emotionally moving in the movement of the falls, maybe even involvement without dominance in the lone small, indigenous figure.

Laura Sewall's ideas about perception may explain my appreciation for Cole's rendering of the landscape of Kaaterskill Falls. She, too, like Shepard, objects to our reliance on the art of perspective, terming it "objective, nonparticipatory perception." Her complaint is that "Our modern Western assumption . . . seems to be that the act of perception happens entirely in the human head, as if the sensible world is little more than a trigger to begin the perceptual process. But could it also be true that the thing seen emanates something that catches our eye, that beckons and calls us out of ourselves?" The act of seeing, then, is a product of the object emanating or reflecting light to be seen, combined with our participation in the act of seeing, a kind of emanation of self. Ideally, that participation leads to a zenlike merging of self and scene, such that "we offer ourselves to that which we see. . . . looking long enough to truly see and value the Other, perhaps looking with 'love eyes.' In the process we surrender the ego, perceiving ourselves in relationship, now woven into the matrix." On three occasions, Sewall refers to this kind of seeing as a "marriage"—between "the inner and the outer worlds," "the sensible world and the realm of personal psyche," and "the viewer and the viewed."[30]

The dramatic light effects in *The Falls of the Kaaterskill*, as in many of Cole's paintings, seem to me an attempt to render in paint the sense of the scene's emanating visibility. The falls and the trees and the rock and the sky are allowed their visual voice, and the carefully rendered detail seems an attempt to give living things their due. And the other side of the vision process seems equally well represented. Cole is not simply a passive recorder of the scene; his senses seem engaged—excited, even—by the scene. I see evidence of sensory participation—or at least that is my sense of it, which may be a purely subjective impression, but since I'm arguing (internally) with those who object to objectivity, perhaps a subjective impression is the best defense.

But beyond the involvement of his senses, Cole seems to bring intellectual engagement to bear on the scene. Sewall says that "Shifting our belief about the nature of vision from one that is largely passive to one that includes our own contribution, our own ocular fire as a source of seeing, suggests that the realm of ideas and imagination is a part of perception."[31] Another common criticism of Cole, targeted especially at his later allegorical paintings, like the *Voyage of Life* or *Course of Empire* series, is that there are too many ideas in his paintings, that he was a kind of moral essayist working with paint. But it is precisely the grappling with ideas that constitutes Cole's engagement of mind with scene. I find in Hudson River School painting, more than in any other kind of landscape art, a sense of something significant going on. In *The Falls of the Kaaterskill* he was dealing with ideas about the place of humanity in the wilderness, the presence of the divine in nature, the immanence of spirit in matter, and most of all the nature of the American character. *The Falls of the Kaaterskill* is not just a pretty picture, but a celebration of national identity. It is about love of country as a formative influence on our character, a recognition that in the land itself is the basis of who we are. It should not surprise us that in the late nineteenth and early twentieth centuries the United States would become the first nation to set aside and preserve wilderness in the form of national parks.

So what does Cole's painting bring to my own perception of the scene—my own seeing? It may not alter (or take the place of) my sensory participation with the scene. But it has a place in the other means of participation Sewall speaks of. Cole's painting is part of what is in my mind, part of what I bring to bear in my perception of Kaaterskill Falls, part of the human emanation that mingles with the emanations of falls, sky, leaves, and rock.

Making our way back down the slope, Jacy feels more secure. At the vantage point below the falls, he exclaims that this has been a "terrific trip!" I feel like an overfilled pool at that moment, joy pouring into me like a swift stream, filling me up and passing onward, billowing mist all around me. The motion and height and roar of the falls, the swirling of the current—it strikes me as miraculous that so much time has passed since Thomas Cole was here, and yet it is all still here. And it is endlessly satisfying to be sharing this with Jacy.

I feel less connected to everyone and everything that night, when Jacy and I, trying to sleep, end up irked by our neighbors, a couple at the next campsite playing their radio. Jacy doesn't like the country songs, and I object to the importation of electronics into the woods. We go to the woods to experience the woods, don't we, so why surround ourselves with that wall of electronic sound that the night sounds cannot penetrate? It's as bad as leaving trash—except eventually our neighbors did turn the radio off, and trash stays even after the depositor has left. Temporary trash, then. Acoustic trash.

Any lessons about love here? Yes, about loving something for what it is, letting down your barriers so that a thing or person or place can get close to you. As opposed to loving a projection of your own life, within a circumference where you radiate only your own experience. I remember again Thoreau's complaint about walking in the woods with other things on his mind, concerns that have nothing to do with the woods, so that he's not really, or not fully, there.

Our neighbors, I suspect, have yet to arrive in these woods.

But maybe I, too, have been guilty of a reluctance to let down all my walls—in my marriage if not in the woods. Judy once told me that she missed me most when I was home, but not really there. Maybe I put up walls in the woods, too, my peculiar ideas about how to go to the woods being part of my projections of self.

But at least I can hear birds singing, insects chirping, my son's regular breathing.

In the morning, after pancakes, I sit on a rock wall next to the lake while Jacy explores the shoreline. I'm playing with some of my leftover Canadian coins and accidentally drop a "loony," a one-dollar coin with a loon on the back, into water a couple of feet deep. It glimmers like memory. Jacy wades in to retrieve it for me.

A couple of weeks later I return to North Lake with my friend and frequent hiking companion David. We drive up from Washington, D.C., where I have been visiting the National Gallery to check out Hudson River School paintings and he has been visiting his brother. David and I, too, walk up to the Catskill Mountain House site immediately after setting up camp. At first we barely pause there, walking south along and under the escarpment, bushwhacking back uphill when our trail peters out. On South Mountain we find the site of the Kaaterskill Hotel, built in 1881 by George Harding. The story goes that the chef at the Catskill Mountain House refused to vary the menu to serve fried chicken to Harding's daughter—so he built his own darn hotel, the largest in the area, with room for twelve hundred guests. It burnt down in 1924.

Returning to camp, we walk through hemlock and balsam fir. My Catskills trail guide reports that the early American botanist John Bartram traveled here in 1741 to see the balsam fir, then called Balm of Gilead, then returned in 1753 with his fourteen-year-old son William, destined to become an even more famous botanist. In his *Travels,* William recalls his first view of a rattlesnake on that Catskills trip. He had taken it for some kind of standing fungus and was about to kick it when his father stopped him. Their guide killed the snake, and the father kept the skin and fangs.[32]

Along the edge of the scarp, overhanging rock slabs offer occasional views of the Hudson River and distant ranges. We can see the Housatonics, Taconics, Berkshires—and I pick out individual mountains, too—Everett and Greylock.

Back at the Mountain House site we run into a daughter and dad duo. She has spiked hair dyed an unnatural shade of red, he an over-hanging belly and baseball cap. They ask us to take their picture and David obliges. Standing with the Hudson River Valley as background, the father, making conversation in a heavy Brooklyn accent, nods to-ward the big sign giving information about the demise of the Catskill Mountain House and asks, "Why'd they ever tear it down? What a shame. This place must have been something back then." Which makes me think, "Back then? What's wrong with the way it is now?"

Next morning, David and I hike up to Kaaterskill Falls, spending an hour or so behind the falls. David ventures down to the pool below the upper falls, to the spot where the Native American stood in the Cole painting. Leaving, we pause by a blasted tree about shoulder high, look-ing over it down to the pool, and everything is waterfall mist and crash-ing water and rainbow rainbow rainbow. To which David says, "This must have been something back then."

At the upper lip of the falls, site of Cole's *From the Top of Kaater-skill Falls*, we spread out to read, write, and snack. In Cole's day there was an observation platform here, now gone, but interestingly his paintings of the site leave out the platform. The scene now, then, is in a way truer to his painting than it was when Cole painted it. Now that's vision.

Mist dampens the pages of our journals, and a wind blows the Zip-loc bag I keep mine in, blows it into the creek and down the falls. There is a moment when I could have snatched it before it hit the water, but the roar of the falls and our proximity to the big plunge gives me pause—and in that pause the baggie is gone. Damn, I've polluted. And we had just been saying how remarkably clear and pristine this place seems. Despite its reputation a century and a half ago as one of America's tourist hot spots, this place still seems wild. We have seen no one else on the trail all day. Around the falls there are no tourist centers or lookouts or souvenir crap—just the falls falls falls.

I make one more summer trip to the Catskills, this time by myself, to hike further along the Escarpment Trail, to Blackhead, Black Dome, and Thomas Cole Mountains. I camp by North Lake again, and visit the place where Jacy retrieved the loony and the shoreside rock where Jacy and I watched a pair of ducks glide toward us. Those seem like excruciatingly lovely moments right now—excruciating because now I am alone and lonely, missing him and my daughter.

Next day I begin the Escarpment Trail at the site of Scribner's Sawmill, where Henry Thoreau and his friend William Ellery Channing stayed when they visited the Catskills—a trip unrecounted in Thoreau's journal, unfortunately, unless some missing pages turn up some day. I pass Boulder Rock, the site of the Kaaterskill Hotel, Artists Rock (where Cole used to bring friends to point out his home in the town of Catskill), Bad Man Cave, North Point (the approximate site of two Cole paintings of North and South Lakes and the Mountain House, both done in the 1840s, when trails were opened up here), Stoppel Point. I find a small crashed plane on the side of the mountain, then reach Dutcher Notch, where I'd intended to camp, only to find signs saying "Camping Prohibited." It is another four miles to the next good site, up and then down Blackhead, and I'm already tired, but I manage to keep my composure. After all, it's a lovely day for a hike, even if the sky is dark and threatening something wet. The trail is in the woods now, with fewer dramatic overlooks off the edge of the escarpment. My attention becomes circumscribed, and I start looking for flowers and berries to photograph. This is typical, I think, of our excursions to the mountains. We begin by seeing large, looking for panoramic prospect views, emulating the aesthetics of landscape art, then eventually shorten our focus and home in on the small stuff along the trail. Perhaps the artistic expression of love of country has followed the same pattern, shifting from appreciation for the panoramic view, in Cole's day, to an eye attuned to the minute in the work of more recent nature writers.

I remember something that David told me on our previous trip, about a paper he had presented at a conference comparing descriptions of Yosemite by John Burroughs and John Muir. Burroughs's descriptions tended to domesticate the place, with images of home and architecture. Muir tended to vivify it, make it seem like something alive. David had said that he can see why in the Industrial Revolution people would prefer Burroughs's imagery, and I had said that perhaps the difference explains the current undervaluing of Burroughs—now our lives are all too domesticated and we want our wild to be wild. But perhaps, too, there is something here about the romantic versus realist sensibility. Burroughs, a Catskills native, focuses on the commonplace (groundhogs, crows) and the close at hand (in essays like "Wild Life about My Cabin"), and even chooses to render the extraordinary (Yosemite) in images of the commonplace. In describing the Catskills, he did not emulate the romanticism of someone like Cole, who sought evidence of the grandness of the nation and its destiny. Nor did Burroughs sketch in dramatic effects that suggest the immanence of God. He just tried to describe what was there, finding even the humble things of this environment worthy of his loving attention.

I see the same impulse in the poems of Pattiann Rogers, full of appreciative detail of everyday nature. In "Geocentric" Rogers focuses on not only the commonplace but the downright unappealing side of nature. The poem is full of images of rot and stench, from the "bilious / reek of turnip and toadstool / decay" to "egg-addled / garbage and wrinkled lip / of orange-peel mold." And yet the poet relishes the "warm seeth of inevitable / putrefaction," concluding that "nobody / loves you as I do" (339–40). This is realism with a vengeance—or, as Roger Weingarten sees it, it is romanticism that encompasses and absorbs realism: "I used to think that the romantic poet was one who believed that roses grew in garbage heaps," writes Weingarten. "After reading 'Geocentric,' I will forever think of the romantic poet as one who sees—with microscopic clarity—that roses *are* garbage heaps."[33]

Clearly Rogers takes seriously Leopold's notion that to see the world as beautiful means that we must also see every essential part of it as beautiful, and there is an obvious lesson about the nature of true love here—that love means accepting the beloved with warts and all, whether we're talking about loving people or nature. But for all her insight into the nature of love and her obvious love of nature, I'm wondering if I can find in a poem like this, or in any of Rogers's poems, something akin to love of country.

I make the climb up Blackhead (speaking of warts and all) and down the other side to camp. I pump water, make dinner, hang food, ponder my topic. A poem by the Mexican writer José Emilio Pacheco bubbles up from my subconscious. Entitled "High Treason," it begins with the startling pronouncement, "I do not love my country." But as the poem proceeds we find out that what he does not love is his country in the abstract, as an idea. At the same time he claims he would give his life

> for ten places in it, for certain people,
> ....
> various figures from its history,
> mountains
> (and three or four rivers).[34]

For me, coming to America was a very long process. Through my teens and early adulthood, I was conscious of the hypocrisy of American ideals—a country that claimed to be the "land of the free" and yet tolerated racism, a country that sang its democratic nature and then seemed to measure a person's worth in dollars and cents. Eventually I came to admire American art and literature and I could see how the high ideals expressed in national documents like the Declaration of Independence had inspired writers and artists and had infiltrated their art, given them something to aim for—or something to explore when the conditions of American life fell short of the high ideals. I saw how those recorded ideals made Americans sure of themselves and confident in their sense of who they are. They know how it is they are supposed to live their lives, have some ideal to measure their nation's actual performance against. Not that America as a nation necessarily does such a great job of living up to its ideals, but at least it has clearly delineated ideals to *try* to live up to, an elevated sense of who we are supposed to be. I compared that to Canada, a culture whose literature generally focuses on the nation's massive sense of confusion in regard to its identity.

And yet, for all my growing admiration—I even made the study of American literature my vocation—I did not love my new country. That came only when I realized that the people I had come to care most about—the people I loved—were American, and so were the places I most cared about—the Adirondacks, the White Mountains, and yes, the Catskills.

Perhaps that is the same process American artists were going through in the early nineteenth century. Writers and artists made Americans care about the actual country—the Catskills first, then the Adirondacks and the White Mountains, then the Rockies. Perhaps that is what contemporary nature writers are still up to—making us care.

I became an American citizen only after living here for thirty years, when I realized that in effect I already was American, and the paperwork would simply be making official what was already true in substance. Perhaps, too, by that time I was willing to accept America with all its faults. The culture might be shallow and materialistic, the politics corrupt, the ideals of the nation sometimes forfeited in the name of power and profit—but here is where I once camped with my friend Pesch and we fell asleep in a meadow, where Duane and I lost sleep to the nighttime scavenging of porcupines, where David and I talked about the merits of John Burroughs, where my son fetched a loony, where Henry Thoreau hiked with his friend Channing, where Thomas Cole stayed out all night in a storm, where I saw a crashed plane. America and me—we share at least a hundred stories.

When I showed up to take the citizenship test (after a useful and inspiring review of the high aims of American government), the examiner started out by informing me that he would not be able to pass me that day, since I was missing some court documentation in regard to the outcome of a legal indiscretion of my youth. But in the course of our conversation, after he found out my profession, we ended up talking about a Nathaniel Hawthorne story set in the White Mountains. The story was "The Ambitious Guest," part of Hawthorne's attempt to commemorate the American landscape through a historical event associated with it, the death of the Willey family in a landslide at Crawford Notch in 1826.[35] We talked about the nationalistic motive behind the story, and I mentioned that Thomas Cole had done a painting there, *The Notch of the White Mountains,* a few years after Hawthorne had written his story. Using his discretionary power, the examiner decided to pass me. At the swearing-in ceremony a few weeks later, a frail and elderly judge congratulated me and the other new citizens, shook the hands of each one of us, and told us how to register to vote. We said our thank-yous in varied accents. Afterward, the Daughters of the American Revolution served coffee and cookies.

In the poems of Pattiann Rogers, there is little overt love of country expressed, little evidence of any sort of jingoistic pride, but I decide that the particularity of Rogers's poems is very much in the spirit of Pacheco's brand of patriotism. There is an intense love of country in Rogers's poems—that is, of the actual places where she lives and of the other living things she shares those places with. In *Dream of the Marsh Wren*, Rogers explains the origin of her first poem "coming from the earth." She was a recent arrival in Texas, homesick for Missouri, where she grew up, and she forced herself, she writes, "to recall every detail I could and to name each detail to myself, to recreate the land with language." This "naming of details of the land . . . this litany" is typical of her poems, noun-heavy as they are with the names of living things.[36] It is those details that bespeak Rogers's involvement with the land, her means of overcoming estrangement in a new setting, her means of participatory seeing and of engaging mind and senses with the world. The earth requires of us that we notice and appreciate the details of life all around us in order to feel at home. What do we get in return? We get sustenance to feed our senses. And we get the opportunity to love. For love, too, is not just a receptiveness to the beautiful, but an act of projection as well.

Rogers writes in "Supposition" of the need to praise, imagining that "the act of praise," occasioned, say, by "the design of rain pocks / On the lake's surface," might become "an emanation rising into space." Or what if praise took the form of light, "affecting / The aura of morning haze over autumn fields"? She imagines "praise and its emanations" being "necessary catalysts to the harmonious / Expansion of the void"—all of which sounds pretty far-fetched, until her concluding supposition: "Suppose, for the prosperous / Welfare of the universe, there were an element / Of need involved" (129–30). Do we have a need to praise? And likewise, as another Rogers poem has it, "The Need to Adore"? Certainly—at least to be fully human we have these needs. These are elements of love and belonging. Is it too much to claim that without nature to encourage and nurture our capacity for praise and adoration, we might be psychically diminished? Nature is not just the far shore the ripples of our love spread toward—it is the surface our love travels upon.

The next morning I make a pilgrimage to Thomas Cole Mountain, by way of Black Dome. I run out of film on Thomas Cole. There is some kind of irony there—visual irony, I guess. In truth, there are no vistas to photograph anyway—the summit is wooded, and where I can peek through the trees there is nothing to see but white stuff, elements of the universal being (clouds) circulating through me and the mountains.

Being visually shut off from the valleys below and the mountains surrounding me makes me feel like I am on an island. A deserted island, for the moment, since nobody else is up on this ridge of the Blackhead Mountains. But neither I nor the mountain is separate from the world around us. The Catskill Mountains, in fact, are not composed of separate masses of upthrust rock. Rather, they are the high remnants of the eroded edge of the Allegheny Plateau, with the valleys and cloves worn down by water and glaciers. Think of an aspen grove—each tree looks like a separate entity, but in truth the whole grove is one organism, sharing a root system.

As a people, our common ground is place itself, common ground in the literal sense. That is where our root system must lie.

If the self is mountain and we are made of resistant rock, love is the stuff that shapes us, cutting the contours of our lives like glaciers have carved the clove that Kaaterskill Falls clatters down. Or maybe the rock of mountains is our past, the no-longer-blank slate (and sandstone and shale and granite) recording the operations of the waters of love—in all its forms.

I retrace my steps back to Black Dome, third highest peak in the Catskills, and snack on gorp at a rock ledge where I can admire the inside of the cloud. The cloud is thick enough that moisture has gathered on my beard as I walked. I think of the flow of water from here, sweat-salted or not, making its way down to North Lake and Kaaterskill Falls, joining with waters from all the other northern Catskill Mountains shrouded in this cloud, and then running to the Hudson to join with waters that started flowing way up at Lake Tear of the Clouds in the

Adirondacks, descending via the Opalescent River. From the Hudson, of course, the cloud's contents might make its way down to New York City and out to the Atlantic. In other parts of the Catskills, from Slide Mountain west, water would run to the Delaware, past where Jacy and I camped last year and saw our first bear, then on past Philadelphia and down to the Delaware Bay. And all along the way, the waters bring life to Indian pipe and painted trillium and balsam fir, peregrine falcon and polliwog, black fly and black bear, redbird and lizard and humming-bird, Pennsylvanian, New Yorker.

This doesn't seem like such a lonely place any more. It occurs to me that where I live in central Pennsylvania, on the western slope of the last ridge of the Ridge and Valley Province, I look across Bald Eagle Valley to . . . the Allegheny Plateau, the same formation I stand on now.

I take out my map, note the contour lines of the terrain I will soon be descending. They are emanations raying out from this high point, ripples spreading. If it weren't for the cloud, I'd think I could see home.

4

ESTEEM NEEDS

Shasta la Vista

These are, first, the desire for strength, for achievement, for adequacy, for mastery and competence, for confidence in the face of the world, and for independence and freedom. Second, we have what we may call the desire for reputation or prestige, . . . status, fame and glory, dominance, recognition, attention, importance, dignity, or appreciation.

ABRAHAM MASLOW, *Motivation and Personality*

When I teach the idea of plot in a fiction class, I draw an outline of a mountain on the board and write in "Exposition" at the foot of the mountain, "Rising Action" on the upward slope, "Climax" at the summit, "Denouement" on the steep escarpment of the far side. Given the similarity to the classic shape of narrative, perhaps it is not surprising, then, that stories of mountain climbing, retracing the upward path of ice-chopped, cramponed steps, often make for compelling reading. The literature of mountaineering is a rich genre, dating back to Edward Whymper's 1872 *Scrambles Amongst the Alps,* or perhaps earlier to Alexander von Humboldt's account of his voyages to the Andes from 1799 to 1804, and including such recent examples as Joe Simpson's *Touching the Void* and Jon Krakauer's *Into Thin Air.*[1] Beyond all other genres, the literature of mountaineering is notable for its invocation of the traits listed in Maslow's first set of esteem needs—strength, achievement, mastery, competence, confidence, independence, freedom. It may be difficult to say why we climb the mountain—beyond the pat answer "because it's there"—but the literature of mountaineering is clear about what it takes to get there. Maybe the answer to the "why" question is "because it's hard," and to get to the top is an accomplishment. It would hardly be worth it if it weren't difficult, and because it is hard we must demonstrate—or develop—that first set of traits that Maslow sees as essential to our self-esteem.

I suppose that mountains have also been the arena for the kind of esteem Maslow mentions in the second set of traits—fame and glory and all that. Certainly Edmund Hillary earned worldwide fame and glory and reputation by climbing Everest, and a few elite climbers continue to do so. But those of us who are not making first ascents, who climb mountains in the footsteps of hundreds or thousands before us— we can make no claim to fame or glory. Perhaps we gain some small reputation among friends and acquaintances for our excursionary exploits (even if they do groan at the sight of our slide projector), but mostly the esteem we get from mountains is not much of a public issue. It is something that comes from within, or something between us and the mountain. And perhaps it has as much to do with humility as confidence, and with the world making sense to us. These are ideas I wish to explore in some of the literature of mountaineering, especially in the mountain writings of one of the climber/writers I hold in the highest esteem, John Muir. But what is it that leads me to conduct my exploration on, of all places, the mountain of my failure?

Flying at thirty thousand feet, higher than Everest, somewhere over the Midwest and its landscape of rectangular agriculture, I am on my way to Mount Shasta—for my third attempt to climb it. Shasta is a 14,162-foot volcanic cone in northern California, snowcapped, partially glaciated. My first try on Shasta came twenty years ago, when I lived in San Francisco. Halfway up, some of our group, all friends from work, were suffering—not so much from altitude as just plain fatigue. Since the outing was more a social occasion (the bonding thing) than a serious climb, we all turned back with the tired ones. My second attempt was my most memorable excursion in the mountains—any mountains. It was in November, several months after the first trip, late in the season to try a big mountain. Peter and I drove through the night from San

Francisco and camped at Sand Flat, at about 6,000 feet. We slept only a couple of hours, getting up at five, intending to go up and down in a day, so we carried only day packs, no tent or sleeping bags. Before we reached Lake Helen, above 10,000 feet, it had begun to snow, which turned into a whiteout, with visibility next to nil. We kept going, figuring uphill is bound to be the right way. But instead of going up the center of Avalanche Gulch, we mistakenly angled up the right side of the gulch, up Sargent Ridge. Got to the top of the ridge, rime in our beards, snow falling fast oh fast—but silently and beautifully too. That, in fact, was the sound the snow seemed to make landing on the hard white crust of the mountain—"silent, beautiful, beautiful too." We got to the top of the ridge and saw on the other side not the slope leading to the summit that we had hoped for, but pure, deep chasm. The ridge was jagged, not something we wanted to try to follow, and the snow kept falling.

We munched gorp, knowing there was not much to talk over, and after taking pictures of the rime dangling from our beards we headed down. Of course, in the whiteout conditions we couldn't see our footprints heading up, couldn't find the iced-over flat of Lake Helen. But we figured downhill must be the right way, so just kept heading down.

We probably erred to the right again, but we knew the important thing was to get below tree line and off the exposed part of the mountain before nightfall. We also knew that it would be safer to miss by going too far right rather than left, because at least to the right we were sure to hit a road eventually.

We got to the trees with the dark after walking for twelve hours, pretty much without a break. To keep our water from freezing, we hugged our water bottles inside our jackets, next to the warmth of our bodies. For five more hours, we walked in the woods. I suggested we bed down under ponderosa pines, but Peter demurred, not so much out of fear that we would freeze as out of concern about getting to work the next morning. Eventually we hit a jeep path and followed it out to the road, way, way downmountain from where our car was parked.

So there we were, eleven at night in a snowstorm on the side of a 14,000-foot mountain, and wonder of wonders here came a car. Driven by young men, teens, probably headed up to the Bunny Flat parking lot to drink beer. They dropped us at the mile marker where we had pulled off the road. Now of course the dirt road we had followed, not much of a road to begin with, was covered with a foot of snow and had blended indistinguishably with the surrounding landscape. The car was a couple of miles in, and we couldn't find it. We wandered around for a couple more hours, exhausted. Peter kept saying the car is near the gully, and I kept saying no, it's over there, and pointing. Finally, we listened to each other and followed Peter's gully in the direction I had indicated and found the car. It was now three A.M. and we had been walking for twenty-two hours.

Peter drove through the snow, guessing where there might be a hint of a dirt road below the wheels. Then we headed south to San Francisco, and got there in time for Peter to get to work. In truth, we were never worried about dying on the mountain—we were just tired and very lost. And we hadn't climbed Shasta.

I'd been out to Shasta one other time, when I was in California for an October conference. But the rangers dissuaded me from climbing then. Not enough snow, they said—the way up is all loose talus, very tiring. I went instead on a pleasant trip to Mount Eddy, a 9,000-footer just to the west. On top of Eddy, I had a great view of Shasta. My eyes followed the path up Avalanche Gulch—the Muir route, the easiest and most popular route of ascent—up to the Thumb projecting from the line of russet rocks called the Red Banks, then up to the broad summit slope. By eye, the climb took less than a minute.

Now, in May, with plenty of snow on the mountain, I'm back for another attempt.

John Muir climbed Shasta twice, once in early November 1874 and then late that same winter, in April of 1875. He had been in the California Sierras for six years by then and had already explored extensively in the High Sierra, working out his theory of glaciation, finding living glaciers near Mount Lyell and Mount Black (now Merced Peak) and climbing such peaks as Mount Dana, Whitney, and Cathedral Peak. He had already become the most accomplished mountaineer in America, and he'd had one of his most famous mountain moments in his first ascent

of Mount Ritter in 1872, recounted in "A Near View of the High Sierra."
Muir said of Ritter that "it is fenced round by steeply inclined glaciers,
and cañons of tremendous depth and ruggedness, which render it almost inaccessible. But difficulties of this kind only exhilarate the mountaineer." The appeal of difficulty—that is one of the sources of the esteem we get from climbing mountains. What is interesting about Muir
is that the challenge leads to little egotism in the overcoming of the
difficulty. Up on Ritter, Muir got himself into a precarious position
hanging on a cliff where he felt he could move neither up nor down
safely. "My doom appeared fixed," he writes. "I *must* fall. There would
be a moment of bewilderment, and then a lifeless rumble down the one
general precipice to the glacier below." Admittedly "nerve-shaken" and
panicky, he managed to calm himself, felt himself "possessed of a new
sense," and some "other self," or "Instinct, or Guardian Angel . . . assumed control. Then my trembling muscles became firm again, every
rift and flaw in the rock was seen as through a microscope, and my
limbs moved with a positiveness and precision with which I seemed to
have nothing at all to do."[2] Even at the moment of self-rescue, when he
exercises the utmost skill and will, Muir takes no credit for himself. As
several commentators have noted, it was not ego that spurred Muir to
the tops of mountains.[3] And once he got there, he tended to be more
impressed with the mountains themselves than with his own accom-
plishments on them. Muir boasted instead of his "leave no trace" backwoods ethic: On declining to leave his name inscribed in a register book
at the summit of Whitney, Muir wrote, "I have never left my name on
any mountain, rock, or tree in any wilderness I have explored or passed
through."[4]

And yet this selflessness seems contrary to what most of us think
of as motivation for climbing mountains. Yes, Mallory said, quite famously, that he tried to climb Everest "because it's there," but the un-
spoken coda, most of us would guess, is something like, "It's there, and
by God I'm going to get to the top of it!" It's a contest of man (usually)
against mountain, person versus peak. The mountain, then, plays the
role of antagonist, the hero's foil. Often it's not so innocent as a contest—it's war, with mountain as foe, the object being of course to conquer. In his classic *Scrambles Amongst the Alps,* one of many moun-

taineering books in Muir's library, Edward Whymper says after one of his seven failed attempts on the Matterhorn that he was "determined to return . . . to lay siege to the mountain until one or the other was vanquished." Clearly he had been infected with what climbers call "peak fever." When Whymper did succeed in making the first ascent of the Matterhorn, in July of 1865, he exclaimed, "the world was at our feet and the Matterhorn was conquered! Hurrah!" Unfortunately for Whymper's reputation, on the descent four of his climbing companions died in a fall. He was assailed in the English press, his egoistic desire for conquest and fame the target of a volley of blame. John Ruskin, who had much to say about the aesthetics of mountain landscapes in *Modern Painters,* questioned the whole endeavor of mountain climbing in part because he felt mountains were best appreciated from some aesthetic distance and in part because, "with less cause, it excites more vanity than any other athletic skill."[5]

The ego-driven compulsion to see mountain climbing as a kind of war culminates in Sir John Hunt's *Conquest of Everest,* an account of the first ascent of Everest. Hunt's narrative, according to Michael P. Cohen, demonstrates "how completely a mountaineering expedition can be conceived and carried out as a military campaign against Nature."[6] And yet I don't want to be entirely dismissive of the driving force of ego in making our way up a mountain. Whymper speaks of mountaineering as a means to the "development of manliness, and the evolution, under combat with difficulties, of those noble qualities of human nature— courage, patience, endurance, and fortitude." The machismo aside, these are indeed admirable traits, not much different from Maslow's list of the sources of esteem. And there is something to be gained from the effort even when we leave the mountain. Of course, in pointing out the value of these qualities off the mountain, Whymper cannot help but resort to the idea that the purpose of courage and fortitude and all that is to defeat some opponent, whether it's a mountain or life: "We know that each height, each step, must be gained by patient, laborious toil, and that wishing cannot take the place of working: we know the benefits of mutual aid—that many a difficulty must be encountered, and many an obstacle must be grappled with . . . and we come back to our daily occupations better fitted to fight the battle of life and to overcome the impediments which obstruct our paths, strengthened and cheered by the recollection of past labors and by the memories of victories gained in other fields."[7]

In the twentieth century, mountaineering has been less often characterized as contest or uphill ego trip. And yet, anyone who has climbed even a modest mountain cannot deny that we take a great deal of pride in reaching topographic tops. I want to explore the nature of that pride, but I think it is safe to reject early on the idea that we conquer the mountain by climbing it. On becoming just the second person to climb Half Dome (which he called Tissiack), Muir experienced "the rare optical phenomenon of the 'Specter of the Brocken,'" whereby his back-lit shadow, half a mile high, appeared on a carpet of clouds below. Such a display on such an occasion might have given understandable rise to some kind of superiority complex, but while still on the summit, Muir dispels any notion of climber as triumphant hero: "When a mountain is climbed it is said to be conquered—as well say a man is conquered when a fly lights on his head. Blue jays have trodden the Dome many a day; so have beetles and chipmunks, and Tissiack will hardly be more conquered, now that man is added to her list of visitors."[8]

I'm not here to conquer Shasta, then. How can we speak of conquering a mountain when it is still there, big as ever, big as life, once we leave? By the same token, Shasta has not conquered me. Because here I am.

I rent a car at the Redding airport and drive to Castle Crags State Park. My friend Sean is already there when I arrive, with a campsite picked out. We set up tents, eat some sourdough bread that I picked up at the San Francisco airport, store our food in the bear bins, then put on shorts and take off for Castle Crags. The path is wide and soft underfoot much of the way up, and the Crags are amazing—fluted rock, spires jammed together, with stunning views of Shasta to the northeast.

Sean is one of three English-professor friends who will join me on the climb of Shasta. Trained as an undergraduate in environmental science, he knows his plants well and drops names like blessings on trailside flowers. He's a strong hiker, and when he peppers me with uphill questions about what I think terms like "sustainability" and "environ-mentalism" *really* mean, I mostly grunt and pant in reply. For his half of the dialogue, among his queries Sean weaves in references to ancient Greek and postmodern philosophy, and I am feeling awed by his lively intellect as well as his conditioning. But by the time we reach the Crags, our talk has settled into comfortable conversation. Up at the Crags, we edge around granite parapets for glimpses of Shasta, a triangular white slab levitating above the horizon. I play with mental comparisons—ice-cream cone? quartz arrowhead?—before settling on the Pyramid at Gaza as the nearest visual analogue.

On the way down we discuss mountaineering literature. What I like about it, I say, is its understatement. David Roberts speaks of a "certain coldness, strikingly similar in tone . . . the coldness of competence" in mountaineering narratives. And Heinrich Harrer praises certain moun-taineering accounts for their "deliberate understatement" or their ab-sence of "uncalled-for dramatisation" or "cheap sensations."[9] Generally, there is not a lot of melodrama or profundity. Rather, mountaineers seem preoccupied with the technical aspects of the climb. They also focus less on the mountain itself than on the conditions of the moun-tain—the rock, the ice and snow, the weather. These almost seem like intermediaries between men and mountains—the technical apparatus on the one side (crampons, axes, pitons, chocks, ropes), the coverings of snow and ice and weather on the other. Even the rock is described as if it is something on the outside of the mountain, like its skin, rather than being the essence of the mountain itself. Perhaps the preoccupa-tion with technique and conditions is simply a way of diverting atten-tion from the climber's ego as motivator. But it also makes for ad-mirable understatement and an interesting tension. On one hand, we are conscious of the very real dangers and the formidable difficulties being overcome in an enterprise where the metaphoric implications about grand human strivings are very clear—and on the other hand we get details regarding route selection and bivouac sites and piton place-ment, and descriptions of snow and rock and weather conditions.

It strikes me that in Whymper's day the mountain was regarded as antagonist, while in later mountaineering writing, at least through the first half of the twentieth century, the mountain seems less a foe and more the arena where the battle takes place, or a testing ground. And the battle was fought, the contest waged, between climbers from different nations. National pride seemed to replace individual vanity as the motivation for climbers as they sought out the most difficult peaks in the Alps, and then new and harder routes to peaks that had already been climbed. The nationalistic motive remains alive today when we speak of an American team or a Japanese team making an ascent. National pride seems a motivational power much like ego, another sort of esteem-driven engine. But some mountaineering writers have been suspicious of nationalism. See, for instance, James Ramsey Ullman's *The White Tower,* a World War II novel in which an American pilot competes with a German officer to climb the Weissturm. They start out as part of an international team, with representatives from Switzerland, Austria, France, and England. The American protagonist is loyal to the others; the German antagonist is not, climbing for the greater glory of the Third Reich, and he pays with his life for the folly of his jingoism when he refuses assistance, a literal helping hand, from the American. Or consider *The White Spider,* Heinrich Harrer's account of the first attempts on the North Face of the Eiger. The plotline builds not just to Harrer's participation in the first successful ascent in 1938, but beyond it to the fulfillment of the "spiritual brotherhood" of a "European rope." To climb a mountain, suggests Harrer, we must recognize our reliance upon one another and make a commitment to one another.[10] Metaphorically at least, for Harrer the climber's essential tool is the rope, symbol of connection. For Whymper, it was the axe, symbol of assault.

And John Muir relied on some bread and tea, a notebook and pencil.

Sean says that the technical stuff and lack of philosophical depth is precisely what he does not like about mountaineering lit. He points out that a lot of early mountaineers were engineers, and he suggests that their prominence led climbers to see the mountain as a problem to be solved—a technical problem. Sean sees that bent as essentially Aristotelian. What he seeks and admires is the spiritual side of the climb, and of the mountain. The mountain as idea as well as rock and ice— the Platonic mountain.

We talk about Muir, who certainly understates dangers on his climbs. I have been toying with the idea that Muir, climbing and writing contemporaneously with Whymper, manages to anticipate the current state of the art of the mountaineering narrative, moving away from the idea of contest against the mountain to a sense of respect for it—respect that has nothing to do with any egoistic self-congratulation. Arthur Ewart, in fact, makes the claim that climbing ethics have only recently caught up to Muir's practice. He calls Muir "a climbing purist," because he approached climbing with a "certain humility" and not as "mere egotistical diversion." Ewart also calls Muir "the founding father of 'clean climbing' in this country," because he left the mountain unscarred by pitons or bolts.[11] But if mountaineering practices have caught up to Muir, mountaineering literature has not. It is true that Muir, like many contemporary mountaineering writers, avoids melodrama, at least in describing the dangers he faces, but he does so not through technical preoccupation or any understatement of his emotional responses. He simply finds being in the mountains thoroughly exhilarating. He doesn't get melodramatic because he is more exuberantly joyful than fearful. It is telling that in revising his writings Muir saw as his main task the matter of "killing . . . the *verys, intenses,* [and] *gloriouses.*"[12] Perhaps his good spirits were simply a matter of physical conditioning. His constant wandering in the mountains must have worked him into incredible shape. Maybe because of his conditioning he was able to slip beyond bodily preoccupation and exercise his spiritual self, to climb the Platonic mountain.

Sean and I arrive back at camp with the dark. We discuss important matters such as where we can find coffee in the morning, then turn in. By flashlight, I read Muir's account of his first climb of Shasta. He walked up from Redding, a two-week hike, in October, finding the mountain covered in its first snow of the year. Going up on November 1 and 2 via Avalanche Gulch, the "Muir Route" that we will follow on the mountain, he seemed conscious of the danger of the mountain: "no labyrinth of peaks and cañons I had ever been in seemed to me so dangerous as these immense slopes, bare against the sky." It was cold—"the frost was intense"—and the snow dry, and "finer particles drifted freely, rising high in the air, while the larger portions of the crystals rolled like sand." He sank in snow to his knees, sometimes up to his armpits, and at times he had to crawl upward on all fours. But the paragraph re-counting all this hardship ends with an appreciative description that dismisses the impression of suffering: "the bracing air and the sublime beauty of the snowy expanse thrilled every nerve and made absolute ex-haustion impossible. I seemed to be walking and wallowing in a cloud; but, holding steadily onward, by half-past ten o'clock I had gained the highest summit."[13]

Muir may wallow in a cloud, but he does not allow himself to wal-low in any misery about the difficulty of the climb. Neither is there a sense of conquest or triumph over hardships, as he understates the cli-max of arriving at the top. In fact, the narrative climax comes back at camp, where in the morning Muir awoke to a "boundless wilderness of storm-clouds of different degrees of ripeness . . . congregated over all the lower landscape for thousands of square miles, colored gray, and purple, and pearl, and deep-glowing white, amid which I seemed to be floating; while the great white cone of the mountain above was all aglow in the free, blazing sunshine. It seemed not so much an ocean as a *land* of clouds—undulating hill and dale, smooth purple plains, and silvery mountains of cumuli, range over range, diversified with peak and dome and hollow fully brought out in light and shade."[14]

In the lee of a boulder, Muir rode out the storm for several days, staking his blankets down and keeping a fire fed while the storm burst into "full snowy bloom." "The wind swept past in hissing floods," he says, "piling snow on snow in weariless abundance." Through it all, he describes himself contentedly "lying like a squirrel in a warm, fluffy nest," examining snow crystals with a hand lens, taking notes, and draw-ing. Down below, meanwhile, everyone had given him up for lost, and Jerome Fay, who would climb with Muir later that winter, was sent up with two horses to "rescue" Muir. In the next couple of weeks Muir climbed Black Butte, a 6,300-foot volcanic cone in the shadow of Shasta, and did a hundred-mile circumambulation of Shasta.[15]

I note the parallels between Muir's account and my climb with Peter—a November climb, amid the winter's first big storm. I'll even give us credit for being Muir-like in staying calm and finding our share of enjoyment amid the storm. But my retellings of our story usually emphasize the possible dangers, which Muir dismisses as inconsequential. I cannot help feeling that Muir got more out of his experience than we did—and not just because he got to the top before the storm arrived.

Sean and I are up at daybreak, and we head for breakfast in Mount Shasta City, a New Age haven. Like Sedona, Arizona, Shasta is reputed to be one of the sacred places of earth, where the "lay lines" of energy that supposedly circle the planet converge, making this a place of great spiritual power. Over a cheese omelet, I giggle over the Mount Shasta magazine, full of ads for self-improvement workshops on "Tachyon Energy," "Angelic Heart Healing," "Pleiadian Lightwork," "Dolphin Brain Repatterning," "DNA Activation and Clearings," "Alchemical Hypnotherapy," and "Structural Integration." Amid all this the ads for numerology life charts, astrological consultations, and aromatherapy seem downright mainstream. Of course, to remind us that we're still in America, there is also a paired offering of workshops on the "Seven Paths to Understanding" and "Using the Energy of Money." Many of the workshops are offered by various "archangels" and "ascended masters." In the advice column I read a letter from a lovelorn Libran who is convinced that he has found his soul mate—but she's a Pisces and so can't take him seriously as a life partner. The Libra is advised to listen to what she is saying and stop being so dismissive of her concerns. I mention to Sean, who is far more sympathetic to New Age ideas than I am, that my ex was a Pisces and I'm a Libra. To which he says, and do you think it's mere coincidence that you happened to see that column?

We get permits for Shasta at the ranger station, but we're not meeting our companions till late afternoon, so we head out to climb Black Butte, once known as "Muir's Peak." On the way up Sean points out the ripples in the landscape that mark the outflow limits from Shasta's eruptions in the past few millennia. Our conversation dwells again on problems of definition. Sean complains about the materialist bent of literary ecocritics, who seem to see things in nature as nature itself. He wants ecocritics to explore their assumptions—what do we mean by wilderness? Ecocentrism? Consciousness?

For my part, I am generally willing to grant scholars' assumptions about what things mean and to follow their ideological paths wherever they may lead. I also wonder if my present inquiry into the question of how nature satisfies psychological needs constitutes an attempt to justify some of ecocriticism's underlying assumptions. When people ask what I'm writing about, my glib encapsulation of my thesis goes something like this: "Nature is good, and I like it." I might add, "and it's good for us, too," but then I'd sound like a cereal commercial. Sean says, OK, you're getting close to primary assumptions—but what is nature? Is the smallpox virus inside you good? And then the classic consideration—are we part of nature, and if so, and if nature is good, is any and all human action therefore good?

My answer is that nature is the place where other living things and their habitat, and not the human-built environment, dominate the scene. We may be in that scene, but our presence is not essential there for the ecosystem to maintain itself. And I'd rather not get microscopic, I say, though I bet someone could write a fine natural history of the smallpox virus.

We also get into a discussion about a rock, and what a rock is, and what there is to say about a rock. It's not just a rock, I say, it's a rock that got there via a certain geologic means, and it has a story to tell about how it got here, if we could read the rocks right—a story in the igneous genre. It has an aesthetic story to tell as well; see how it blends with the leaning yellow flower nearby (which I can't identify), and look at how it fits with the whole geographic scene here, indicative of a certain climate and topography.

What I'm thinking amid all this discussion is that, boy, Sean sure keeps my mind on its metaphoric toes. He is like a geologic force of the intellect, raising little mountains for the mind, challenges and queries that require some adroitness, and maybe, too, something of the intellectual bulldog, in following an argument step by step through uphill terrain. With Sean, my mind is getting its exercise.

Further up Black Butte there is little vegetation, just piles and piles of loose gray and purple-tinged scree, making one big pile. My guess is that this volcanic cone is so young, in geologic time, that there simply has not been sufficient time for the rock to decompose into dirt, or for dirt to blow up from the surrounding forest and lodge in crevices to make soil. At the top, rocks are stacked to make a four-walled windscreen. Inside the enclosure, on a large, flat rock, someone has painted a yellow smiley face, two feet in diameter. I'm not sure if the spirit of the smiley face here, staring up at blue sky, is insipid degradation or inspired whimsicality. But the rock makes a good backrest while I munch gorp, swig water, and read the rest of Muir's "Near View of the High Sierra."

When Muir reached the top of Ritter he gloried in the view, looking west, north, east, and south at the surrounding mountains, seeing everywhere glaciers, streams, and canyons. At first, he says, an observer from such an "all-embracing standpoint" as Ritter is "oppressed by the incomprehensible grandeur, variety, and abundance of the mountains." But further study reveals "their far-reaching harmonies." The canyons, "however lawless and ungovernable at first sight they appear, are at length recognized as the necessary effects of causes which followed each other in harmonious sequence—Nature's poems carved on tables of stone." Muir recognized glaciers as the stylus employed by Nature in these "compositions," and he perceived the mountain landscape as a work in progress. The wilderness may look "motionless, as if the work of creation were done." But in truth, "in the midst of this outer steadfastness there is incessant motion and change" in the form of glacial scouring, avalanches, lakes, streams, all part of the "eternal flux of Nature."[16]

A couple of mysteries of Muir's prose give me pause. First is the way he manages to merge the scientific with the ecstatic. Muir's description of the landscape as viewed from the summit of Ritter emphasizes the shaping work of glaciers. In this view, he was bucking the view of the California State Geologist, Josiah Whitney, who believed the Sierra Nevada to have been created by a great cataclysm that led to a sudden subsidence of the valley floors. Whitney dismissed Muir's ideas as the rantings of "a mere sheepherder, an ignoramus." Whitney's protégé Clarence King chimed in by calling Muir an "ambitious amateur" prone to "hopeless floundering" as a geologist.[17] They were wrong, Muir was right. In fact, King's attack on Muir's geologic credentials may have stemmed from a mountaineering dispute. In *Mountaineering in the*

Sierra Nevada, King gave an account of climbing "the sharp terrible crest of [Mount] Whitney" in 1870, an account full of derring-do where honeycombed snow and a "cavernous cliff" threatened to "give the deathfall to one who had not coolness and muscular power at instant command."[18] Within a couple of years it became apparent that King had climbed the wrong peak. He returned to climb the real Mount Whitney in September of 1873, about six weeks before Muir climbed it. In his description of the area, published in the San Francisco *Daily Evening Bulletin,* Muir pointed out that Mount Langley—the peak King had mistaken for Whitney—"may easily be ascended to the very summit on horseback." Regarding the ascent of the real Whitney, Muir suggested that "travelers who dislike climbing" might prefer King's southern route over his own more daring eastern approach, which had turned King back on an earlier attempt.[19]

Perhaps Muir's uncharacteristic one-upmanship in regard to King stems from competitive mountaineering juices, or perhaps it is intended as remonstrance for King's attempt to elevate the self by exaggerating the difficulties of ascent. Or maybe he simply wanted his scientific claims to be taken seriously. What strikes me even in the exultant prose of "A Near View of the High Sierra" is that Muir's account of landscape formation is so firmly grounded in reason. In *Studies in the Sierra* he is even more careful to lay out his theories with logic as inexorable as the progress of glaciers themselves. And yet, Muir is typically regarded as one of the great mountain mystics, his climbs considered classic ascents of the transcendent. Is it simply a function of his language, rhapsodic as opposed to objective, exalted as opposed to flat, that allows the impression of mystery to persist in his mountains even when their means of coming into being are rendered apparent?

No wonder he feels exalted—to look down at the world and to come to understand the making of mountains—and to perceive the evanescence of it all. It's the outlook of a god. Which leads to my second question. From that high prospect, perceiving order amid apparent chaos, how does Muir avoid the arrogance seemingly inherent in the view from the highest point, the impression of taking dominion? Is it because he has just demonstrated his humility on the ascent, by showing that his salvation was really none of his own doing?

And now I think I've got it, the explanation for the persistence of both mystery and humility despite his position of comprehending the world from on high. What Muir comes to understand, what he dwells on, is the power of the landscape in its constant flow. It is not the human imagination, capable of taking it all in, that he celebrates, but the creative force of the world. For himself, even as he understands, he allows his mind to be boggled by it all—he allows himself to be awed.

To the west, I find Mount Eddy. To the east, Shasta. Its snowed slopes splay out like a twirling dancer's skirt. It is Muir's "snow bloom," a white blossom rooted in forest, with a short stalk of rock.

When we leave Black Butte, the smiley face looks up, positively beatific.

We meet Michael and John at the trailhead at Bunny Flat in the late afternoon. John, who is finishing up a book on volcanic mountains, has driven from Colorado, and Michael, author of *The Pathless Way*, an intellectual biography of Muir, from Reno, Nevada. Michael is the most experienced mountaineer among us, having worked as a guide in the Sierras in his younger days, but he has never climbed Shasta. Sean has been up it three times—and I of course have been on the mountain twice without setting foot anywhere near the summit. We spend an hour exchanging hellos, changing clothes, and arranging packs, then we're off. Perhaps because I've been worried about my physical performance on the mountain, I start off moving way too fast, given the altitude. Perhaps I'm trying to prove something to myself, or to my friends. My pack, full of winter gear, more than I'll need, is heavy. But the day hikes I've taken the last few weeks, and the climbs of Castle Crags and Black Butte the last couple of days, seem to have gotten me in reasonable shape. Still, as Michael points out, we are all officially middle-aged, and the snow is soft and sloppy in the late afternoon warmth. It takes us two hours to get to Horse Camp, about twice as long as we expected. The area is snow covered, but the spring is running, and we find an excellent campsite on solid ground under red firs. The evening is busy with chatter and chores—set up tents, fetch water, make hot chocolate, prepare day packs for tomorrow's climb.

John and I share a tent, and by flashlight I read aloud Muir's account of his first Shasta climb and his first encounter with a Shasta storm.

At 1:30 in the morning we hear climbers clank and crunch past our tent, flashlights bobbing. They gather in the flat, and a guide cautions them to stay together on the way up and not to worry if the pace seems slow. "We know how to get you to the top," he says. Another asks repeatedly, "Everyone had their ginkgo? Who needs ginkgo?" This seems almost surrealistic, a disembodied voice in the dark pushing ginkgo, of all things, but we find out later that because ginkgo thins blood, it can fend off the headaches that often come in the thin air of high altitude.

Winds arrive as soon as the group leaves, and the nylon of our tent crackles furiously. We get up at 4:00. I try to get my stove going, a heavy-duty mountaineering stove made for high altitude that usually roars like a welding torch. But I overprime it, or perhaps the nipple is gunked up since I haven't used it in years, and liquid gas leaks out at the valve. And of course the leaking gas catches fire, seething blue around the bottle and leaping orange a couple of feet up. I can't shut the fuel flow off because the valve is on fire. John and Sean and Michael, their voices urgent, are saying stand back, but I pick up the whole stove, flames and all, run over to the snow, and drop the stove, still burning. I heap snow on the burning valve till the flames there are snuffed, at the same time leaving the fire at the burner going. Then I bring the lit stove back to our cooking area, somewhat abashed at my difficulties. My companions are chuckling, perhaps at my stupidity for picking up the burning stove. Or is it nervous relief and they are really impressed with my courage, quick thinking, and creativity in dousing the stove? Am I gaining their esteem, or losing it?

We start walking at 5:30, later than we had hoped. Ideally, climbers should summit and be well on their way down before midday sun softens the snow, and that means starting in the wee hours, the wee-er the better. But it is not long before we realize that sun may be the least of our concerns today. The wind gusts stronger the higher we go. Ice pellets blown off the ridges sting our faces and compel us to lean low and forward. We make our way up the rise in the gulch called Spring Hill, both gravity and the airstream conspiring against our upward progress. But I feel good physically, moving steadily.

I'm thinking still about the stove, and about one of the sources of esteem we find in the mountains—the satisfaction of comprehensibility. Or to use the terminology of Rachel and Stephen Kaplan, coherence and intelligibility. In their landmark study *The Experience of Nature,* the Kaplans identify coherence and legibility, along with complexity and mystery, as the sources of our interest and satisfaction in nature. By coherence they mean the ability to make sense of a landscape; complexity refers to the variegated interest of a landscape, its plenitude of things to exercise our senses and intellects on. Legibility is the ability to read and understand the landscape, in essence to render its complexity coherent. And mystery refers to a landscape's ability to keep us intrigued because there is always more to be observed and deciphered, something presently hidden beyond the next ridge, something new to encounter in the next life zone.[20] A mountain is an especially rich environment for these appeals—complex because it has been the setting for some remarkable geologic event, and because its upward projection creates a variety of life zones; mysterious because it is, literally, on a different plane of existence (the diagonal and occasionally vertical as opposed to the horizontal), because it has so many sides to it, so many levels, and because its conditions make it the realm of the nonhuman. And yet (and here are the sources of esteem and comprehensibility) its height also provides a vantage point from which we can perceive order in the surrounding landscape, thus providing coherence. And the process by which we succeed in reaching those heights offers a kind of intellectual clarity. On a mountain, the things you must pay attention to work on a scale that is compatible with our understanding. Maybe because a mountain, at least above tree line, presents the nicely stripped-down, bare bones of an ecosystem, we can see how all the parts fit together, including the topography and weather as well as the biota. For Muir on Ritter, rising above the clutter of everyday life, even the geologic history of the Sierra became clear in his vision.

We live most of our lives in a world we do not understand, and the frightening thing is that we accept our lack of understanding. I know that there are people who understand how a TV works, or a radio, or a computer—but I don't and most people I know do not. Similarly, we don't really understand the workings of the vast social institutions that engulf us. The effect of this is a sense of helplessness. It's not just that we feel small in the face of these forces around us—we feel incompetent. Or worse, we accept our lack of understanding as the norm.

But out in the woods or on a mountain, even the technology we use is on a small enough scale that it makes sense. I melt snow to get water. I pump fuel into the tubes that lead from container to the stove. But the liquid fuel must be preheated to turn to gas, so I spill some in a little metal cup at the bottom of the stove, let it burn to heat the fuel line, then open a valve to release the gas. As it burns, the fuel line is continuously heated and turns the liquid fuel into the gas that burns at the burner. I can see how it works—just as I can see how the mountain makes its own weather, how its winds keep alpine plants low to the ground.

Of course, even knowing how a stove works, I managed to set the thing afire this morning. But at least I understood the process.

Following the contours of the gulch and the tooth marks of the crampons that have gone before us, we arrive at 50/50 Flat, halfway between base camp and Lake Helen. Gusts freshen. Each step is higher satisfaction. I know how to climb a mountain—step by step.

In *Touching the Void,* Joe Simpson talks about the repetitive pleasure of climbing—swing the ice axe, feel the chop take effect, sink crampons into the shelf you've just cut. (On Shasta, the ice axe is not needed to cut steps, but only for self-arrest in the event of a slip.) After he and his friend Simon reach the summit of Siula Grande in the Peruvian Andes, a storm hits, and then disaster when Simpson falls through a cornice and breaks his leg. Simon tries to lower him down the mountain on a rope, but when Simpson slides over a cliff and into a crevasse, his friend can't hold the weight and has to cut the rope. Left for dead, Simpson manages to crawl out of the crevasse and saves himself by, first, reducing the impossible task of returning to base camp into small, accomplishable chunks, so that he "thought only in terms of achieving predetermined aims and no further." Then he finds a new pattern of movement to adhere to: "Place the axe, lift the foot forward, brace, hop, place the axe, lift-brace-hop, place-lift-brace-hop. . . ."[21] Just as one climbs a mountain a step at a time, he descends a four-part lurch at a time.

This repetitive motion, too, is part of the satisfaction of comprehensibility. On a mountain we see how the summit can be reached. It may be hard to get there but we can see what it would take to do it. Comprehensibility is a kind of mastery, of one's own experience if not of the mountain. We may be humbled by a mountain, but we may also have an elevated sense of what we can accomplish. Mountains expose the simplicity of life—to reach a goal requires a certain number of steps. You may be tired and out of shape, the conditions may not be perfect, but you know that to get there, you will need to take those steps in order to reach the top. In *Into Thin Air* Jon Krakauer explains the appeal mountains held for him as a young man: "Achieving the summit of a mountain was tangible, immutable, concrete. The incumbent hazards lent the activity a seriousness of purpose that was sorely missing from the rest of my life."[22] We experience clear and recognizable accomplishment in climbing a mountain. There is a summit to reach, a clearly definable point at which we can claim success in our endeavor. And that is satisfying. In the rest of our lives we rarely have a sense of when we have reached some sort of summit. Isn't that, in fact, what Maslow's hierarchy is all about? Once we're well fed, we want security. Then we want love, and then esteem, which maybe we get from being promoted to vice president or associate professor, only then we want to make president or full professor, and meanwhile trying to make that happen we've let our love life go down the toilet—and we haven't even started talking about self-actualization yet, besides which, I'm famished, then after I've eaten I notice again that I need to lose a few pounds or so, or more, and now my self-esteem is sinking again.

But on mountains we actually reach the top on occasion.

Well, on some mountains some people do. For the rest of us, there is all the more mystery to savor.

Above 50/50 Flat we move out of the shadow cast by Green Butte Ridge. The sun rising above the ridge begins to shrink the shadows cast by ridge and spire lining the gulch. To the southwest we see the jumbled towers of Castle Crags. And the wind is, literally, picking up. Michael is right behind me, and we share observations of things blowing down the mountain—stuff sacks, plastic bags, a foam pad, a snow shovel—then a whole tent, poles and all. We meet a steady stream of climbers heading down, some who camped at Helen and some from the group that left Horse Camp at 1:30, made it to Lake Helen at dawn, and then turned around. They all say that the wind is even worse up there, and they all say "nobody's climbing the mountain today."

While we wait for Sean and John, I take pictures. Seen through the viewfinder, it's a beautiful day. The spires of Casaval Ridge seem etched with exquisite clarity against a sky of deep, rich, pure blue. I'm already thinking of the effect of those pictures—of people seeing them and saying, "you couldn't climb Shasta on a perfect day like that?"

And in its way it is perfect. The wind is not cold or bitter, just forceful. Giddy-making. We have the sense of being caught in something extraordinary. "Climb the mountains and get their good tidings," said Muir. "The winds will blow their own freshness into you, and the storms their energy, while cares will drop off like autumn leaves."[23] Those fresh winds are blowing away the cares of plenty of climbers today. Of course it's also blowing away their loose gear, and the climbers themselves. We get up to Helen around 9:00, and the wind is indeed even stronger there. We huddle in the rocks to snack, and then I admit what everyone else has already accepted—that we will go no higher.

"Climb the mountains and get their good tidings." Just what does Shasta, expending so much breath on us, have to say today? This morning's sermon seems a familiar one on the virtue of humility. Mountains constantly remind us of their power, constantly command respect. Actually, they don't give commands—that would mean they take some interest in our activities. They simply *require* respect, or we require it of ourselves if we don't want the mountain to kick our ass—or if we don't want to kick ourselves in the ass via the agency of the mountain. Which makes the mountain what, a giant granite boot? No, that can't be right—clearly we want to get past the *foot* of the mountain.

Forget the personification. We're not wrestling with the mountain, and we don't defeat it by arriving on top. Yes, we absolutely experience exhilaration there, the epiphany of the apex, but if there is any conquest involved, it is of some inner foe—doubt, fear, weariness. And the mountain can defeat you in so many ways—turning you back in the whiteness in which you have lost your way, sapping your strength with its steepness, sometimes killing with its cold or its thinly oxygenated air. But there I go personifying again. It's not malevolent or concerned. It's just there.

If the mountain makes us feel small and humble, and we are anything but conquerors when we make our way up it, isn't that the opposite of esteem? No—because there's pride, and self-confidence, involved in the measuring of self against the tall gauge of the mountain. The mountain may seem like a resisting force on the way uphill, or as the immovable object that cannot be overcome with our all-too-resistible force—but sometimes, by the exercise of our skill and will, the resistances can be overcome. I think of Harrer's account of the first ascent of the Eiger's North Face. Caught in an avalanche on the way up, he and his team survived only because one of his rope mates had the presence of mind to drive in a piton at the last second, hastily and loosely, and then protected it from the falling rock and ice and snow with his severely buffeted hand. "The miracle and mercy were none of nature's fashioning nor the mountain's," says Harrer, "but were the result of man's will to do the right thing even in moments of direst peril. Who can say we were merely lucky?"[24]

Harrer is making the point that the mountain is a testing ground of our character. For Harrer, climbing is about building a better self. The esteem we get on a mountain comes from mastering the appropriate skills and having the courage and fortitude to put them to use under adverse circumstances. Skill and will. He calls the North Face of the Eiger "the extreme test not only of a climber's technical ability, but of his character as well." Later he objects to the idea "that this extreme testing of oneself is the mainspring of mountaineering," but his objection is to the perception that the test is of oneself, for the most important character trait that climbing should reveal is our commitment to our companions. If the climber "thinks first of his rope mates, if he subordinates personal well-being to the common weal, then he has automatically passed the test."[25]

Like Whymper, he sees carryover value in the traits developed on the mountain: "I have no doubt whatever," he says, "about the invaluable contribution a difficult and, in the eyes of many, an incredibly dangerous climb on a mountain can make to a man's later life." He credits his experience on the Eiger with giving him "the strength, the patience, and the confidence to cope with apparently hopeless and dangerous situations" that he would encounter after the mountain.[26] (For an account of some of those situations, see *Seven Years in Tibet*, Harrer's story of his World War II escape from a British internment camp in India and his journey across the high Himalayas to Tibet, where he befriended the young Dalai Lama.)[27]

Strength, patience, and confidence are fine things, but it may be that we are more in need of learning something about the virtue of humility these days. Fortunately, the winds and storms and vertical slopes of high mountains have something to say about that as well. But I'm not sure the purpose of going to a mountain is to hear what it has to say so that we can remember the lesson when we return home. Perhaps down there, in the horizontal realm, is where we do our homework, mere preparation for the real test. Up here is where we put into practice what we have learned about life, and about ourselves.

On the way down, wind at our backs now, I ask Michael how we get esteem from climbing mountains. He dismisses the conquest idea, though he speaks respectfully of how that had motivated an earlier generation of climbers. He says climbing is a craft, and we get satisfaction from doing it well. And the satisfaction is at its peak not after having done the climb, but in the doing of the climb. I mention the idea that we gain esteem by climbing because the mountain offers a clearly defined goal—but one that is hard to reach. To accomplish the goal you have to overcome fatigue and your own physical limitations. I'm also thinking, and the mountain has to let you. There are times when the utmost will and skill will not be sufficient. Maybe the goal then has to be in finding satisfaction anyway.

Michael says of course you like to get to the top—that's what all the work is for.

Now that the wind is more aid than hindrance to our progress—or regress—or retreat—I wonder if it has actually let up, if we should turn around and head back up. But then Michael shows us his pants pockets, full of ice and snow blown in from the wind following us, ushering us down. Besides, it is too late to try to summit now. The sun has softened the snow sufficiently that we seek out rock outcrops to walk on. We're back at camp by 10:30 and discuss our options. Nobody else feels like hanging around, baking in the sun, in order to try again the next day. Sean suggests that we drive down to Mount Lassen and climb that as our consolation prize. Lassen's about four thousand feet shy of Shasta, but it does have more active volcanic vents.

Everybody's cheerful, happy with each other's company and our morning walk in the face of the wind. I'm the only one expressing any disappointment, but I'm pleased to be among friends and already I'm looking forward to Lassen. We're packed up and on the trail an hour later, back at the cars by early afternoon.

But once again I have not gotten to the top of Shasta. Strike three. Am I merely unlucky? Lacking in skill or will? Or just readily receptive to the mountain's message about the virtue of humility?

At least we were turned back by what one ranger said were the strongest winds he had ever seen at Lake Helen—sixty miles per hour. What I will not get from this failed attempt is esteem in the eyes of others from stories of my mountain conquest, but that should have nothing to do with my self-esteem. I did my best, and I enjoyed myself. I tried to follow Muir, if not up the mountain, at least in terms of finding beauty in extreme conditions.

In town we eat at a Mexican restaurant, then John gives us a tour of Mount Shasta City's spiritual-mending boutiques, which he has visited often while researching his book on "Volcanoes and our Inner Lives." In the Soul Therapy Center, I lift from a shelf a contraption like a long dangly earring with gemstones and crystals hanging on a copper-wound wire. Lo, it's a "Sacred Geometric Vajra," also known as an "Etheric Weaver." Neither name enlightens me as to its purpose. A woman named Life or something—one of the resident New Agers that

John calls "Shastafarians"—comes over to help. She holds the doodad about a foot over my open palm and it swings in hovering rings that are slow to diminish. Supposedly it is responding to some sort of spirit energy, but I'm never quite clear just what the swinging is supposed to indicate about that energy, and I suspect that the woman is doing some minute twirling where she holds it pinched above my palm. In another room, we see a pyramid-shaped framework made out of what looks like white PVC pipe. It's an "Ascension Meditation System," about the size of a bed, made out of painted copper. The idea, I gather, is to lie inside and absorb the spiritual benefits of "pyramid power." I think of the volcanic cone of Shasta and all the stories John has told us about mysterious civilizations inside the mountain—like the white-robed Lemurians who live in golden chambers, or the Yaktayvians, whose exquisite giant bells can sometimes be heard on the slopes of the mountain. One legend has it that the lost continent of Atlantis is inside Shasta.[28] To lie inside the pyramid, then, would be to place oneself in the beautiful and peaceful realm of one of these mystical peoples.

In the "I Am" Reading Room, we are invited into the inner sanctum of the Violet Room, where we sit on hard-backed chairs facing a light with a revolving purple lampshade. We are supposed to feel energized, but I for one get downright sleepy. Still, when we leave the woman is delighted to have perceived just what we needed—even when we ourselves didn't know it.

That evening we camp at Castle Crags. We buy a bundle of wood, and I stack some in the stone fireplace and douse it with stove fuel. Too much fuel, as it turns out—a touch of the match sends flames ten feet high with an audible whoosh. But once again I emerge unscathed from my incendiary misadventures. And once again the guys are amused.

Around the fire that night, I ask Sean why he seems so willing to grant the assumptions and beliefs of New Age adherents but is so keenly skeptical about the claims of philosophers and literary critics. The difference, he says, is that critics are playing the game of rationality, and the rules of that game—the very foundation of it—involve disputation as a means of honing arguments and arriving at truth. But faith is another matter.

I fall asleep thinking of Shasta and the pyramid in the Soul Therapy

Center. The spiritual seeker wanting to enter the mountain, the mountaineer wanting to stand on top of it—are both looking for the same thing? If that thing at the heart of the mountain is inner peace, then maybe there is a kind of logic to seeking inside the mountain. But my sympathies remain with the mountaineer. Peace, I hope, is not hidden in some place we only hear or dream about, a mystical place buried under real rock; it's in a high place that may be hard to get to but is still part of this world. The path to understanding calls upon our inner resources, but it leads upslope in the physical world.

But that night I dream Shasta is a giant bell swaying in the wind.

Next morning we wake and eat and pack, then say good-bye to John, who is heading up the Oregon coast to camp with his wife. The rest of us drive south and east to Lassen. The trail begins at about eight thousand feet, angles up through snowfields and then onto volcanic dust and dirt and rock. Lots of switchbacks and columns of weirdly eroded and sculpted rock. Signs along the trail inform us that Lassen erupted over 150 times in 1914–15. It's a "plug dome" volcano, meaning that the top was plugged and extruded lava pushed up the summit and then spilled out under it.

We encounter some wind going up, but nothing like what we experienced on Shasta. At around ten thousand feet Sean gets energized and talks up a storm, including a rambling description of Emily Dickinson in climbing regalia and her Mazamas mountain club membership card—but no hat, which is unnecessary since "everything reflects off her." I'm entertained, but still mulling over Muir's first experience on Shasta. Interesting that the climax of the essay is not the summit—the top is not anticlimactic but preclimactic. This is actually typical of some classic mountaineering texts. In Thoreau's "Ktaadn," it is his description of the Burnt Lands after he descends from the Table Land of Katahdin that sparks his most elevated rhetoric—directed at "vast, Titanic, inhuman Nature," where he yearns for "Contact! Contact!" with "rocks, trees, wind on our cheeks! the *solid* earth! the *actual* world!"[29] In Simpson's *Touching the Void*, the accident that gives rise to the most dramatic action comes amid a storm during the descent of Siula

Grande. Similarly, Krakauer's *Into Thin Air* climaxes not at the summit of Everest, but during the storm that strikes on the descent, stranding climbers between the summit ridge and their high camp, and on the South Col within a thousand feet of camp. Perhaps this pattern of deflating the apparent climax is in the vein of understatement that I find typical of mountaineering accounts. Perhaps it is a narrative strategy, to keep the rising action of the plot moving beyond the expected apogee. Or perhaps it is because climbers are typically just too damn tired at the top to get very excited. Harrer on reaching the top of the Eiger addresses the question of what he and his companions felt at the moment of victory: "Joy, relief, tumultuous triumph? Not a bit of it," he says. "Our release had come too suddenly, our minds and nerves were too dulled, our bodies too utterly weary to permit of any violent emotion."[30]

Like Krakauer on Everest and Simpson on Siula Grande, for Muir, too, the climax is a storm, which he finds exciting rather than threatening. So, hey, on Shasta we simply experienced the usual climactic event, the storm, before instead of after the summit. A premature climax.

But esteem for Muir has nothing to do with measuring himself against the mountain. Even the storm is not exciting to Muir because it is a kind of test that he survives. He does not for a moment talk about it as life threatening or even spirit challenging. Rather, he is rendered ecstatic by the storm. It is the mountain itself he is interested in, in all its moods and meteorological manifestations, not his performance on it.

So how does that qualify as esteem? Maybe again, as in our need for love and belonging, we need to look for the principle of reciprocity. The mountain has given Muir so much—see Maslow's whole hierarchy—and it ends with him esteeming the mountain, giving esteem, not just getting it. To receive "recognition, attention, importance, dignity, or appreciation" (Maslow's sources of esteem) from our exploits on the mountain, we must first bestow these upon the mountain.

And me on this trip? Is its frustration of my desires leading me to greater or lesser appreciation for Shasta? Is it taking on ever-greater importance for me? Michael says that among climbers a repeated failure to climb a certain summit usually initiates a "vendetta" against the mountain. But maybe I have to find a way to climb *with* the mountain. The wind blowing into our faces—seen in one light it was a force to struggle against. Seen in Muir light, it was the mountain coming to us.

We emerge on a shoulder of Lassen. Beyond the crumbling and still-charred rim of the summit crater we see Shasta, photogenically framed by two pillars of Lassen rock. Shasta seems to float on the horizon. I stand on a rock and hold my ice axe in midair, and Sean takes my picture from such an angle as to make it appear that the point of the axe is planted in Shasta's summit. Then I turn my head sideways and thumb my nose, and Sean moves the camera so as to place Shasta just beyond my extended and wiggling little finger. I imitate Arnold Schwarzenegger, confusing the tag lines of two separate films: "Shasta la Vista, baby. I'll be back."

The last part of Lassen's summit ridge requires some scrambling, and then we're there. We sit on purplish cleft boulders jumbled at the summit. The remains of the far rim of the caldera, partially dismantled by the 1914–15 eruptions, have left blackened, sooted, craggy rocks.

The snow is soft on our way down, and we skid and slide giddily, joking about a ranger we met earlier who was flagging the trail so people wouldn't cut new trails through the snow and cause more erosion. He expressed concern about damage "to the resource." Somehow I can't see John Muir climbing a resource.

Sean and Michael depart after our climb, and I camp at the only campground in Lassen National Park open this early in the season. I'm camped by a huge Douglas fir, sharing the site with a Steller's jay. I can hear West Sulphur Creek hissing below, some birds calling cheerfully. Eating dinner, I decide I'm officially sick of sourdough bread. And of salami and cheese. And gorp. How did Muir remain content with his Spartan menu of bread and tea for weeks at a time?

When Muir left the Shasta region almost two months after his November ascent, he visited friends near the Yuba River and had an experience later recorded in one of his most famous essays, "Wind-Storm in the Forest." He climbed a hundred-foot-tall Douglas fir to ride out the storm "like a bobolink on a reed" amid a "wild exuberance of light and motion." This exuberance captures the attitude of most of Muir's "Stormy Sermons," as Michael calls them, including his Shasta climbs.

Tom Lyon has observed that Muir believed the "primary fact of nature" to be "flow," already evident in his account of his first summer in the Sierra:

> Contemplating the lace-like fabric of streams outspread over the mountains, we are reminded that everything is flowing—going somewhere, animals and so-called lifeless rocks as well as water. Thus the snow flows fast or slow in grand beauty-making glaciers and avalanches; the air in majestic floods carrying minerals, plant leaves, seeds, spores, with streams of music and fragrance; water streams carrying rocks both in solution, and in the form of mud particles, sand, pebbles, and boulders. Rocks flow from volcanoes like water from springs, and animals flock together and flow in currents modified by stepping, leaping, gliding, flying, swimming, etc.[31]

In his Stormy Sermons Muir doesn't content himself with observations of nature's flow; he seeks it out, revels in it, finds a way to go with the flow. Wind, snow—these are elements of the flow. And reed, bobolink, man, fir, we're all fellow travelers caught up in the flow: "We all travel the milky way together, trees and men; but it never occurred to me until this storm-day, while swinging in the wind, that trees are travelers in the ordinary sense. They make many journeys, not extensive ones, it is true, but our own little journeys, away and back again, are little more than tree-wavings—many of them not so much."[32] The slopes of Shasta yesterday, then, were but a branch of the tree of my life, and I got a good ride there, even if it was just a little tree-waving. This is classic Muir, downplaying the storm and any hint of his courage in braving it, finding it all exhilarating.

The jay flaps back and forth between the ground around the picnic table and a low branch of the Doug fir. I tilt my head back to find a likely branch for storm-riding. Wouldn't it be cool to climb up there and leave my book of Muir essays a hundred feet up? If only the book could climb by itself.

Muir on that branch—it's the quintessential Muir moment. Ritter and Shasta were other branches on that tree where Muir rode out storms—where he sought out storms and immersed himself in them. From there he could perceive the flux and flow of the natural world, and could place himself within that flow; from that precarious vantage point flowed the exuberant language with which he sketched his mountains. Can it be coincidence that just before this trip I encountered a book called *Flow: The Psychology of Optimal Experience*? This is one of many works by the contemporary psychologist Mihalyi Csikszentmihalyi (say CHICK-sent-me-HIGH-ee) about those satisfying moments of total absorption in experience, where self-awareness seems to fall away and we feel at one with the world or the activity of the moment. These are experiences of exhilaration that all of us recognize, and they are the moments that serve as climactic events in all sorts of stories, including our life stories. Among the elements necessary for flow to occur, says Csikszentmihalyi, are these: "a challenging activity that requires skills"; "the merging of action and awareness," such that our "attention is completely absorbed by the activity"; "clear goals and feedback," like winning a game (or getting to the top of a mountain); "concentration on the task at hand," a concentration so intense that we momentarily forget any worries or cares not relevant to the present activity; "the paradox of control," where we feel a (sometimes surprising) capacity to handle a difficult or risky task; "the loss of self-consciousness," or "the loss of the sense of a self separate from the world around it"; and "the transformation of time," or its disappearance.[33] Think of Muir momentarily stuck on the cliff on Ritter and suddenly finding the skill to make his way up the rock—Muir on top of Ritter witness to the ancient (and yet ongoing) processes of mountain-making, perceiving how all the Sierra grandeur within his sight came to be—Muir on Shasta so caught up in the storm that he wanted to spend a week in its midst—these are high granite branches where Muir chose to put himself in the position of hanging on for dear life, bending with the wind along with all the other possessors of dear life. Muir's scientific contribution to the mountain realm was to perceive mountains as part of the dynamic flux and flow of all nature. His literary contribution was to place himself within the flow and to describe how it feels to be caught up by it all.

Muir's wild ride in the wind came at the midpoint of his winter of storms, culminating in his second Shasta trip in April and May of 1875.

Actually, he climbed the mountain twice on his second trip, once on April 28, with a party surveying the summit, then again two days later, with Jerome Fay, to take barometric measurements. Most of his account focuses on the second of these ascents, when Muir encountered more storm and peril than, perhaps, even he bargained for. Again, Muir downplays reaching the summit—"The slight weariness of ascent was soon rested away."[34]

On top Muir saw a bee, and then a storm hit—or as Muir casually puts it, the storm "began to declare itself shortly after noon." The clouds, "with delicious tones of purple and gray," were thick: "they impressed one as being lasting additions to the landscape." Then the understatement ceases: "the storm became inconceivably violent" and the temperature dropped below zero. The wind "boomed and surged amid the desolate crags," and thunder, "the most tremendously loud and appalling I ever heard, made an almost continuous roar."[35] Muir was confident he could find his way down, but his companion insisted on stopping at the volcanic vents on the summit plateau. Muir stayed with him, though he thought it a bad idea to breathe the noxious gases of the fumaroles and to let their clothes get wet.

They were caught in a whiteout, as Peter and I had been on our November climb. Only more so. Two feet of snow fell on Muir, double the amount Peter and I saw. And it did not fall gently on that night. Muir says that "the storm-blast laden with crisp, sharp snow seems to crush and bruise and stupefy with its multitude of stings." This sounds like the ice pellets we were pelted with on our climb yesterday. And yet, still, in the middle of a dire situation, Muir sees beauty. He calls the snowflakes "crisp crystal flowers," again delighting in the image of snowfall as flora, and recalls that "The touch of these snow-flowers in calm weather is infinitely gentle."[36]

Through the night Muir and his friend lay in the hot springs, broiled on the underside and frozen on top where they lay exposed to the storm. Michael Cohen suggests that Muir's "overnight bivouac became a geological excursion" recapitulating Shasta's geologic history. The cold might have reminded Muir of the work of the glaciers on the mountain, and the thunder sounded like "the fires of the old volcano . . .

breaking forth again," still engaged in building the mountain. Muir seemed to see himself as a kind of Shasta, and life itself as a volcanic process, "a fire, that now smoulders, now brightens, and may be easily quenched." His own fire and light were not to be extinguished quite yet, but clearly Muir felt some trepidation up on Shasta. And still, he claims that the pain of being simultaneously "frozen and burned" could not fully deprive him of his "capacity for enjoyment."[37]

The following day they made their way down the mountain, finding only light snow down below, until Muir arrives at the narrative climax with one of his "how beautiful" passages: "How beautiful seemed the golden sunbeams streaming through the woods between the warm brown boles of the cedars and pines! All my friends among the birds and plants seemed like *old* friends, and we felt like speaking to every one of them as we passed, as if we had been a long time away in some far, strange country." In fact, the frostbite Muir contracted on Shasta would affect his gait for the rest of his life. But that night he gazed through a bedroom window and "saw the great white Shasta cone clad in forests and clouds and bearing them loftily in the sky. Everything seemed full and radiant with the freshness and beauty and enthusiasm of youth."[38]

He had just been "[f]rozen, blistered, famished, benumbed" up there, and yet at the end of the day he is gushing with enthusiasm, holding the mountain in the highest esteem.[39]

And there I was earlier in the day thumbing my nose at Shasta.

Csikszentmihalyi equates flow with "optimal experience," which Maslow called "peak experience" and which I'll discuss further in my next chapter, on self-actualization. But the idea of flow seems relevant to the need for esteem as well. By flashlight I read Muir's "Mountain Thoughts," and I immediately find a passage that conveys the essence of the esteem Muir found in the mountains. The mountain for Muir is neither the conquered foe nor a high measuring stick by which we take vertical stock of our growth. You get as big as the world not by standing on top of it or by standing next to it, but by letting it in and by letting yourself flow out to it. "Wonderful how completely everything in wild nature fits into us, as if truly part and parent of us," he says. I admire the wordplay there, Muir riffing on Emerson's "I am part or particle of God" (in "Nature") and Thoreau's version, "part and parcel of Nature" (in "Walking").[40] Muir says nature is "part . . . of us" but also "parent of us," within us but also that which engenders us, nurtures us, raises us. "The sun shines not on us but in us. The rivers flow not past, but through us, thrilling, tingling, vibrating every fiber and cell of the substance of our bodies, making them glide and sing. The trees wave and the flowers bloom in our bodies as well as our souls, and every bird song, wind song, and tremendous storm song of the rocks in the heart of the mountains is our song, our very own, and sings our love."[41] Rapturous stuff—Muir feeling good about the world and about himself. Which makes sense, the world and the self being indistinguishable. In a letter to his friend Jeanne Carr he expressed something similar: "I'm in the woods woods woods, & they are in *me-ee-ee*."[42]

Is this mysticism? Yes, by God, of course it is. But this is getting close to the crux of the matter. Why do we feel good in nature—good about ourselves, among all other things? Is it not precisely this melding of self and world that is at the heart of both religious experience and nature writing? Over and over this theme of oneness, of merging, is repeated—perhaps by none so melodiously as John of the Mountains. And yet as I say this I know how naive it all sounds to our culturally trained ears. Oneness? Merging of self and world? More New Age woo-woo. Well, sure—but it has been the woo-woo of all the ages, hasn't it, and we just don't want to hear it. Hindus call it *moksa*, Buddhists seek it through mindfulness, Mihalyi Csikszentmihalyi calls it flow. And it is not the stuff of rationality. But this absorption of self in the world, the falling away of self-consciousness, is not the humility of finding oneself small in comparison to the mountain. And it is not some sort of diminution or loss of self. Rather, it is a kind of addition: One self plus one world makes greater oneness. It is overflow—of ecstasy, joy, rhapsodic bliss and enthusiasm and appreciation, a swelling up of the self, an expansiveness attained by glorying in the all-around, the deep breathing of taking it all in and letting it out again.

Those traits that Maslow identifies as the means by which we earn esteem—strength, confidence, achievement, and so on—all that seems a long way from this idea of mystical oneness. And yet perhaps it is the mystical connection that earns our ultimate admiration. To fit with the world we inhabit, comfortable not just in our own skin but in our surroundings—that accomplishment we would likely take over even fame and glory. For that sort of esteem must come from within. For the archer who really appreciates his bow, who knows all that it is capable of, to be one with his bow must be supremely satisfying. So, too, for the hockey player with the puck, the artist with his brush. And the climber with his mountain.

In "Mountain Thoughts" Muir spells out for us the route of access to the mystical realm. He speaks of the "Song of God" sounding all around us and of being "absorbed in the harmony." Then he lists, in some detail, the auditory "wonders" that surround us in the mountains:

> Crystals of snow, plash of small raindrops, hum of small insects, booming beetles, the jolly rattle of grasshoppers, chirping crickets, the screaming of hawks, jays, and Clark crows, the "coo-r-r-r" of cranes, the honking of geese, partridges drumming, trumpeting swans, frogs croaking, the whirring rattle of snakes, the awful enthusiasm of booming falls, the roar of cataracts, the crash and roll of thunder, earthquake shocks, the whisper of rills soothing to slumber, the piping of marmots, the bark of squirrels, the laugh of a wolf, the snorting of deer, the explosive roaring of bears, the squeak of mice, the cry of the loon—loneliest, wildest of sounds.

All this is followed by an apparent non sequitur: "One is speedily absorbed into the spiritual values of things. The body vanishes and the freed soul goes abroad."[43] But wasn't he just talking, in delighted concrete detail, about the realm of the body? Where did the comment about spiritual values come from? And the answer, of course: Things. The physical world. In the process of becoming absorbed in the things, we enter, or are absorbed by, the spiritual realm. And here, I realize too, is the way Muir's mysticism differs from that of the New Age mystics in the town of Mount Shasta. At least judging by their language, their mysticism is not grounded in the real world, or at least in its concrete, sensory details. It is too quick to enter the ethereal. What exactly is "structural integration" or "DNA activation"? I don't know. But I do know the croak of jays, the whisper of conifers, and the pelt of wind-driven snow.

Hence the appeal of storms: "Only in the roar of storms do these mighty solitudes find voice at all commensurate with their grandeur."[44] Why does Muir delight in taking all that a storm can dish out? Because that's when you really hear what the mountain has to say. And if you can absorb that, then you are taking in the mountain. You are in the storm, and the storm is in you.

Next morning I try to drive to a trailhead to hike into Bumpass Hell and its steam vents, fumaroles, and boiling mud springs. But the road to the trailhead is snowed in. So I try a hike up Brokeoff Mountain. But nobody has hiked up there yet this spring, and I can't find the trail through the snowfields on the forested lower slopes. So I drive back up to Lassen.

More Muir thoughts: What his Stormy Sermons are about, then, is letting the mountain in, storm and all. The storm, in fact, is the mountain manifesting its right of ingress. Those who seek to conquer want to be on top of the mountain, those who want to measure themselves want to be in its proximity, but—atop or beside—both are really shutting the mountain out. So, too, those who try to keep the mountain elements from touching them close. But Muir opens himself up to the elements, lets them in. And they are in him, and he is in the mountains mountains mountains.

Up on the Summit Ridge I pause at the view of Shasta again. Do I declare a vendetta, or just appreciate that Shasta delights in showing me such varied moods? Or should I have an elevated sense of my self-importance? Shasta's summit lies amid a "harmonic convergence" of the lay lines of earth, and yet the appearance of my life force seems to be sufficient to make all meteorological hell break loose up there. Assuming, that is, that hell's the abode of wind and snow.

I am hiking strong today. Yesterday with Sean and Michael, I felt like the slow poke, and it took us over three hours to reach the top. Today I'm there in half the time and feeling good. Settled in the granite semblance of an armchair, I read Muir's "An Ascent of Mount Rainier"—a mountain I did manage to get to the top of, with my friend Peter, on my first try, not long after our failed Shasta climb. Muir writes, "one is inclined to guess that, apart from the acquisition of knowledge and the exhilaration of climbing, more pleasure is to be found at the foot of mountains than on their frozen tops."[45] I peek over the top of the book at the luffed jib of Shasta. I remember Michael saying yesterday that the highlight of mountaineering was not the top but the middle ground, where the top crags may frame the scene above, but there is other stuff in the foreground—intermediate crags, boulder heaps, alpine flowers, a trail winding upward. On top, the whole landscape becomes background. Which is where Shasta is now.

But if I am trying to congratulate myself on avoiding the overrated pleasures of summits, Muir offers only so much solace. His comment on the appeal of the lower slopes of mountains is followed by this: "Doubly happy, however, is the man to whom lofty mountain-tops are within reach, for the lights that shine there illumine all that lies below." In his account of "Glenora Peak," Muir says, "It is hard to fail in reaching a mountain-top that one starts for, let the cause be what it may." Muir failed to reach Glenora on his first attempt, when his companion fell and dislocated both arms within minutes of the top.[46] But after his three ascents of Shasta, Muir seemed content with its lower slopes. He returned to the mountain four more times, in 1877, 1885, 1888, and 1898. On the 1877 trip Muir served as guide for two great botanists, America's Asa Gray and England's Sir Joseph Hooker. Afterward, he visited Lassen. From here, he undertook a series of river adventures, rowing down the Sacramento River, then the Middle Fork of the Kings (running out of food for four days there), then the Merced and the San Joaquin before visiting the Strentzel family near Martinez. There he commenced a courting of Louie Strentzel that three years later led to marriage.

I move like snowmelt down Lassen, in a state of pure delight, each turn in the descending switchbacks summoning up a synonym for delight. Rapture. Exhilaration. Ecstasy. Yes, I am even feeling some *verys*, *intenses*, and *gloriouses*. Partly I am so pleased with myself for managing a hike a day on this trip—up Castle Crags and Black Butte, to Horse Camp and Lake Helen, now Lassen twice. I have ventured out on several branches of this California tree, even if not all the way up to the top branch. Partly I'm just feeling good physically because of those hikes. Mostly it's the mountain in me.

A couple of hours later, driving through the park en route to the airport and my flight home, I stop by the outlet stream of Hat Lake, on the northeast slope of Lassen, devastated by mudslides during the eruptions of 1914–15. On a grassy bank exposed to the sun, I clean my crotch and armpits with a wet bandanna, then rinse off with water poured over my head, water so cold it makes my eyeballs ache, like when you eat ice cream too fast. I hang my bandanna, the one with the constellations in blue on a night sky background, on the branch of a whitebark pine, which in Muir's day was known as flexilis pine.[47] Equipped by evolution for dealing with heavy snowfall, the branch droops but holds under the weight of the wet bandanna.

A few days later, at home, I'm still thinking about not making it to the top of Shasta, thinking of the wind, and relating that to another topic much on my mind of late, a woman, A. I said to her before the trip that no matter what happens between us, this (meaning the beginning of a relationship) has been great—to feel excited and giddy and romantic and falling—to feel the pangs of uncertainty like some chivalric lover. It is true that this, like so many other relationships, may not keep progressing, and is not likely to arrive at the apex of marriage (and it doesn't)—but that doesn't make it worthless. Even the storms of anxiety are worth savoring, for they tell me I'm still alive inside, and still climbing.

And now, head-on, a gust of she hasn't called and stinging ice pellets of what does it mean. Pause for balance—then take another step. Up ahead, on the wind-driven plateau above the outcropping of rocks, I may need to turn around, but for now let's see how far I can get.

A few weeks later I see Sean and John and Michael at a conference. We share photos and memories of our climb, then make plans for another trip to Shasta the following May—not a vendetta exactly, but a highly motivated return visit.

5

SELF-ACTUALIZATION
Song of Bald Eagle

What a man *can* be, he *must* be. He must be true to his own nature. This need we call self-actualization.

It was found that self-actualizing people distinguished far more easily than most the fresh, concrete, and idiographic forms from the generic, abstract, and rubricized. The consequence is that they live more in the real world of nature than in the man-made mass of concepts, abstractions, expectations, beliefs, and stereotypes that most people confuse with the world.

ABRAHAM MASLOW, *Motivation and Personality*

1

JANUARY

So here is my project for this first year of the new millennium: to consider the role nature plays in the process of "self-actualization" on territory very close to home—my own nature, or piece of it, humble Bald Eagle Ridge, whose western slope I live on—while pondering our literature's greatest epic of the self, Walt Whitman's "Song of Myself." Whitman's poem has fifty-two parts, and I propose to consider them one at a time, a year of Sundays on the trail, recording my observations in the form of a weekly journal. I want to put into practice the advice of Whitman's first biographer, John Burroughs: "The walk you take today through the fields and woods, or along the river-bank, is the walk you should take to-morrow, and next day, and next." And to heed Thoreau's advice as well: "Books should be read as deliberately and reservedly as they were written." Whitman's "Song of Myself" went through many revisions after it first appeared, untitled, in the first edition of *Leaves of Grass* in 1855. It was "A Poem of Walt Whitman, an American" in the second edition (1856), then "Walt Whitman" by the third edition (1860). The division into fifty-two sections, or "chants" as Malcolm Cowley calls them, was introduced in 1867, and the poem became "Song of Myself" only in 1881. Along the way, the poem itself was constantly being expanded, reshaped, and tinkered with.[1] I won't take quite that long to read "Song," but still I intend to progress at the deliberate and leisurely pace of a chant a week.

Why consider the poem Whitman's Song of Self-Actualization? Because in it Whitman, or at least his persona Walt, exemplifies the traits Maslow identifies as the marks of the self-actualized. In addition to feeling "physical contentment" and "safety, peace, security," a sense of "belongingness" and of being "loveworthy," being comfortable in terms of "self-reliance, self-respect, self-esteem"—in other words, being satisfied in terms of physiological and safety needs and the needs for love and belonging and esteem—the self-actualized are blessed with "serenity, peace of mind, . . . kindliness, sympathy, . . . Healthy generosity, Bigness, . . . Tolerance of, interest in, and approval of individual differences . . . greater feelings of brotherhood, comradeship, brotherly love, respect for others." They are "More profoundly democratic" and demonstrate "honesty, genuineness, and straightforwardness." The self-actualized also move "toward [a] larger and larger, more and more inclusive and unitary philosophy or religion," and they are capable of an "increased perception of connections and relations; awe; . . . thrill, sensuous shock, delight, . . . [and a] sense of symmetry, rightness, suitability, or perfection." They enjoy "more transpersonal and transhuman cognitions" and the "more frequent occurrence of ecstasy, peak experiences, orgasmic emotion, exaltation, and of mystic experience."[2]

Because he thought psychological health had received less than its due in his profession, Maslow devoted much more attention to self-actualization than to the other needs, to the point of focusing an entire book on the phenomenon of "peak experiences," the cultivation of which he seemed to regard as both the sign and the goal of self-actualization.[3]

"Song of Myself" can be read as a treatise on self-actualization. Though he offers no details or explanations, Maslow includes Whitman on a list of personages whom he regards as possible cases of self-actualization—along with other literary types like Ben Franklin, Ralph Waldo Emerson, Frederick Douglass, and John Muir.[4] Why go to the mountain to read Whitman's "Song"? In large part because the poem is about Walt being "true to his own nature" and "living in the real world of nature"—and about the conflation of those two natures. Partly, too, in order to follow Whitman's own recommendation about how to read his poems. He wanted *Leaves of Grass* published as a pocket book "to induce people to take me along with them and read me in the open air: I am nearly always successful with the reader in the open air."[5] I propose to consult "Song of Myself" as a trail guide on the way to peak experience, or as a poetic cairn marking the upward path.

My route up Bald Eagle Ridge follows old logging roads and jeep trails up around a wooded knob, along the ridge (with views of Tussey Ridge, Mount Nittany, Happy Valley, and Beaver Stadium) to a flat, open spot, then back down. Along the way I cross a narrow stream three times and pass through hemlocks, rhododendron, laurel, oak, hickory, maple, past blackberry bushes, wild grapes, blueberries. The whole loop, about two miles and a vertical rise of about seven hundred feet, takes about an hour and a quarter on a good day—meaning when I'm in decent shape and there's not much snow or mud or undergrowth.

On January 2, 2000, a balmy fifty degrees—this millennium seems much warmer than the last—I climb with my son, Jacy, aged nine, going on ten. He delights in the patch of ice by the relay tower, crawls across on hands and knees after he slips, laughing. Not quite halfway up we find a hollowed leaning hemlock with piles of scat pellets spilling out of it. A mystery. The pellets have obviously fallen from something that spends a lot of time up inside the hollow trunk. Something sizable— the pellets are an inch long, of a thickness somewhere between a pencil and a finger. We guess raccoon, and I find myself wishing I knew more about dung. We find a few clusters of late withering grapes fallen from trailside vines. At the top, in an open dirt area where four-wheel drives and all-terrain vehicles coming up from the east must turn around, and maybe park for the view, we play "hide-the-water-bottle."

On our way down we race on the steep parts, tugged by gravity, slipping on mud, holding hands. Near the bottom Jacy announces that there are 7,200 seconds in a hockey game.

It's a wonderful hike. Not much has happened, but thinking it over, I see that it has been quality time with my son. I'd go so far as to say it qualifies as one of Maslow's "peak experiences," where we find all our needs satisfied, when we feel satisfied with life, with ourselves. But in truth I haven't been all that conscious of my self as self. I've been focusing more on Jacy, and on the laurel and rhododendron and hemlock, and the leafless oak and black birch, and the mystery pellets. And Whitman? He starts off "Song of Myself" with the claim, "I celebrate myself, and sing myself / And what I assume you shall assume."[6] Many readers, those who don't love Whitman, find this arrogant and immediately off-putting. My defense is to point to the next line: "For every atom belonging to me as good belongs to you." He's sharing himself. And I wonder just what I have to share with the world. Maybe it's what Thoreau says, that "A writer a man writing is the scribe of all nature—he is the corn & the grass & the atmosphere writing."[7] Maybe I can be the part of Bald Eagle that is capable of pondering the mountain and recording it; maybe I can be nature appreciating itself. Too often we try to appreciate nature by distancing ourselves from it; we step back to look, to view from some aesthetic distance, and we forget that we should also be in the picture, recording from within.

Walt loafs at his ease, observing summer grass. I'm starting in winter, watching a mountain. But there is still some grass on the track up near the top, some of it still green since it has been so warm.

Walt says, "I, now thirty-seven years old in perfect health begin." I've got a few years on Walt and no longer feel in perfect health. I've got that nerve inflammation in my foot from backpacking. Tennis elbow lingering from last summer. A muscle strain in my rotator cuff from throwing the football with Jacy earlier in the day. In general, out of shape. Too much blubber on the belly—well, Walt had that, too. And my legs quiver on the uphill. Among other things I want to accomplish in this year of once-a-week hiking is to get my leg jello to set into muscle.

On the idea of being nature writing: Walt ends part 1 with "I harbor for good or bad, I permit to speak at every hazard / Nature without check with original energy." He harbors nature—it is safely at port in him. And he permits it to speak, unhindered by preconception— "Creeds and schools in abeyance." OK, I'll try that, too.

2

Out at 9:20, after muffins and juice and a quick read of the Sunday paper.

Six grouse erupt out of the rhododendron slick above the trail forks and the clearing at the first stream crossing, just before the droppings tree. The grouse took off one at a time, not in a concerted flurry, and all in different directions—most uphill, though, and only one directly over me. Several left after I stopped to look. Another one up on the ridge-top trail. The Droppings Tree, I now see, is a pine, not a hemlock. It's just off the trail at the top of the stream bank. Below, right by the side of the stream, is a hemlock, and some of its lower branches reach over to the pine—so I saw those and thought they were from the leaning tree with the droppings. Some fresh scat has been added to the pile.

Tracks of four-wheelers frozen today.

Went up the steep trail. Thought of how apt this project is—a day a week on the mountain. Nature is about a seventh part of our lives, along with the arts (for me, especially literature), sports and physical activity, family, romance, work, friends. All of these can help us meet our psychological needs, but nature gets less than its due in the lives of most of us—maybe along with the arts. Which doubly justifies this venture.

Let's see what Walt has to say today. "Houses and rooms are full of perfumes, the shelves are crowded with perfumes"—but he will not let himself be intoxicated by them. Instead he goes outside, and though "The atmosphere is not a perfume . . . It is for my mouth forever, I am in love with it" (25). This really is in large part a nature poem. Of course, that should not be surprising since Whitman considered nature both the source of poetic inspiration and the measure of its greatness. John Burroughs's *Notes on Walt Whitman, as Poet and Person* included a section on Whitman's poetic philosophy, ghost-written by Whitman himself. In this statement on the "Standard of the Natural Universal," Whitman says that poems must be measured by "the standard of absolute Nature," and that "every true work of art has arisen, primarily, out of its maker, apart from his talent of manipulation, being filled fuller than other men with this passionate affiliation and identity with Nature."[8] Is it any wonder, then, that the Poet-Persona of "Song of Myself" seeks out nature, seeks to fill himself up with it, to absorb it, become it? "I will go to the bank by the wood and become undisguised and naked," he says. "I am mad for it to be in contact with me."

Well, I'm enjoying my hike this morning, but I'm not quite achieving that level of ecstasy. Walt delights in "The smoke of my own breath. . . . My respiration and inspiration, the beating of my heart, the passing of blood and air through my lungs." The focus here is on the self, on what's happening with him—then the next line is immediately about contact with the world he inhabits: "the sniff of green leaves and dry leaves." He's taking in the wild. Then—"The sound of the belch'd words of my voice loos'd to the eddies of the wind"—giving it back.

And now I see I need to bring Walt with me on my hikes. I should have read that aloud up on top and given some of my voice to the world.

Wonderful coincidence—Walt is talking about connecting with the world, and a few lines later he's talking about reading—more of the kind of connection I want to make. Right after asking, "have you reck- on'd the earth much?" (not enough, old friend, but let's go together and reckon), he asks:

> Have you practis'd so long to learn to read?
> Have you felt so proud to get at the meaning of poems?
>
> Stop this day and night with me and you shall possess the origin of
>   all poems,
> You shall possess the good of the earth and sun, (there are millions of
>   suns left). (26)

What is the origin of all poems? The earth. And the self. But Walt does not want us to learn of earth and sun solely from his poem. He urges us to make our own direct contact:

> You shall no longer take things at second or third hand, nor look
>   through the eyes of the dead, nor feed on spectres in books,
> You shall not look through my eyes either, nor take things from me,
> You shall listen to all sides and filter them from your self.

OK, Walt, I'm listening. In your words I hear the flurried wing beats of grouse.

3

Cold, ten degrees Fahrenheit, a dusting of snow from two days ago up here on the mountain; it's mostly melted down in the valley.

In chant 3 of "Song" Whitman says, "There was never any more inception than there is now." Inception, the beginning. I assume he's talking about life:

> Urge and urge and urge
> Always the procreant urge of the world. (26)

A day like today makes a good test of our confidence in constant inception. This is not the summer season Walt seems to be in, loafing on the grass. This is mid-January. The beginning of the year, yeah, but is this not the time of year when life pulls the covers over its head, heads for a burrow, and makes itself scarce?

Well, no. Today's hike was gloriously full of encounters, much of it in the form of tracks. Unidentified bird before the hemlocks, lots of deer, and something like a small dog. Could it be fox?

The mystery of Scat Pine deepens (and so does the pile of scat), but now I'm getting more information. Lots of fresh droppings atop the snow. They seem to be dropped inside the hollow part of the trunk, then roll out. Lots of urine on the snow inside the hollow, and a trail of urine leading from the trunk to the stream bank. I see a deer print there, but this does not look like deer scat, and of course I doubt that a deer would arrange himself so his rear end was all the way back into the hollowed trunk—or that he would return there for every evacuation. I reach up inside with my hiking stick—hollow at least four feet up. So something up inside is the source of the scat. The lack of prints makes me think bird—but that has got to be one huge bird. Owl maybe? But nesting inside the trunk?

Other tracks—four-wheeler tires. Clearly these trails get active use, though I've yet to see any jeeps out here.

A tree has fallen across the steep path. I head up there, then take a side trail towards the southerly knob. Surprise a grouse, then see his tracks—three pronged, larger than I would have expected. Here's how we learn to read the wild—we see the grouse, then its tracks, and from then on we know the track as sign of grouse. Maybe we hear the flurried wing beat reverberate in memory.

So, too, with reading the alphabetic tracks of a poem. Experience helps flesh out the symbols.

I detour off the knoll-crossing path to get to the highest point of the ridge, take out *Leaves* and read section 3, chant it to the woods: "Clear and sweet is my soul, and clear and sweet is all that is not my soul." I admire Whitman's enthusiasm. I know what it is to see the world as "clear and sweet," but I have trouble feeling so celebratory about myself. Me? With all my flaws? Clear and sweet?

But it is a good thing to recite to the woods. The high point here is nothing special—just an indiscriminate part of the woods. A view to the west, to the Allegheny Front, some laurel, but mostly hues of gray and brown of vine and bark, underlain by white. Neutral tones. "I am satisfied," I read, "I see, dance, laugh, sing" (27). I speak, I see, I breathe, and I feel, at this moment, pretty darn clear and sweet. I also feel as though I am giving something to this place, these woods, packaged in the carbon dioxide of my exhalations—take them in, trees. Wait, don't they need their leaves to do that? You, mountain laurel—this verse is for you.

This section of the poem has more references to sexuality. When Walt says it is time to "go bathe and admire myself," he includes "every organ and attribute of me . . . Not an inch nor a particle of an inch is vile, and none shall be less familiar than the rest." Yes, even the naughty bits. Maslow points out that "self-actualizing people tend to be good animals, hearty in their appetites and enjoying themselves without regret or shame or apology. They seem to have a uniformly good appetite for food; they seem to sleep well; they seem to enjoy their sexual lives without unnecessary inhibition and so on for all the relatively physiological impulses." Or as Thoreau put it in regard to Whitman's poems, a little bit shocked but all in all approving, "It is as if the beasts spoke." Maslow, too, seems to be at least somewhat ambivalent about the enjoyment of hearty appetites. Elsewhere he says that "a healthy man is primarily motivated by his needs to develop and actualize his fullest potentialities and capacities. If a man has any other basic needs in any active, chronic sense, he is simply an unhealthy man."[9] So go ahead and be a good animal—just don't enjoy your hearty appetites too much. Sounds like Maslow was not wholly free of inhibitions himself. His is a halfhearted endorsement of physiological impulses.

Whitman, though, appreciates his appetites with whole heart. He bewails the dawn departure of his "loving bed-fellow" and wonders if he, Walt, should "scream at my eyes" because they cease to follow the form of his lover departing. And because they "cipher and show me to a cent, / Exactly the value of one and exactly the value of two, and which is ahead?" This is an honest song of the self, in which he yearns for a companion, yearns for sex. Amid the world's procreant urge, "always sex." Certainly there is value in going alone to these woods, into this world, seeking oneness. But we can do the math—two is greater than one.

Like Walt, I too would like to share my life. But I am also glad for the experience of reading aloud and alone to the silent woods. That, I think, will become tradition.

Looking at the scat by the pine, at the tracks of deer and grouse and jeep, at the print of my own boot soles, I hope that I am giving something of myself here, not just taking. The scat, the jeep tracks, the footprints left (and right)—not an inch nor a particle of an inch is vile.

Coming down, I see three deer, running. Rounding a bend, they lean into the turn like bicycle racers. Soon I see that their prints mark their speed. The hooves have penetrated through the snow to the frozen earth and scuffed it, leaving dramatic splashes of earth in the snow. The tracks leave the path near where it joins another. The deer crossed the second path and, I presume, climbed the bank over that one, but I lose the tracks. Have I disrupted their lives? Or given them essential practice in evasive maneuvers? I urge them on—and urge and urge.

4

Brought my cross-country skis up the mountain today. I knew it would be too steep to ski up, but I figured I'd take one of the side logging roads and go along the ridge. I get up halfway, to Mystery Scat Pine, then try the skis, but the snow, three or four inches worth, is too powdery; my skis scrape on the rocks and bring a shrieking halt to any attempt at gliding. I go a few hundred feet and turn back, leaving the skis propped up against a tree, and hike up with the aid of the poles. I go up the Knoll Trail I came down last week. Flush two grouse. See many deer tracks and about three dozen places where deer had scuffed through snow to get at ground foliage or lain down. They follow the same paths I do, it seems.

I read chant 4 of "Song" at the top of the ridge. Walt says that all the things outside ourselves—our childhood, nationality, the books we read, the company we keep, even our connections to others that may make us anxious or sad ("The real or fancied indifference of some man or woman I love"), all the stuff that's in the news—all these may influence us, me, "but they are not the Me myself" (27). The "I" may take all these in, may change as a result, but there is still an "I" that does the taking in, that is something more than the sum of all the things that influence us.

So I am not just a few inches of powder and a paperback *Leaves of Grass*. And it is not even what we do that makes up the "I," it seems. Walt describes himself as "Both in and out of the grave and watching and wondering at it." So he's part player of life, part observer? I'm the guy who hikes up Bald Eagle every week and reads poetry to the woods— and also the guy who reflects upon that, observes the practice?

I told someone, an attractive woman, over dinner this past week that I read poetry aloud in the woods. "Cool," she said, and I said, "It *is* cool." She tittered because it seemed I had inappropriately taken over the prerogative of sending compliments my own way, but I intended really to say that it was a cool thing that I had stumbled upon, as if it was something outside myself. Or maybe I wanted to appear in her eyes as the kind of guy who recites poetry to ridge tops, in which case I was seeking validation from externals and no longer doing it to give something to the world. Or for myself, the real Me myself that is defined by something other than how we're molded or seen from the outside.

None of which makes me clear about who that "Me myself" is, or who or what I am. But enough of this intellectual lint gathering from the depths of my navel. Maslow says that self-actualization involves "less projection and ego-centering" and "more reality-object-and-problem centering," and I suspect that Whitman, too, is less interested in looking exclusively inward.[10] Self-actualization is not about being absorbed in the self, but about figuring out how to allow for the self to be absorbed in the world.

Like Walt, "I witness and wait." It is early in the year.

5

Snow falling, precipitation gone sailing, flakes in full trim, tacking southeastward. About six inches on the ground, but too powdery to try skis with all those rocks underneath. I'm also realizing, though, that if it were crusty enough to keep my skis off the rocks, I wouldn't be able to handle the downhill.

See lots of deer tracks again, and a four-wheeler has been through some of the trails. Its tracks make the walking easier.

Whitman today meditating on body and soul. After all, he's the self-proclaimed poet of both, ain't he?

> I believe in you my soul, the other I am must not abase itself to you,
> And you must not abase itself to the other. (27)

It is tempting to consider the "Me myself" from chant 4 as soul, but here Walt says that no, he is body as well as soul, and the self is not restricted to one or the other.

Watching the snow, I think of the familiar association of soul with heaven, body with earth. Snow, angel stuff, brings heaven to us in parachutes of psychic rations, spiritual first aid floating down to the war zone. On my way down, the snow stops, the bank of clouds shifts, and sun streams down. That, too, is heaven-sent. I just needed the reminder of snow to appreciate all that arrives from above. Gift-wrapped water and air.

But I don't want to dissolve into the air and become all soul. Walt cautions us against devaluing the body. He asks soul to "loafe" with him on the grass, and then he and soul get it on:

> I mind how once we lay such a transparent summer morning,
> How you settled your head athwart my hips and gently turn'd over
> > upon me

And parted the shirt from my bosom-bone, and plunged your
    tongue to my bare-stript heart,
And reach'd till you felt my beard, and reach'd till you held my feet. (28)

Obviously he is remembering a human love, but the referent for the
"you" here is soul. Walt won't let us divorce soul from our natural and
physical selves, and he won't deprive soul of desire.

I realize how little I've devoted to sex in my own musings here. I
wasn't sure if it belonged with physiological needs or the need for love,
but clearly it is as much a part of all our needs as is nature. Walt goes on
to say in the next few lines, "a kelson of the creation is love," one of my
favorite lines—so much so that "Kelson" was one of the names my ex
and I had considered for our son. A kelson is the line of timbers on the
inside of a ship, above the keel—it holds things together, helps steady
the part that keeps the ship on course.

After his sexy encounter with soul, Walt seems to enter the more tra-
ditional spirit realm, where he perceives "the peace and knowledge that
pass all the argument of the earth" (I suppose here he invokes the power
of intuition), recognizes his connection to God ("the hand of God is
the promise of my own") and to other people, and sees the power and
necessity of love. But he won't let the discussion get too ethereal or abstract, returning at the end to small details of the physical world—
"leaves stiff or drooping in the fields," and "heap'd stones, elder, mullein
and pokeweed." The ordinary, the commonplace—these, too, are the
stuff of the soul.

In Walt's kosmos, the body is not the starting point in ascending any
hierarchy of needs. It is right there at the top, sharing space with the
spirit, inseparable. The earth, I think, extends at least as far as the
moon—so gravity and the tides tell us. And the sky begins at our feet.

6

FEBRUARY

I said to Walt, what is the snow, my feet scuffling through eight inches
    of it, his book in my fanny pack,
And he said, funny, I was going to ask you the same question.
I have told you about the grass, that it is democratic stuff that grows
    everywhere for everyone alike,

That it is "the flag of my disposition" made of "hopeful green stuff,"
And "the handkerchief of the Lord" and "the beautiful uncut hair of
  graves,"
By its sprouting reminding us of life's vitality
And of the miraculous in the common.
So you tell me about the snow, I wouldn't want to hog the conversa-
  tion.

I said, Walt, maybe snow is your own beard, still growing long, long
  after you've lain to rest,
Or your bleached bones, resurfacing, reminding us again of the purity that underlies dirt
(And what is dirt but another name for the earth we love?).

It is a crisp clean sheet spread out on the year's new-made bed.
But look, already, there's a wrinkle here and there, left by track of deer
  and jeep,
And the rill's familiar crease down the mountain.
By spring, I know, the restless year will have kicked the sheet clean off
  the bed.

Or I think the snow is a new-stretched canvas, and God a painter al-
  ready sketching in His annual masterpiece,
Or an account book accumulating debits and credits,
Or a blank journal page on which I write at the top of Bald Eagle, my
  hiking stick a stylus, "A DEAD WHALE OR A STOVE BOAT," because
  I've been reading Moby-Dick.
How long before those words will be covered up, or blown away, or
  melted away?
An hour? A day? Long enough to mystify or delight some passerby?
And now I think that gravestone epitaphs are also a kind of writing in
  the snow.

Maybe the snow is the white whale, meaning everything and nothing,
  nature or God or our emptiness where we struggle to see something, insist on it,
Or Frost's white spider on a white heal-all, and the "design of whiteness to appall."

Catch a snowflake on your hand, and it disappears in the act of
    catching.
It's a parable for science, perhaps, and a lesson on the ephemeral.
I think of Burns's snow falling in a river,
"A moment white, then gone forever."[11]

My snow, Walt's grass—like Melville and his whale, we wonder, "Surely
all this is not without meaning." Among the higher needs identified by
Maslow (and usually incorporated into the drive for self-actualization)
are cognitive needs, our intellectual curiosity, the desire to know and
understand the world around us. How often we look to nature for lessons on life, on the self. "Particular natural facts are symbols of particular spiritual facts," said Emerson in "Nature," outlining the transcendental method—to look closely at nature in order to learn about the
self. I suppose I could attribute the symbolic logic of Melville, Whitman, Frost, and myself to exposure to transcendentalist ideas. But the
notion predates an early nineteenth-century philosophical movement.
Shakespeare speaks of finding "tongues in trees, books in the running
brooks, / Sermons in stones." In eighteenth-century America Jonathan
Edwards in *Images or Shadows of Divine Things* read nature incessantly
as a kind of scripture. Mountains for him represented the path we take
to heaven. The way up is difficult; it is much easier to head downhill.
But once you get to the top, don't get too self-satisfied or prideful.
Lightning strikes those high places. For Edwards, nature is where we
read the mind of God, and of course he was trained to look at things
symbolically.[12] The Bible itself is full of parable, and what a preacher
does is interpret. Thus the origin of literary criticism. Some of us still
feel we are engaged in sacred work.

Maybe those who looked to nature for insight into the mind of God,
or to see what the hand of God has wrought, started a habit of mind
that persists even in those who look to nature for secular parables.[13]
Maybe we sense that out there is a reality uncorrupted by our own self-
reflection. Maybe we look to nature to perceive universal laws that per-
tain to all of life, ours included. Maybe it's a habit of mind that dates
back to our evolutionary past, when our chances of survival were enhanced by our ability to read the land. Which way did that deer go? How

can I take advantage of the topography here in order to take my prey? We are the end products of those who were most skilled at reading nature.

Maybe reading literature should be valued for requiring the exercise of the quintessential human talent of reading, interpreting, making sense of things. Surely all this is not without meaning.

I remember a backpacking trip on the Appalachian Trail in Virginia's Grayson Highlands, awaiting the zen moment of "packlessness"—that instant when you first cease to be aware of the pack on your back, which usually takes a couple of days to arrive. It involves becoming accustomed to the weight, accepting the weight, finding a rhythm that allows you to carry the weight without being conscious of the weight, and it involves a falling away from self-awareness. As long as you are focused on the self, on how you feel, you are aware of the weight.

The idea in falling away from the self is to become more fully aware of what is outside the self—in the Grayson Highlands, phenomena like wild horses reclining in a meadow, a rock outcrop chunking into the sky like a butte, fringed phacelia wearing a white crown. On Bald Eagle, silver sequins bejeweling new snow.

And of course we're talking metaphor here. The weight of the pack represents the burdens we carry in life, and the object is to carry them gracefully, to forget about the weight as burden. And of course as soon as you recognize that you have achieved "packlessness," you lose it in the moment of recognition. It's the snowflake in your hand all over again.

Maybe we indulge in this sort of extravagant symbol-reading in nature simply because there we have undistracted time at our disposal, on our hands and on our minds, and all around us, as opposed to it bossing us around in the assembly-line routines of the clock-world. And given our evolutionary propensity for making sense of things, our minds wander in that direction, reading whatever appears before us, or around us. Maybe our minds get stimulated to engage in the reading of symbols when our senses become engaged. Is it too much to say, then, that we are most fully alive in nature, where there is a greater range of sensory stimulation?

Walt's grass, my snow—both speak to the key lesson of life. The world is "hieroglyphic"—read it if you can—and "the smallest sprout" and short-lived flake alike attest that "there is really no death."

7

The woods are crackling today, with ice dripping off branches and clattering on crusty snow. I have been away for almost a week at a conference in Reno, and much weather seems to have visited while I was gone. Snow level is down—must have had some warm days. It's crusty, so it must have melted by day and solidified by night. Then an ice storm must have come yesterday, tinseling the trees, most of the tinsel falling in today's high thirties. Lots of downed branches, finger sized low on the mountain, whole thigh-thick trees up high. On the trunks and branches, the ice tubes are starting to separate from their living molds, turning from translucent to milky and falling away like shedding snakeskin.

Whitman continues on the death theme at the start of chant 7—"it is just as lucky to die" as to be born (29). Maslow speaks of the peak experience allowing us to become reconciled to death and evil in the world, to accept them as part of existence. In the peak experience, he says, "Evil itself is accepted and understood and seen in its proper place in the whole, as belonging there, as unavoidable, as necessary, and, therefore, as proper."[14] There is plenty of death brought by the ice in the woods today. And is it lucky? An acceptable and reconcilable evil? Well, the downed branches mean more sunlight getting through to sprouting stuff on the ground come spring. And I suppose ice storms have helped make these trees what they are. Take the whole "radical scheme" of this "deciduous business," as Annie Dillard calls it.[15] Think of the damage the ice storm would have caused if there were still leaves on the trees. As it is, these trees knew enough to shed their leaves just in time. And as it happens, all that decomposing leaf-stuff builds more nurturing soil. As the woods lie fallow, amid all the things falling down and dying with the season, nature constantly reaffirms life.

Walt calls "The earth good and the stars good, and their adjuncts all good." That's the kind of sentiment that makes me see "Song of Myself" as a nature poem. But he goes on to stress that he is "not an earth nor an adjunct of an earth." Rather, he is a people person, "the mate and companion of people." After a week being social, talking about ideas that matter equally to me and new acquaintances, making music into wee hours with friends I see but once or twice a year, giving more hugs and handshakes and smiles in a week than I usually dispense in a season, I think I understand. It's not that running to the woods, or walking there, is escapism. But I decide to rethink my policy of trying to go up Bald Eagle by myself whenever possible. The important thing is to go there—all the better if I can share the experience with someone, for that, too, is an experience of the self. I doubt I'll be as gregarious or as expansive as my graybeard friend, but I need not go isolato.

One line throws me in this section—a wonderful line. I "am not contain'd between my hat and boots," says Walt. So he's more than the body. But is he referring to soul, surrounding the body like an aura? I'm picturing the self as a web, lines leading out from the self like trails, connecting to friends like Mike, blowing riffs on the harmonica on "Like a Rolling Stone"—and Cindy, who walked with me up the hills outside Reno just far enough to touch a tree and scrape up enough snow for a snowball—Ann, who showed me some yoga positions in a "salute to the sun." My kids. My colleagues.

The threads of affection that connect me to all these are part of me, the part that cannot be contained between hat and boots. But surely there are also threads connecting me to the one ruffed grouse I surprised today, to the overhanging branches of berry brambles encased in ice tubes that I whacked with my hiking stick in order to knock off enough ice for the stalks to lift up a foot or two to let me under and through, to the deer whose body heat wears circles through the snow and down to the grass below where they bed down, and to the denizen of Mystery Scat Pine, still leaving fresh droppings at the foot of the hollowed-out trunk. And to Bald Eagle.

Which reminds me—saw two bald eagles at Pyramid Lake in Nevada last week.

During peak experience, says Maslow, "the whole universe is perceived as an integrated and unified whole"; we comprehend "that the universe is all of a piece and that one has a place in it—one is a part of it, one belongs in it."[16] I'm remembering the long solitary strand orb-weaver spiders sometimes shoot across trails, paths in air that they walk along in order to move from web to web, or that they send out in order to start a new one. The threads of connection stretch far.

8

A few inches of snow fell this week, followed by freezing rain, so every step crunches. I won't be surprising any creatures today. Where a thicker crust has formed, thunder's underfoot. Under the hemlocks below the road, though, the snow is still soft. The sleet must have been caught in the needles.

Ice still glazes the topside of deciduous branches, windowpane thick, substantial enough to make the twigs inside look like the ice's shadow.

Purplish arrowy fronds of sumac fruit point up, signaling aspiration.

At the top I stop crunching steps, get out "Song of Myself"—chant 8 has the first catalogue, a series of one-line vignettes representing city life—when I hear someone else's crunching approach, another human figure in blue, hatted, passing through hardwood silhouettes. He doesn't see me, and I don't call out. First person I've seen up here.

Whitman speaks of a suicide sprawled on the floor, fallen pistol nearby—a babe in its cradle, the "blab of the pave," a fistfight—an unglorified view of city life. In his accepting heart, Walt notes it all, and in the face of what is not good or beautiful, he forebears disapproval, offers sympathy (30).

I follow the path across the knoll down to its intersection with the ridge trail to find the footsteps of the man I saw pass by. Several sets of footsteps line the path, all the same size. Large. I follow them to where I usually turn down the mountain. His prints go on to the open flat spot just beyond the next rise. I follow the prints, intending to offer a greeting. My only fear is that he'll turn out to be the landowner and will view my presence as trespassing. Or that he'll be afraid of me, appearing out of the winter woods. But we have the mountain in common, the bond of our prints overlain on one another.

At the flat spot the prints turn down a track that heads down the other side, to the southeast. The man must take one path up, walk along the ridge, go down another. I like the thought of the two of us, unknown to each other, ascending the ridge from opposite sides. He must have seen my tracks up here, maybe my message in the snow a few weeks ago—"a dead whale or a stove boat." Who knows, maybe he stood in silent wonder while he watched me pass by one day.

OK, he's probably no alter ego. But he must be a kindred soul.

9

Walt moves from the city to the country, sees himself helping out with the haying, "stretch'd atop of the load," his "hair full of wisps" (30). The ripples of his empathy roll out to all the shores and regions of America.

The snow has melted off Bald Eagle. Jacy walks with me today. Just before we enter the hemlock stand, he imagines our hike as a kind of football play, and he calls the signals: "Hut-hut-HIKE!" And off we go.

Jace is curious about the pile of mystery poop by the leaning pine. And it is an amazing pile now, several inches deep, spreading out over an area about twelve square feet.

Up near the top, I compliment Jace on keeping up with me. He points out that I may have longer legs, but he has more energy. "You calling me old?" I ask. "Well," he says, "you are the one who likes to take naps on the couch."

We go to the flat where off-road vehicles come up from the other side of the mountain. I sit on a log to read about Whitman's hayride, and Jacy wanders around to check out the views. I'm thinking of Whitman's widening circles of empathy. I see my son fifty yards away and I couldn't feel more connected. I know I feel that kind of connection to nature at times, too—that I'm a part of all this, and it infuses me with joy when I take it in. It is in search of those moments that I have taken on this project of searching for myself on the slopes of Bald Eagle. But I also know that I don't feel that kind of communion with much of the human community outside my family. And I know that much of the human community finds it odd, or sadly deficient in us, that "tree-huggers" can feel such compassion for and connection to nonhuman nature. I think of someone like Thoreau, who seemed so much more capable of loving nature than of loving people. I want to believe that if we learn to love nature and care for it, that helps us do the same for others. I'm not sure which is closer to the center—that center where we love ourselves—and maybe for different people the levels or rings of love come in a different order. But I guess what I want to learn or to perceive is an art of love that doesn't stop with my boy, now walking towards me ready to play "hide-the-water-bottle," or the grouse that we flushed on the way up, or this mountain or the creek that runs down it. Let all this be the center from which the concentric rings of empathy, caring, and love emanate.

Or maybe that circle that is me is not at the center, but at some outer edge.

10

MARCH

Incredible day—seventies and sunny.

Just said goodbye to the kids. Couldn't talk them into joining me on the hike, though they wanted to play outside in the woods. I'm sitting on Bald Eagle's Bald Spot, the four-wheeler flat. In the previous two sections Walt has gone from the city (and the "blab of the pave") to the country, and now he's in wilderness, a lone hunter "Wandering amazed at my own lightness and glee," then a sailor (30). Then he's at the wedding of a trapper and a "red girl"—"his luxuriant beard and curls protected his neck, he held his bride by the hand" (31). The trapper is coarse and rough through and through, but also tender and loving.

Then Walt speaks of a runaway slave making his way north through the wild, so the wild is the path to freedom, but a hard path, and the slave is "limpy and weak," with "galls" on his body. Walt pours him a bath, gives him clean clothes, feeds him, puts him up for a week so he can recuperate.

I like the progression from city to country, building up to wilderness—but still the theme is human connection. "Ah, love, let us be true / to one another!" said Matthew Arnold. It's what Melville says, too, in the image of Queequeg and Ishmael joined by the "monkey-rope" as Queequeg clambers on the back of the whale for the purpose of inserting the blubber-hook. Says Ishmael, "this situation of mine was the precise situation of every mortal that breathes; only, in most cases, he, one way or another, has this Siamese connection with a plurality of other mortals." (Is the sin for which the men of the Pequod pay the fact that the line of connection to the nonhuman is the harpoon line, which kills as it connects?) And it's what Hawthorne says in showing us that the "unpardonable sin" is to dissociate from our kind, and E. M. Forster, too ("Only connect.").[17] The wild is a good place to set that lesson. What an ecosystem tells us is that all living things connect. And one thing that I've always liked about the woods is that when you do meet another person there, it tends to be a friendly encounter. Eyes meet, greetings are exchanged—not like the visual aversions of city streets, where we look up at second floors, or down at our feet, or at some invisible wall a few inches in front of us, or if eyes do meet, you quickly draw the blinds so nobody can see inside.

But if the wild is the appropriate setting for connection, why am I out here by myself? All I can say is that I'm ready to share.

Shorts and T-shirt feel fine today. And yet it's early March, season of big snows around here. Next week will be my last hike of the winter.

I think again of the mountain-slope pattern of a plot diagram. On the lower slopes of the narrative, the setting out, we have exposition, introducing the principal characters and the setting. Characters: me, Walt Whitman, the mountain. Setting: me, Walt Whitman, the mountain. Of course, the exposition also introduces the problem of the narrative, which goes something like this: What can we teach each other or reveal about each other, me, Walt, and the mountain?

The answer to that question will be a long time coming, but there are more immediate goals I might consider along the way. Each season can be a stage in the overall plotline, propelling the narrative onward, upward, forward. Of course, along the way I can also seek the soul of each season, which is an implicit subtext of any place-based account of the year. Have I found winter's essence? Was it the ice storm encasing branches in silver sheaths, the brambles drooping over the trail with the weight? The mystery creature holed up in the hollow of Scat Pine? The snow where I scrawled the whale-catching incantation from *Moby-Dick*? Whitman's lessons on death and connection?

Some soul-of-the-season haiku:

With his son and a book
a man climbs a mountain
in new snow

Among leafless oaks
on Bald Eagle Ridge,
a man reads poems aloud

11

A colleague shot himself a few nights ago. Who knows why, but one story is that his kids told him recently that they are getting a "new daddy," since his ex is planning to remarry. I've spent some time the last few days learning to play the Lucinda Williams song "Drunken Angel," about a friend of hers who committed suicide. Also tried writing a song of my own, the only decent part of which was the refrain:

> You didn't take your life,
> you didn't lose your life,
> you just gave it away to the wind.

He wasn't a close friend, but I'm having trouble coming to terms with the suicide, trying to make sense of it all. I'm asking not only why, but how could he. How could he do that to himself? How could he do that to his kids? To everyone who knows him? Somehow Walt's claim that "there is really no death" rings hollow right now (28). But other lines come back to me from the catalogue of chant 8:

> The suicide sprawls on the bloody floor of the bedroom,
> I witness the corpse with its dabbled hair, I note where the pistol has fallen.
>   (30)

When I'm upset, it's harder to get motivated to go walking, but that also seems to be when it does the most good.

Chant 11 of "Song" is the erotic description of the twenty-eight young men bathing, and the woman, aroused, watching behind a curtain and in her imagination caressing their bodies, her hands like water dripping down their skin. It's about physical love, and her loneliness, and these days I am coming to know more about the latter—and specifically what I'm lonely for is physical love. Say it—spell it out—SEX. But not just the sex—all kinds of intimacy. I'd like to bring a lover up here, to share it with her. But I realize that this mountain is becoming very special to me, and I wonder if I should save it for someone special, like I'd save the deepest and most intimate parts of my self.

No—this mountain is nothing I built or need to hide away because it's too personal. It is my meeting ground, where I come out from within to meet the world.

The cold—around freezing—numbs my fingers now.

I note that Walt's scene of the peeping woman uses images from nature to express sensuality. Again, the connection, I think, is in the savoring of the sensory that we most often feel in these two realms. Nature, love, and sex—these are the things that delight our senses, pure and simple. Trace words back to their roots, says Emerson, and they come from nature. We imitate its sounds, we try to encapsulate its principles in word-making zephyrs of breath, in sinuous maneuvers of rooted tongue that direct our meaningful breaths over the obstruction of teeth like quartz and loam of lip. Or maybe our language is simply lacking in abstraction in talking of nature because it is the realm of the concrete. There it is, undeniably there, defying abstraction. Does this have anything to do with an acquaintance killing himself? Maybe a walk in the woods doesn't explain why. But it explains why not. As Maslow puts it, "Peak experiences can make life worthwhile by their occasional occurrence. They give meaning to life itself. They prove it to be worthwhile. . . . I would guess that peak-experiences help to prevent suicide."[18]

Even without love in our lives, we can go to the woods to feel alive, satisfactorily so even if not always ecstatically so.

12

My first early morning hike, prebreakfast. Big excitement today! The mystery of Scat Pine is solved! A large porcupine, built like an ankylosaurus with an attitude. He (She? It?) was in the stream when I got to the pine. Built more on the horizontal than vertical, its quills splayed out sideways. Face and body black, but quills very blond at the ends— a good portion of them, not just the tips. So blond that—and this will sound weird—they looked greenish, like ferns in sunlight. There were some fallen pine boughs in the stream, and hesheit blended in very well down there.

Hesheit either didn't hear me or had no flight response and walked right up the bank towards me. I stepped back so as to be out of his way when he got up. He came up a fallen log, which explains why I didn't see tracks in the snow very often—the log was either bare or iced up most of the time. He looked almost dainty coming up, passed within a foot of my toes, and turned the corner into the opening at the front of the tree and scratched his way up the hollow.

A really big porky. And beautiful. A self-actualized porky, caught up in a peak experience where, says Maslow, "fear disappears."[19]

Whitman today describes men at work—or rather boy and man, the butcher-boy sharpening his knife, chattering and dancing "his shuffle and breakdown," the blacksmith hammering, "overhand so slow, overhand so sure," unhurried, "each man hits in his place," while Walt admires "the lithe sheer of their waists" (32).

Interesting how nature poets—I'm thinking of Gary Snyder writing about loggers, or Robinson Jeffers in regard to fishermen in "Boats in a Fog"—admire physical labor.[20] More awareness of the satisfaction of the body, I guess—and not just sexual satisfaction. They celebrate being healthy and in the open air. My porcupine—as unhurried and right in his place as Walt's blacksmith. A calm rhythm to his movements. Or maybe he's like the butcher-boy with his sharp knife—with a multitude of knives. No, more like the blacksmith. Secure in their defenses, they need no honed flight response.

It's spring. I'm on the lookout for the soul of a new season.

13

Up to Bald Spot with a friend, Scott, visiting from Reno to give a reading on "Love and the Wild" at my college. I show him Scat Pine—now Porky Pine. On the way up we talk about readings for an environmental studies class. Scott waits patiently while I read aloud and take notes.

Walt writes admiringly of a black man at work, a "picturesque giant" with "polish'd and perfect limbs" (32). But Walt says "I do not stop there," and he goes on to exult in his role as "caresser of life wherever moving," "absorbing all to myself and for this song." The black man holding the reins, oxen that "halt in the leafy shade," the ducks he startles on a "distant and day-long ramble"—all these he takes in, not just with the senses, as we "take in" a view, but with the mind, with fellow-feeling, with sympathy (33).

The ducks have "wing'd purposes," and he calls the "tufted crown intentional." Intentionality and purposefulness are not reserved for us.

Those are qualities we share with the things of the world, which in fact are not things but . . . but what? Living things? Us?

I consider that some may take offense at the lumping of "the negro" with oxen, duck, tortoise, and jay. But surely Whitman's point is not to diminish supposed "lower forms," nor to lower himself in finding commonality with all, but to exalt. Exalt all. Maslow says that during peak experience, "There is a tendency for things to become equally important rather than to be ranged in a hierarchy. . . . This same kind of total, non-comparing acceptance of everything, as if everything were equally important, holds also for the perception of people."[21] Thus the origin of Whitman's democratic spirit, rising above the prejudices and social hierarchies of his day.

Some great lines in this section—"do not call the tortoise unworthy because she is not something else." Life seems to progress at a tortoise pace sometimes—but we should love it for what it is. Remember the contest with the hare.

Another great line: "the jay in the woods never studied the gamut, yet trills pretty well to me"—the gamut meaning the musical scale. We are not superior musicians for knowing or inventing the scale, or for having a capacity for book learning—or book writing.

Listen to the jay trilling pretty well. Singing of the soul of spring? Actually that's a chickadee I hear now. Listen to the rising stream-sound of the west-born wind filtering through leafless stalks and boughs. I take it in. I give it back. I'm breathing.

14

APRIL

Walk up with Susan, a friend visiting from Maryland, talking of five-year life plans, mutual friends and acquaintances.

Crow cawing—ah-ha-ah-ah, ah-he-ah-ah-ah-ah—circling around the north end of Bald Spot, then heading southwest along the ridge.

Chant 14—this is one of those sections that convince me that "Song of Myself" is nature writing, starting with the "wild gander" flying through the night, sounding out "*Ya-honk*" (33). Walt is skilled at rendering in words the sounds of the natural world.

In moose, cat, chickadee, Walt says "I see in them and myself the same old law." Here the lesson of connection, to render his insight in ecological terms, or of oneness if you want to get zen about it. Or to put it in an American context, he extends the principle of natural law, ultimate source of our rights, says Jefferson, to all living things. I'm not sure if Walt is anticipating environmental ethics, expanding the concept of rights beyond the human to other species and to places, but he's certainly expressing the sense of life's commonality that underlies considerations of environmental ethics. The egocentric self gives way to the ecocentric. Or as Maslow says, "Normally we perceive everything as relevant to human concerns and more particularly to our own private selfish concerns. In the peak experiences, we become more detached, more objective, and are more able to perceive the world as if it were independent not only of the perceiver but even of human beings in general. The perceiver can more readily look upon nature as if it were there in itself and for itself, not simply as if it were a human playground put there for human purposes." This seems true of Walt, except for the part about becoming "detached" and "objective." He is anything but. His tactic is to perceive nature in and for itself but to include himself as part of it, or to extend the self to include nature, to remain involved and subjective even as he moves beyond self-concern. In so doing he exhibits another trait of the self-actualized amid peak experience: "moving toward the perception of unity and integration in the world," so that "dichotomies, polarities, and conflicts of life tend to be transcended or resolved."[22] One such polarity is the binary opposition of human versus nature; another is the self versus the world around us. These dissolve in Whitman's song.

"I am enamour'd of growing out-doors," says Walt, praise for the Wide World which is now dripping precipitation on this page—and Walt's. (I lift my face, await the first cool drop, the sky scattering droplets freely forever.) "Song of Myself" is a poem of growing outdoors. He admires men that "taste of the ocean or woods," whose lives are not just rooted in the outdoors but seasoned in it.

Susan points out the parallels with Snyder's "Axe-Handles" in Walt's description of mauls and of men working with tools.[23] They both sing of appropriate technology that connects us to the world rather than distances us or allows us to dissociate ourselves from it.

15

Been sick with another chest cold, and haven't been out in a week and a half.

A week ago we had an inch of snow on the ground, which melted in a day, but still—that's the stuff of winter. Today, it's in the eighties.

A vulture circled me on my way up. Supposedly they find their meals by scent, but I swear they've scoped me out visually quite a few times. They may not have great vision—though hawks and eagles do, so why not vultures?—but they must use both sight and smell.

This section is another of the great catalogues in "Song of Myself," Whitman's attempt to cram all America into his poem. But it doesn't feel cramped—it feels expansive. The long lines are litany, tracing the activities of Americans from contralto and carpenter to prostitute and bride and old and new husband. And yet, for all the length of the lines and the savoring of multitudes of details, there is something of the spirit of haiku here—each line a quick observation of the physical world, an observation without moral or aesthetic judgement, so the prostitute is as beautiful and worthy of note as the bride, and each line looks outward.

Maslow says that the peak experience is "ego-transcending, self-forgetful, egoless, unselfish . . . . more object-centered than ego-centered."[24] How, one might wonder, can a poem that announces in its very title its preoccupation with the author's self make a claim to ego-lessness? (Not that Whitman would make that claim, but I will on his behalf.) The self in Whitman's "Song" serves as the center of perceptions that radiate outward. But the self itself emanates out of that center and along those rays of perception. The boundaries of self dissolve into the space where self and world interact with and engage each other. Vision extends the self as far as the objects it takes in. At the same time the selfness of the things of the world radiates as well, and Whitman's a protophenomenologist:

> And these tend inward to me, and I tend outward to them,
> And such as it is to be of these more or less I am,
> And of these one and all I weave the song of myself. (36)

He absorbs all he sees, absorbing not just meaning noticing, but a taking in that is literal, a kind of imbibing. And in his self he flows out to all, not just in yearning, not necessarily reaching out in the sense of lending a hand, but in the active exercise of empathy. The inward warp and the outward woof—that is the essence of the weaving.

So today I am new buds all over the mountain, clouds coming in now, the spiraling vulture, the desert-colored grass emerging from a circle of rocks from an old fire pit on Bald Spot, and a plane droning over the next valley.

Another vulture just took off from a sapling nearby, wings rustling like new fabric.

Sun on the back of my neck.

All these the warp to the woof of my notes, my reading aloud, my delivery of Walt Whitman to Bald Eagle Mountain.

16

At Bald Spot. Striped maples budding on the way up via Steep Trail. Gray day after a week of rain, making up for less snow than usual this winter.

Whitman writing in place here—celebrating geographic diversity. He is southerner and Yankee, "A Kentuckian walking the vale of the Elkhorn" and "At home on Kanadian snow-shoes or up in bush" (36). He is old and young, foolish and wise, "Stuff'd with the stuff that is coarse and stuff'd with the stuff that is fine." I'm tempted to say, "as are we all," but maybe the truth is that we are not. We shut out parts of ourselves; we are exclusive in our selfness. But where we resist parts of life and experience that we don't identify with, or try to, Walt absorbs it all, takes it all on. He takes it all *in*, too, and gives it back: "Breathe the air but leave plenty after me." Maybe that should be the credo of our culture, akin to the backpacker's "Take nothing but pictures, leave nothing but footprints." We don't need to be ashamed of our place on this earth, and we can put resources to use, as long as we leave plenty for the next person. Or civilization. Or species. "Breathe the air but leave plenty for the next living thing." Maybe this is the middle ground of conservation, lying between preservation and progress.

(I remain troubled by the phrase "living thing." I don't want to reduce that which has life to a "thing." It is telling that our language doesn't have a word for the concept of something alive that does not in-volve saying "thing." We've even internalized a possibility like "liver.")

What strikes me in this section is how Walt's identification with oth-ers—other Americans, that is, from farmer to Quaker and prisoner to priest—includes an awareness of place. The section ends:

> (The moth and the fish-eggs are in their place,
> The bright suns I see and the dark suns I cannot see are in their place,
> The palpable is in its place and the impalpable in its place.)

An ecological lesson here—everything has its place—that applies to Kentuckian and Canuck, lepidopteran and roe. A transcendental lesson as well—the physical and the spiritual, too, have their place, and Walt delights in both.

The wind rustles stalks of budding bushes all around me. I straighten up from my hunch over notebook and breathe deep. The first blond grass at my feet is now knee high. Tendrils radiate from the main stalk in the form of tributaries leading to a river, but the current is re-versed—here it's a river reaching out, pushing tributaries further out. This leaf of grass has grown significantly since last week, in its space be-tween rocks in a fire ring. I'm thinking that this is a good place to write, and I'm seeing everything in its place on this Earth Day when I flash on the name of this mountain—Bald Eagle. Where there are no more bald eagles. Or so few I have yet to see one.

We have breathed the air of Bald Eagle, of the Ridge and Valley country, but we have not left plenty after us. Time for us to give back. Exhaled CO_2 inspired by a steep incline or shaped into oral utterance of poems is a start, but something more, too.

17

Hiking up with Jacy, seeking the source of our stream. To go up the mountain we take the trail that leads out of the yard and then cut through the hemlock stand. But if we stay on the trail another fifty yards we come to the stream, the lower reach of the same one we cross sev-eral times in climbing the mountain. The kids and I like to peer under rocks there, looking for red-backed salamanders (lead-backed form). The stream there is narrow enough to step across, and fast moving. It leads eventually to Bald Eagle Creek, which makes its way to the West Branch of the Susquehanna, which leads to the Susquehanna, which leads to the Chesapeake Bay.

Jacy and I bushwhack after the stream crosses the marsh at the foot of the Steep Trail. Tough crossing over fallen saplings, the aftereffect, I suppose, of the ice storm in mid-February.

And we find the source! Which is actually multiple sources in the form of several spring seeps in the woods a couple hundred vertical feet from the top. Jacy explores while I read.

Walt says his "are really the thoughts of all men in all ages and lands, they are not original with me" (37). And "If they are not just as close as they are distant they are nothing." Here I am, very different from Whitman, over a century later, in a different place, and seeing there is something in his words that fits here.

> This is the grass that grows wherever the land is and the water is,
> This the common air that bathes the globe.

Jacy and I have come up today to do stream observations. Last week we tested the water down by the house, finding it neutral in terms of acidity, with very high dissolved oxygen content. In short, a healthy stream. My well water was not so good in terms of dissolved oxygen, suggesting something consuming the oxygen—something like bacteria. So I installed a filter this week.

I'm thinking of this stream, and thoughts, and poetry. The stream has been fed by seeps and drainage all the way up the mountain. But ultimately we did find a source, the spot where the water that becomes the stream first issues from the mountain. Walt says he is not the source of his ideas—but he must be somewhere up near the top, where the flow is pure, and where it moves quickly. His poems are leaves of grass, and the water that sustains them are what—his words? The ideas that he doesn't take full credit for? Is Whitman like a channel that those words find their way down? Here I am on Bald Eagle, checking sources. Having found them, I will remind myself to drink deeper down below.

I teach Jacy a bit about haiku, then I ask him what he thinks of the Whitman I just read aloud. He says, "I don't know."

18

Gorgeous sunny day, in the sixties. High Point, the grassy knoll—a grassy spot on the ridgeline trail, higher than the Bald Spot that I think of as the top, just because it's open like a summit. But in truth the trail descends to the Bald Spot from here. A robin chir-weeking nearby. Maybe at me? Or is he celebrating the day and the season?

Last week of school this past week. And I've been stressed. Actually, more than that—outright depressed. A combination of things, among them feeling alone in the world. And the kids, whom I usually consider reason enough for my being romantically unattached, are not very fond of me these days. They prefer to be at their mom's house for now. Not much overt complaining to me, but when they talk to her on the phone they whine about wanting to be with her. When I asked them about it, they said they cannot stand me when I'm upset. In my mind, I hadn't been particularly angry with either kid in recent weeks. Maybe I've been impatient. Annoyed. Curt. Behavior learned from my father, most likely. But I don't remember ever being unable to stand him.

Their comments hurt—and I've vowed to be more patient, kind, calm. I feel as though I need to earn their love and affection back, and maybe that's not a bad thing. I wrote their words down, put the note by my bed, to remind me to do better—and of the consequences of not doing better.

So what's been making me especially stressed, depressed, impatient lately? Huge changes, none of which have made their way into my Bald Eagle journal. I guess I have not really been going up the mountain to get inside my self at all, since I've left so much of what's inside out of these pages. Suspecting dietary sources for some health concerns in our children, my ex and I have put the kids on a gluten-free diet, which is very difficult to accomplish since almost all prepackaged food has gluten somewhere in it. Gluten is in wheat, so that means no store-bought bread, muffins, or cookies, and wheat seems to be used as filler in things like sauces and frozen foods. Then a few weeks ago we pulled Jacy out of school to start homeschooling, with both me and my ex sharing the job of teaching, and it's hard to find the balance between parent and teacher, or between letting him explore his own interests and imposing some structure. By requiring certain tasks to be accomplished, I seem to have become the bad cop. Which is part of what has made me less fun to be with.

I've also been dismayed by an unsuccessful class at school. And one particularly unenthusiastic student who has made it plain how worthless she considers the subject, the class, and me. On my plotline, I am thoroughly enmeshed in the part of the narrative where complications are introduced and confronted. And down in these dumps I am further dismayed by the realization that I have nobody to talk to about it all. All I can do is take a walk and hope that, as Thoreau says in "Walking," the woods can bring me back to my senses.[25]

Oh well, let's see what Whitman has to say today. Maybe I can talk to him.

Yes, he does have something useful for me. He plays his "music strong," he says, not just to the victors, for "battles are lost in the same spirit in which they are won" (37). Yes, it is "good to gain the day," but, affirms Walt, "I also say it is good to fail."

Is it good to feel as low as I do these days? Maybe it teaches empathy, which Walt is so full of. Maybe pity. Maybe an appreciation for the time to mull over low thoughts, for they go deep.

The trip up the mountain must take us back down. And it takes mental and physical effort to go back up each time.

I'm beginning to feel like Sisyphus without a stone.

19

MAY

Been a couple of weeks—I was in England's Cotswolds for a week in there—and now it's a different world on Bald Eagle, lush and green and overgrown, with bugs and high weeds and heat and sweat to make arms and legs itch. Have to start wearing a bandanna to keep sweat out of my eyes on the uphill haul. Have I missed the change of the season by being away? Or has being away enabled me to notice the changes?

The thick undergrowth makes the mountain very different from what it was two weeks ago, and of course very different from the meadowy Cotswolds. At the same time, I was conscious there of how voyagers to America a few hundred years ago could have been reminded of home—similar looking plants and similar climate, though this is hotter in summer and colder in winter.

Let's see what Walt has to say today. More of his democratic urge: "This is the meal equally set, this the meat for natural hunger" (37). This hearty morsel of a poem—no, it's not a morsel but a multicourse banquet—is for all. And it feeds a "natural hunger," which could mean a hunger for things that come naturally to us, like the yearning for freedom and respect, but maybe, too, is the hunger for nature. From his invitation to feast, delivered to "the wicked just the same as the righteous," he says his poem is "the press of a bashful hand . . . the float and odor of hair," a kiss, "the murmur of yearning." And then there's a blend of Walt with the world—"This the far-off depth and height reflecting my own face, / This the thoughtful merge of myself and the outlet again." The distant height—of a mountain like Bald Eagle?—is a mirror of the self. And the poem is about all that that self takes in, and it is "the outlet again" of all that. He takes nature in, and he gives it back.

Again and again, I find breathing at the heart of this poem. Is that just because I'm always reading at the top, while I'm catching my breath after the uphill walk? And of course I think of the reading, too, as a kind of breathing—as inspiration is a literal breathing in.

Walt as poet is like a force of nature, having his purpose just like April showers do, or "the mica on the side of a rock." His purpose is to astonish, like "the daylight" or "the early redstart twittering through the woods." Or like this photosynthetic crescendo issuing from the slopes of Bald Eagle, the unidentified birdsong all around me, the shadow of my twitching hand on the page, something moving off in the brush.

On the way down I find an owl feather on the trail.

20

Just a few days since my last visit, so I'm not so stunned by the explosion of greenery. But still I can see that there are spots on the trail that in a few weeks will be uncomfortably high with weeds, and the striped maple saplings on the Steep Trail will be high and overhanging enough to make me stoop.

Writing this at the high point of the Steep Trail, just before the turn onto the Ridgeline Trail. Great sunny morning. Chant 20 has one of the great patches of "Song"—the "I exist as I am, that is enough" part (38-39). Walt's "foothold is tenon'd and mortis'd in granite," he says— like on a mountain, sole to rock? Go deep enough, and there is rock under all our steps.

A gray squirrel just walked within a few paces of me.

Walt is "hankering, gross, mystical, nude"—earthy, we might say. And he points out that whatever he says to us, whatever wisdom he offers, we must "offset it with [our] own / Else it were lost time listening to me." I listen, I read his words atop the ridge, and I offset Walt's Song of himself with the song of Bald Eagle.

"I wear my hat as I please indoors or out"—not subject to convention.

"I find no sweeter fat than sticks to my own bones." And why not— ain't he a man? Isn't it good to love oneself, corporeal part and all?

Walt says, "To me the converging objects of the universe perpetually flow." Matter is fluid, it seems, and time, too, which is why he can wait "ten thousand or ten million years" to come to his own. This sense that everything flows through him may sound like the epitome of ego-tripping, especially when he proclaims a few lines later, "I know I am deathless." But rather than proclaiming godlike status, Whitman is probably simply pointing out that he is made of atoms. In 1847 Whitman had enthusiastically reviewed Justus Liebig's *Chemistry in Its Application to Physiology and Agriculture,* which theorized that when an organism dies, its atoms rearrange themselves into new chemical compounds that form the basis for new life, in the process eliminating any disease that had contaminated the original organism, thus creating, in David Reynolds's words, "an ongoing resurrection and a democratic exchange of substances inherent in nature."[26] Hence Walt's earlier statement that "every atom belonging to me as good belongs to you." No wonder he can say "whether I come to my own to-day or in ten thousand or ten million years, / I can cheerfully take it now, or with equal cheerfulness I can wait." Why not—his atoms aren't going anywhere.

In pondering the flow of everything in the universe towards him, Walt writes, "All are written to me, and I must get what the writing means." This, too, takes away some of the apparent egocentrism of the passage. He doesn't claim to have written the words, or to understand them quite yet. His emphasis on the self trying to read what the world is saying does not seem so far removed from our postmodern sense that we are always involved in what we perceive, and that where we are "situated" (ethnically, economically, socially, and so on) affects what we make of the world.

Today, the world's writing seems clearer than usual. I have come back, I think, from my depression of a couple of weeks ago. The Cotswolds did me good. I'm troubled by the kids' diminished affection for me lately, but that has been a good wake-up call for me, to earn love every day with continued kindness. And to keep my damned lousy temper in check. My mantra must be, "I am holy." Maybe that's part of what Walt is getting at. Certainly Allen Ginsberg thought so in his discordant contemporary reworking of Whitman's "Song" in "Footnote to Howl," where he says everything is holy.[27] And why not—we may have in us atoms from Shakespeare, from Whitman; heck, we may have atoms from Adam, and from the eroded granite that once was part of the much higher upthrust of Bald Eagle Mountain. None of it is going anywhere. We use it for awhile, then give someone or something else a turn.

In holiness, of course, there is an awareness of the blessedness of existence. Up on Bald Eagle, I sit content.

21

Been away in the Catskills, searching for John Burroughs's Woodchuck Lodge and Slabsides with my friend David. Given Burroughs's friendship with and admiration for Whitman, we were interested to see that at Woodchuck Lodge, lilacs bloomed at the edge of the front porch and climbed the railing.

Coming up the mountain, I find weeds and grasses knee-high now in several places, waist-high on the Ridgeline Trail. This is the season of profusion—laurel coming into bloom, blackberry blossoming, some purple and white flowers spreading new petals down by the stream crossing. I surprise a quail family coming round the shoulder of the mountain onto the Ridgeline Trail. Three or four babies flail off into the woods, and the mother flies out towards me, pulling the old wounded-wing routine and squealing piteously. It all seems very Whitman-like.

For all his recognition of the role of death in life, and his acceptance, even celebration, of it, there's a springlike spilling-forth and bursting-out in Whitman, a blossoming of thick-scented words. It's the leaf of grass with swollen grain head, bursting, distributing seeds with wind-gust and breeze.

Another great section of "Song"—the "poet of the Body" as well as the Soul section, and "poet of the woman the same as the man" (39). And again, the movement of the section seems to go from human-centeredness outward to all the Earth. His is "the chant of dilation," opening up, expansiveness, encompassing all. Some beautiful nature writing here: "I am he that walks with the tender and growing night," the "mad naked summer night" he calls it, sounding like one of the Beats there (or they like him). And more, a night-song now:

> Earth of departed sunset—earth of the mountain misty-topt!
> Earth of the vitreous pour of the full moon just tinged with blue!
> . . . .
> Far-swooping elbow'd earth—rich apple blossom'd earth!
> Smile, for your lover comes.

I know I am projecting, but I cannot help feeling as though Bald Eagle's blackberry blossoms are a kind of welcoming smile from the mountain—not for me alone, but not excluding me either.

Walt's breathless celebration offers an ecstatic, empathic exchange of carbon dioxide and oxygen between writer and blackberry bush. These words are formed in its tangled image, and that of winding trail, too, bursting into blossom on this page, and this page trying to take it all in, and to give something back.

22

JUNE

Surprise another quail family on the way up—the momma not as freaked out as the one last week, but she kept my attention on her by staying fairly close to me and approaching the trail whenever another of her brood fluttered out of the brush ahead.

I pluck a leaf of grass on the Ridgeline Trail, the top foot of it, with budding grain, to use as a bookmark.

Blackberries already giving up their blossoms, leaving hard brown berries-to-be. After the flower comes the fruit.

Here Walt's "blurt" is about the sea and evil and vice and his acceptance of all. To the sea he says, "Dash me with amorous wet, I can repay you" (40). I know I'm far from the sea, but this makes me realize I should come up here in rain, as the last section reminded me to come at night—to repel no season or time of day or circumstance of the mountain.

The "influx and efflux" of the sea remind Walt to accept both sides of the equation of life:

> I am not the poet of goodness only, I do not decline to be the poet of
>   wickedness also.
> What blurt is this about virtue and about vice?

Together virtue and vice make a balance. And yet for Walt, that balance makes something wonderful, not neutral:

> The minute that comes to me over the past decillions,
> There is no better than it and now.

Now is the moment of perfect balance. And now. And now, when the breeze hisses in the trees like surf, when the sun drops thick rays through humid ninety-degree air, when the brush is high enough to block the view of the surrounding mountains, Nittany, Tussey, and the Allegheny Front, and of Happy Valley. "The wonder is always and always how there can be a mean man or an infidel." Well, I suppose I've been both myself. These are the times when I have forgotten to weigh the perfect balance of a given moment. A mountain, where one slope meets another and earth gives way to sky, is a good spot to read that scale.

23

About six P.M. Rain's on its way to Bald Spot. Rusted bottle cap by the fire pit next to my foot, my rump on a trunk. Red berries coming out on a bush along the Ridgeline Trail, and more grass stalks waist high and growing fast. Saw grouse and babies down on the path leading out of the yard.

This section is Walt's acceptance of "Reality," which he "dare not question," "Materialism first and last imbuing," and his celebration of scientists and mathematicians, the "lexicographer," chemist, and grammarian, those who work with fact and hard-and-fast rules. But of these Walt says, "I but enter by them to an area of my dwelling" (41). With his words he seeks not to represent Reality, but to penetrate it—or to represent that part of Reality that goes beyond fact or measurement or categorization. Leftover transcendentalism, I suppose.

With his "word of the modern," he seeks to add to the "Endless unfolding of words of ages" (40). All this serves as a reminder that you need not reject science to call yourself a poet, even if your purpose is far from scientific, and you need not reject facts to call yourself a mystic. But the facts are there not just to be accepted, but to be pondered and explored.

And so, too, Walt's words. I should consult a field guide to identify those red berries. But where can I find a field guide to poetry?

24

No flurries of grouse display this morning. Is their birthing season over?

Regarding Porky Pine: The porky must not be there much any more—the scat underneath is turning to light brown earth, no longer in pellet form except at the outer ring of the circle of scat. I guess the pine was just winter quarters, now visited only occasionally, if at all.

Blackberries coming out on the ridgeline—hard green pellets where the blossoms were. That small red berry, as yet unidentified—looks like poison to me for some reason. Probably the red, a warning sign.

This is another of the great sections of "Song of Myself," and it's one where we clearly see Walt celebrating the self, and indicating that he means that self to be representative, a self expanding outward in empathy to encompass all ("Through me forbidden voices"). And we see here what I take to be a pattern—the circles of empathy extend first to the downtrodden of humanity, to topics normally excluded from literature (sex, death), but the extension reaches out ultimately to the natural world. He encompasses that too, absorbs it, tries to express it. "Through me many long dumb voices"—including those who don't speak human language (41–42).

In all my previous readings of "Song of Myself" I'd thought of Whitman's concerns as America first, then humanity, and finally nature as a means of expressing those other concerns. Not so. Much of the poem celebrates life at the level of physiological needs. Walt is "Turbulent, fleshy, sensual, eating, drinking, and breeding." He says, "I believe in the flesh and the appetites," and "copulation is no more rank to me than death is." I go back to my observation that physiological needs are those we share with other living things, so what Walt celebrates is what all life has in common.

My seasonal plan seems to fit now—starting in winter, the season of death, and leading now to spring's massive upwelling of new life. Much of my trail winds through what has become high grass and weeds. Thankfully this area is not known for an abundance of ticks.

At the start of this section Walt sees himself as "a kosmos, of Manhattan the son." And now I see the logic of my centering this song-essay on Bald Eagle Mountain. It too is a cosmos, where we can see all of life, a place that takes all life unto itself.

More of Walt's celebration of the physical self: "The scent of these arm-pits aroma finer than prayer." Time to check my own.

Well, I don't think much of prayer either.

But in truth I do like the scent of my own armpits. I understand Walt here: To hate your own scent is to reject part of your self. Yes, we need to accommodate our self to the society around us at times, and the world around us too, so we should not assume that our armpit stench ought to be the object of universal worship. But alone, yes, duck your head down, lift your arm, and sniff appreciatively. Then you're on your way to loving yourself, and maybe the rest of the rank world, too.

Two spots where I see the outreach-to-nature pattern: First, the "Through me many long dumb voices" stanza, where Walt progresses from "prisoners and slaves" and "the diseas'd and despairing" to "Fog in the air, beetles rolling balls of dung." And in the ecstatic "it shall be you" stanza, beginning with Walt's human self—his blood, breasts, brains, "the spread of my own body." Then he extends the litany of all to parts of him that "shall be you." Among the items: "Firm masculine colter it shall be you." The glossary in the back of my text tells me that a colter is "an iron blade attached to the front of a plowshare" (504). So if he is colter, we are the earth. And in fact, that's what much of the rest of the stanza asserts. We are everything from "timorous pond-snipe" to "Trickling sap of maple, fibre of manly wheat" to "sweaty brooks and dews." And more:

> Winds whose soft-tickling genitals rub against me it shall be you!
> Broad muscular fields, branches of live oak, loving lounger in my
>   winding paths, it shall be you!

Was that you, Walt, brushing against my legs on the ridgeline path? This is the kind of inhalation exultation that blends ecology and zen, one saying everything is connected, the other saying we can merge with the all. We call this oneness. Maslow calls it "peak experience."

These moments don't last forever, of course. We stay on the summit only a short while, then we head back down the mountain. And Walt will retreat and advance like waves on a Long Island shore, or like the seasons.

One more line of "Song of Myself" as nature poem: "A morning-glory at my window satisfies me more than the metaphysics of books." But it's nice to have both, especially when the book gives instruction on noticing morning-glories.

25

Last day of spring. Shaded woods on the way up, thick with morning damp, a wonderful rich, rank smell. If this were fall, I'd say it is the aroma of decay, but here we are at the climax of spring, and it's the smell of what, growth? Does growth have an odor? The fragrance of life itself? The sweet smell of process? Whatever it is, it is rich and satisfying.

Laurel on ridgeline now past bloom. Berries swelling—sampled one, just one, near-ripe blueberry. Blackberries now recognizable but small and hard and not yet ready to release from the clasp of the blossom cup.

Time to look back over the last few months and think of those moments and events that can make up my spring-essence haiku. Recovering from the death of a colleague—finding the springs at the source of the stream, the springs at the source of spring—the blackberry blossoms announcing future fruit. I take a breath, deep—thank you, plants—and here's a little something for you:

Rhododendron leaves shimmer—
a man reads a poem—
breathing takes place

> Vulture's lifting wings rustle—
> raindrops plat on a page—
> warp and woof.

The stream's source—
spring seeps
high on a mountain.

> A leaf of grass
> with budding grain-head
> serves as a bookmark

Talked with a friend from Minnesota last night. She is involved in a project gathering and preserving seeds of native prairie plants—painstaking, careful, and glorious work. She says restoration is her core value. She is trying to find ways to give back to earth, taking as little as she can and eating low on the food chain, no meat or dairy. I know I've been puzzling over what I have to give back to the earth. I imbibe great draughts of air and laurel scent and the occasional blueberry—add it all up and it's a whole mountainfull of nature—and what do I give back? I read a poem to the mountain once a week?

But maybe that's enough of a gift, after inhaling deeply of life, to let it out in a burst of song. Is this pen capable of harmony? Is my life melody? And if so, what does that make the mountain? Rhythm?

Certainly Walt is one of the deep inhalers, gulping down life in large, hearty swallows. That's one of the things I admire about him—he breathes deep. And while I admire those who engage in restoration efforts, I don't believe restraint should be our guiding precept in life. Yes, I want restraints upon industry, the large-scale takers who give little or nothing back to the earth. But if your way through the woods leaves the woods as they were when you return home, then we should take in as much as we can.

First lines of the section today are about taking in and giving back:

Dazzling and tremendous how quick the sun-rise would kill me,
If I could not now and always send sun-rise out of me. (43)

A few lines later Whitman talks of his song: "With the twirl of my tongue I encompass worlds and volumes of worlds." If each breath takes in the world, his words, sung, spoken, recorded, give out all he takes in. After all, he is large, and he can spare a few worlds. This world fills us up—that's what we need to do, let it fill us up, to overflowing, so that when we open our mouths the world can issue forth again. This air we breathe is shared stuff, and plants and animals live in reciprocity.

And yet, Walt is more than his words, he says. He chides speech, for it "conceive[s] too much of articulation." For "Writing and talk do not prove me," he says. He is more than a man made of words. To Speech, he says, "I refuse putting from me what I really am, / Encompass worlds but never try to encompass me." Is he larger than a world then? That would be the height of anthropocentrism. Or is he expressing his sense that words can celebrate and sing and exult, but they cannot capture or contain—not even one man who is full of this world's delicious hot air, full of life, full of himself.

These words don't contain or circumscribe Bald Eagle, they don't even add to it. They have flowed from the mountain through me, been filtered there and likely diminished to human scale, and out my pen.

The section ends with Walt taking a brief vow of silence: "With the hush of my lips I wholly confound the skeptic." Who could believe that he can still his tongue? But the next section begins, "Now I will do nothing but listen."

More blueberries on the ridge once I start looking for them. A week from now—bonanza!

Sudden realization partway down the mountain: It is not enough to give words, no matter how many worlds they give utterance to. Walt gives himself: "Walt you contain enough, why don't you let it out then?" It's not just words he's got in him. So the question is how to give of himself. He'll start by lending an ear.

26

JULY

Summer: rising action. But I'm sick today—cold, sore throat, feeling crummy. Hard to get motivated to walk, but still the walk itself is fine once my legs get going. Still surprising lots of grouse, though no more of the wounded-wing routine. I guess the young are off on their own now.

Here is where Walt does nothing but listen. I'll try, too, from where I sit on Bald Spot.

To the left and behind is a bird, tweeting in sets of threes—onetwothree onetwothree onetwothree, first note the highest. Another species further to my left—one two onetwothreefour—again, first note the highest. Flies buzz behind and around. Bushes in front of me rustle in breeze. I sniff sniff sniff.

Lots more birds, more distant, all around. Amazing that we don't hear all that unless we listen. Walt mentions "bravuras of birds" (44). But most of his are city sounds.

Feeling lousy, I don't do justice to Walt in my reading to the mountain.

Second bird to my left now making a sound more like a trill than a distinct four-note call. But the opening one two stays the same. Or is it a different bird over there now?

Walt's focus on listening again places us in the realm of the physiological, the senses, which he is sure to include in his accrual of all to his self. For him the senses are a stream of connection, mostly to others of his species—"I hear the sound I love, the sound of the human voice." On my Bald Eagle excursions I hear too little of that, which is a comment on the state of my self these days—too disconnected from others of my kind. Though I remain eternally hopeful.

27

Fourth of July. Another day when I had trouble getting motivated to walk up here to Bald Spot, but feeling great pleasure once I'm on my way. One of the first times I'm really conscious of excitement at seeing the mountain change. Tiger lilies are blooming by the road, and rhododendrons along the stream going up to Porky Pine. And a spiky spear-shaped white plant—white round BBs blooming into snowflakes on the spearhead, half the spearhead abloom—lots of them on the south end of the Ridgeline Trail. Also blackberries ripe there—ate a couple dozen—and blueberries and huckleberries ripening by the summit approach. More coming in the next few weeks, too—have to start bringing containers so I can make the kids blueberry pancakes.

Walt talking about form and sensitivity here:

To be in any form, what is that?
Round and round we go, all of us, and ever come back thither. (45)

What is that about? Life is life, no matter what form it takes? Berry, crow, earthworm, bear?

But then he suggests we need "higher" forms. He's glad he's not a "quahaug in its callous shell," for he is aware, in his human form, of "instant conductors all over" him, so that to "feel with my fingers" makes him happy, and "To touch my person to some one else's is about as much as I can stand." So just as in the last section he celebrates sound, here he dwells on the glories of touch. Just as I've been glorying in taste—of blueberry, huckleberry (darker blue, seedier, tarter), and blackberry. Actually, I think those are really black raspberries.

And given my overlong celibacy, I think I can sympathize with what he says about the touch of body to body. Outside the pages of this journal, my love life is full of sparks going nowhere. I'm like a Fourth of July sparkler, fizzling. Or a short circuit, connections not being made even after a spark is generated.

I'm wondering if this would be a good spot to watch the fireworks show at Beaver Stadium. It would be if they had Fourth of July in December—too much brush and foliage this time of year, blocking the view of the stadium. There is only a circumscribed glimpse or two at the south end of the Ridgeline Trail.

28

Still no bonanza of the black raspberries, just a dozen or so good ones, but the blueberries are coming into their own. Brought a cup with me today. Another sunny, not humid day. Nights have been cool—into the forties last night. Still have the sniffles.

In this section Walt is ravished by touch. It reads like a rape scene. "On all sides prurient provokers" assault him, "Behaving licentious toward me, taking no denial" (45). They unbutton his clothes, and his other senses abandon him—"They bribed to swap off with touch and go and graze at the edges of me," leaving him helpless before the "red marauder" of touch.

But who are the "prurient provokers"? I take them to be in part the touching organs of others, the skin of lovers, but maybe, too, the feel of summer sun and gentle breeze caressing on the marriage bed of my cheek. Or a berry, soft and dimpled, received in my fingers, the stalk's gift, the tug of the transfer almost imperceptible.

Walt gives in:

> You villain touch! what are you doing? My breath is tight in its throat,
> Unclench your floodgates, you are too much for me. (46)

It's all very sexual, of course, and maybe this is a lustful encounter. But still the imagery remains tied to nature. The senses "graze" at the edge of his being and "stand on a headland." So he is the landscape, the senses living things.

Even if nature is just playing the role of metaphor here, it's telling. Here are the two areas where our senses operate most intensely—in sex and nature. Again I think of the scope nature gives us for the exercise of our senses—the varieties of things rubbing against us as we walk, from zephyr to weed stalk, the range of things to hear and see, some close, some distant.

Or maybe it's just the "procreant urge" we find all around us in nature—those berries I savor are seeds of the blueberry bush. And a berry is a mechanism for seed dispersal via the agency of bird or bear. Or me.

29

Deer in the hemlocks, berries on the ridge. Blackberries (black raspberries?) ripening now—nice payoff in big berries for each pluck. Some are quite tart, and I learn that if it needs to be pulled off, the berry will be sour. The ripe ones come off with the gentlest of tugs, a process of almost beckoning the berry into your fingers with a firm surrounding touch. Ah, the wonders of manual dexterity—to pick berries with enough pull to get them off (so to speak) yet not enough to squish them. Not "villain touch"—remarkable touch.

As it happens, Walt is still on the topic of touch in this chant: "Blind loving wrestling touch, sheath'd hooded sharp-tooth'd touch!" (46). And yet he's worried about it leaving him—must be the touch of a lover he's missing. He speaks of "Parting track'd by arriving," as the lover's touch comes and goes. Homoerotic imagery is evident in his description of "Landscape projected masculine, full-sized and golden." But note again how he couches sexual content in natural images. Missing his love makes him see his lover in a "masculine" landscape. And this mountain? Don't we usually think of mountains as feminine? As in *Tetons* being French for breasts? Ah, but here in spring, everything, it seems, springs to attention, like an erection. The bushes shoot up and shoot their seed in the form of berries. Whitman says, "Sprouts take and accumulate, stand by the curb prolific and vital."

He is describing nature in these lines—that is, the natural image is not metaphor but the actual thing being described. The metaphor is the idea that all this is phallic. The transition comes in the fourth line (of six) in this section: "Rich showering rain, and recompense richer afterward." There he's talking about the lover's arrival, and he's finding compensation in his departure. Maybe the rain is his tears of sorrow, but there's a richness that follows. The image, of course, evokes the seasonal cycle, and that's when he shifts to landscape description.

In midsummer on Bald Eagle, here we are in the season of richness, "perpetual payment of perpetual loan." Time to cash in a few more berries. Or deposit them into my gullet.

Remarkable how Whitman plays with the idea of gendered landscape here—not maternal, giving birth all over the place, but engorged. Emily Dickinson does that kind of landscape gender reversal too, wishing she were a boat mooring in the harbor of a lover in "Wild Nights! Wild Nights!"[28]

And of course all this bursting life is really the product of both male and female. Of course nature is erotic. No wonder our senses are so "engaged" out here.

30

AUGUST

Been humid, hot, and rainy lately. I'm out here before the heat of the day, not up to seventy yet, but humid enough to bring out a good sweat on the way up.

Recent changes—cobweblike things on the lawn. Work of spiders or a fungus of some kind? Indian pipe peeping out on the first stretch of trail. ("Chlorophyll?" they say. "We don't need no stinking chlorophyll!") I found out the name of the tall, eight-foot weed stalks with yellow-cupped buds on the top foot or so—common mullein. The white-flowered ones are, I think, black cohosh. Surprised one grouse this morning. (Where have all the others gone? Deeper into woods? Bellies of owls?) And one deer. Berries aplenty on the ridge. Discovery—the best blackberries are the smaller ripe ones, not the mondo grosso ones, which are always a bit sour and wooden tasting. The lesson? Size isn't everything? More like, appreciate the small things in life. Ten small fish may be better tasting than one big one. Maybe we learn more from 138 chipmunk sightings than one bear encounter—if we pay attention.

What does Walt have to say on the subject, or any other?

Yup, he's on target—first line of this section: "All truths wait in all things" (46). A few lines later: "The insignificant is as big to me as any." Or as Maslow puts it, "the sacred is *in* the ordinary." This, he says, is "The great lesson from the true mystics."[29]

Then Walt offers an argument against rationality:

Logic and sermons never convince,
The damp of the night drives deeper into my soul.

Maslow points out that rationality is incompatible with peak experience. To be "completely rational or 'materialistic' or mechanistic" leads one to view "peak- and transcendent experiences as a kind of insanity, a complete loss of control, a sense of being overwhelmed by irrational emotions."[30] But it's not simply letting go of reason that Whitman recommends; rather, it's a kind of coming to our senses. He celebrates not pure instinct but common sense:

> (Only what proves itself to every man and woman is so,
> Only what nobody denies is so.)

Maybe he's suggesting something closer to the original meaning of common sense, from the eighteenth-century Scottish enlightenment philosophers, whose ideas were influential in early America—that common sense is an actual sense, like sight, hearing, touch, taste, smell. So too are aesthetic appreciation and morality, and they are all allied, so that a failure to appreciate the beauty of what we take in through our senses is a moral failing—a deficiency of one's sense. Or senses.

Whitman will not neglect the common and the physical. He rejects Cartesian dualism, which divides body from soul and says that real human nature is found in the soul. Walt says, "soggy clods shall become lovers and lamps." The clod is a lamp because it brings enlightenment as surely as sunshine—or a French philosopher.

A wonderful line about a man and woman soon follows: "And a summit and flower there is the feeling they have for each other." They are mountaintop and thistle, rock and bud, mutually nourishing. Maybe, too, the material and the ethereal? There's something spiritual about a flower—its upward aspiration, its invisible essence of fragrance, its miraculous appearance amid clod and rock, springing from some seed embedded in the earth. But of course it's also material, physically there, and a mountain perhaps is equally spiritual.

Walt says of the man and woman, "And they are to branch boundlessly out of that lesson"—the lesson of the summit and flower.

I feel growing in me an awareness of Bald Eagle as habitat—for deer, grouse, porcupine, cohosh, mullein, thistle, blackberry. And at my feet where I sit on a log at the Bald Spot, leaves of grass.

I see a wood turtle on the way down, offering lessons about patience and taking your time. I lean on my walking stick and watch for ten minutes. He gradually pokes out his head, cranes upward to try to see me better. I kneel slowly to make eye contact. He has circular pupils. I hope to watch long enough to see him walk off, but he outwaits me. When I stand to go, he retreats inside. I tap on his shell and say, "I know you're in there!"

Jewelweed, bugbane, thistle, cohosh, mullein, yarrow all in bloom.

31

Got the kids to join me today. They often resist the steep climb, but I bribed them by giving them each a leaf to serve as a ticket good for one piggyback ride. Of course, along the way they started picking up other leaf "tickets," then pointed out that the trees were full of them. But they showed mercy and cashed in only a few.

Some blackberries and blueberries still on the ridge. We see three wood frogs on the way up.

Walt is again sympatico with today's observations in this great section: "I believe a leaf of grass is no less than the journey-work of the stars" (46). Everything is perfect (and yes, it is a glorious day today, sunny-clearblue sky, puffywhite clouds, seventies cool), and he mentions the "tree-toad" ("a chef-d'oeuvre for the highest") and the blackberry ("fit to "adorn the parlors of heaven"). "And a mouse," he says, "is miracle enough to stagger sextillions of infidels." Maslow speaks of a "freshening of experience" in the peak experience, when "the miraculous 'suchness' of things can break through into consciousness. This is a basic function of art."[31] That's what "Song" reminds us to do, to notice the world around us, celebrate it, become awed. Aesthetic needs are another of the higher needs (along with cognitive needs) that Maslow identified without actually integrating them into a specific slot of his hierarchy, but when he says that art is a means of achieving peak experience, the implication is that aesthetic sense is a subset of self-actualization. And nature, it seems, is not just a suitable outlet for our need for beauty, but the vehicle by which we convey the essence of the beautiful. Art can remind us to notice the miraculous in the commons of nature, but just as often nature is itself the emblem of the miraculous.

Among the miracles Walt says we should be thankful for is the "hinge in my hand," which "puts to scorn all machinery." That hinge is capable of recording what I've thought about here, and what Walt Whitman thought, too. With the gifts of memory and hinged hand and dexterous fingers, I, with Walt, can "call anything back again when I desire it"—from "plutonic rocks" to mastodon and the buzzard that "houses herself with the sky," snake, elk, auk. "I follow quickly, I ascend to the nest in the fissure of the cliff." Again, what I find so remarkable here is the prominence of nature in the poem. Here it is the substance of the whole section, and this is one of the most celebratory sections. How have we ever thought of this as anything other than a nature poem? Because he calls it "Song of Myself," and we've assumed the human status of that self as automatically separate from nature? Because we have assumed that nature must function transcendentally, as symbol (merely) of self or spirit? And that therefore it is not valued for itself? Maslow says the self-actualized "live more in the real world of nature than in the man-made world of concepts, abstractions, expectations, beliefs, and stereotypes that most people confuse with the world."[32] That real world is Walt's subject here, an absolute valuing of nature for itself and of Whitman's capacity to notice it and follow it. Of course in his noticing he frequently explores levels and layers of meaning. Is that somehow opposed to the valuing of nature in and of and for itself? I remember a student once responding to a discussion about regarding nature as a storehouse for symbol. I had suggested that to render nature as symbol is a kind of use, so again we are valuing nature for what it can supply us, as resource. Her objection was that if we take lumber from a forest, the forest is eventually gone. But if we take meaning from it, the forest is still there when we're gone.

These woods, Walt's words—still here.

32

Hike up with Jace, talking about animals—the weights of the biggest bears and of jaguars, who would win if the Chicago Bears really were bears playing against the Jacksonville Really Jaguars.

Humid and sunny. We see several daddy longlegs, two toads, a fawn, big fat ball-shaped mushroom, red-tailed hawk. We hear grouse.

And of course Walt writes about animals in this section (I swear I don't plan these instances of propinquity): "I think I could turn and live with the animals" (47). Question to Jace: "Could you live with the animals?" His response: "Well, it might be neat, but there would be a few disadvantages, such as heat and cold. 'Cause we don't have fur." Pondering how early humans dealt with extremes of temperature or with predators, I point out that our ancestors probably did have more hair until they had gained sufficient dexterity to do more with tools, like make clothes. I also point out that we must have relied on skill with language to cope with predators. We could say, "Hey, Charlie, watch out, there's a lion stalking you. Why don't you climb that big tree there, and Joe and I will sneak up behind him with our spears." "Right, Beano. Can do."

But I digress. Walt praises animals for their acceptance of their lives; they don't bewail their sins or complain about their lives or "make me sick discussing their duty to God," or offer oblation before one another or their creator. Is Walt seeing in animals traits he wishes to nurture in himself? He, too, is totally accepting of the state of things, of one's life condition, and of course he is so far from self-subserving that he sings this celebratory song of the self.

Perhaps that is what he's getting at when he says that animals "bring me tokens of myself." I think of the Pattiann Rogers poem "Second Witness," where she wonders what she doesn't know about herself "From never having seen a crimson chat at its feeding / Or the dunnart carrying its young?"[33] But Walt says we should not define ourselves solely by examining the tokens of ourselves dropped by animals. He rides a "gigantic beauty of a stallion," but then says, "I resign you, stallion, / Why do I need your paces when I myself out-gallop them?" Ultimately, then, to live with the animals may not be enough. Maybe because we have something to say to ourselves, to each other, in our own language. Among them: Look at what we can learn about living from animals.

33

Just back from a backpacking trip in the Catskills, and I'm impressed with the rigors of the climb up Bald Eagle. It's a steep and long-enough haul to evoke a good sweat and strain, even compared to the rugged Catskills with full pack.

Tree trunk on tree trunk scraping from breeze catching leaves—not a moan or groan, too high pitched for that—squeal, squeak, whine, creak. Protesting something—but what? This is a breezy, sunny, not-too-humid morn, the forest feeling the burden of full leaf in August, ready to lay that burden down about six weeks from now.

A lengthy catalogue in this chant, almost six pages, much of it sights and sounds of a walk. "I am afoot with my vision," says Walt, and it is a vision that encompasses city, farmland, wilderness. Among the wilderness sights: "the rattlesnake suns his flabby length on a rock," "the panther walks to and fro on a limb overhead" (48). He sees a settler girdling trees to clear the land, crops of persimmon, corn, flax, buckwheat, rye. He is:

> Scaling mountains, pulling myself cautiously up, holding on by
>   low scragged limbs,
> Walking the path worn in the grass and beat through the leaves of
>   the brush.

Sounds like the Ridgeline Trail. Then he shifts from the rural scene back to the city and out to sea, "Where the she-whale swims with her calf and never forsakes it," and "Where the fin of the shark cuts like a black chip out of the water" (49).

Lots of close observation: "where the geese nip their food with short jerks." Niagara is a "cataract falling like a veil over my countenance." If that refers to Bridal Veil Falls, does that make America the bride, and him America?

Walt includes human scenes as well, from "the cot in the hospital reaching lemonade to a feverish patient," to a lovebed:

> I turn the bridegroom out of bed and stay with the bride myself,
> I tighten her all night to my thighs and lips. (50–51)

Sexy stuff. All this at a pace evocative of a walk—"I tread day and night such roads." Whitman's cataloguing flows at a hiking pace—not a stroll, more measured and fluid and energetic than that.

His point here concerns empathy: "I am the man, I suffer'd, I was there." He is the shipwrecked soul, the mother burned for a witch, the hunted runaway slave. But more than half of this section is composed of nature catalogue—he is the basking rattler, the feeding goose, the "winter wolves [that] bark amid wastes of snow and icicled trees," and "the yellow-crown'd heron [that] comes to the edge of the marsh at night and feeds upon small crabs." Onward, outward—containing multitudes.

To slip out of the self, then, to merge with the all around, is not to lose the self but to gain the world. It's not a shrinking of the self as consciousness of self leaks away, but expansion.

I see delicate fluffs of milkweed seeds, like droplets in a vegetative cloud, ride the winds across the clearing.

34

Cool, sixties, evening. First day of school. Glorious weather. Uneventful hike—several grouse on the ridge, and some bear scat. Saw a small bear on the road the other day. Big spiderweb above Porky Pine.

This section tells "the tale of the murder in cold blood of four hundred and twelve men" massacred in the Mexican War (53). Seems a long way from the slopes of Bald Eagle, though I guess this ridge, too, has seen violence. Surely brave blood has fallen here. Bald Eagle was once called Muncy Mountain, after the Muncies, whose name means "the wolves" and who were called the "Delawares of the Mountains." There was also a Chief Bald Eagle at some point. In the 1700s the Muncies were driven from their main village north of Lewisburg and forced further and further west by white settlement. While the ridge has survived without much development, the Muncies have not. Neither, for that matter, have the wolves or the bald eagles.

All this reminds me that history, too, is part of a place. Walt's empathy, expansive historically as well as geographically, extends even into the past.

35

Overcast morning, getting humid—will probably rain later.

A grouse up on Ridge Trail doesn't flap off right away, so I watch for ten or twenty seconds. Lots of itchies on legs from overhanging brush. Lots of ragweed in open spots. In a few weeks this hike will be hell for my hay fever.

I've been reading Laura Sewall's book on seeing and the need for receptivity.[34] Seeing receptivity as a kind of taking, or taking in, I've wondered what I can give back to this place that I've been so busy taking in.

But maybe the problem is we give too much of ourselves, till we end up imposing ourselves on the land. Think of sight as a projection of self outward, seeing what we want to see or are predisposed to see, versus taking in what is there, letting it react upon us. We need to give less and allow ourselves to be given to, allow the world to give to us—to allow ourselves to take in more, and be taken over. What we do typically is give so much that we take over. All this sounds paradoxical, but it makes sense to me, for the moment at least.

Walt today gives us the story of a sea fight, featuring John Paul Jones, he of "I have not yet begun to fight!" A story from Walt's "grandmother's father the sailor" (54). The American ship, the *Bonhomme Richard,* damaged by cannonball, afire, the powder magazine threatened by the fire, the ship presumed to be sinking, but the captain, "serene," will not surrender, and by midnight, "in the beams of the moon," they win the day.

Well, no sea battles have erupted here on Bald Eagle Ridge, nor any land battles that I know about. But perhaps the patriotic pride and interest in the past are relevant, and certainly the lesson in persistence is. There are days I don't feel like doing this hike, but each time I do I feel as though I've won the day.

36

SEPTEMBER

Hot, muggy day, with Susan, discussing the Internet and intellectual property rights, which reminds me that, legally speaking, we are trespassing on the mountain. Maybe there is a kind of freedom on the Internet that we don't enjoy in the real world. There, you can wander where you please.

Walt writing of the aftermath of the sea fight: "Formless stacks of bodies and bodies by themselves, dabs of flesh upon the masts and spars"—lots of gory detail (55).

And thunder over the Allegheny Front on this humid day, like cannon from a foe's ship.

More gore: "The hiss of the surgeon's knife, the gnawing teeth of his saw, / Wheeze, cluck, swash of falling blood, short wild screams, and long, dull, tapering groans." What's all this got to do with Bald Eagle

Ridge? Maybe this is Walt's turn to show us the grief and pain that are also part of life. The season turns here on Bald Eagle in time with Walt's shift in mood. The growth on the trail is about as lush as it has been all year, but the blackberries have shriveled and hardened on the vine, and the vines themselves have withered and browned.

And the high-stacked clouds to the north are billowed sails, bringing cannon-rumble nearer. I've always wondered about the pulses of grief and pain in "Song of Myself." It's such an optimistic poem, and you would think that once Whitman had made the point that pain can be included in his song, incorporated into and absorbed by the healthy self, that he'd be done with it. Why not show us the self emerging from pain, progressing through the stages of grief toward acceptance and on into the state of joy? Why have pain recur so often in his "Song"? But of course the recurrence is more true to life, isn't it? No matter how happy or "self-actualized" we may be, we don't leave grief behind forever; to pretend that we could would mean becoming callous about emotional trauma, and Whitman is far too empathetic to recommend that sort of petrification. No, the poem's vacillations of pain suggest that we cannot close our hearts to the pain but must open ourselves to it, recognizing it and accepting it, seeing that it, too, is a necessary part of living deeply—and that it doesn't last forever.

Amid all the human atrocity Walt describes, there are still significant references to nature—"a few large stars overhead, silent and mournful shiny." That's the pathetic fallacy at work there, with all nature sharing in the human emotion, but it shows how we look to nature at times of trauma. We find there, if not solace always, at least something consonant with our deepest feelings. If we see the world as sympathetic in our darkest moments, that is one more reason to cherish it.

And there is redemption, too. Amid the amputations and groans and bits of wayward flesh, Walt speaks of "Delicate sniffs of sea-breeze, smells of sedgy grass and fields by the shore." Walt's beloved coast seems to beckon, and if the sea whispers that "low and delicious word death" (as he says in "Out of the Cradle, Endlessly Rocking"), he can still take in a deep and fragrant gulp of living shoreline.[35]

37

A great, cool and breezy, blue-sky, end-of-summer-but-feels-like-early-autumn, low-humidity day.

I'm wondering about my tactic of starting out most entries with a description of weather. There was a time in my life when I thought that sort of thing the most trivial of empty chitchat. Why waste time discussing weather when there are social issues to sort out and the state of the soul to attend to, and life is short? Now I think weather-talk is an appropriate first step in noticing the world around us. If you are aware of the weather, it is likely that you feel the need to accommodate yourself to it because you intend to be in it. When my plans entail more than moving from house to car to office and back, I had better care about the weather.

To notice the weather is to be mindful of the world you are entering into outside your door. To be mindful of the world's feel on your skin.

My soul-of-summer haiku:

Trills and calls and whistles—
ya-honk and squawk and caw—
birds don't sing, they chat.

> The names of flowers—
> jewelweed, cohosh, yarrow—
> like spoken fruit

Jewelweed, bugbane,
thistle, cohosh, mullein,
yarrow all in bloom

> Fireworks of flowers blooming
> and berries exploding
> on the tongue

Tugs gentle as wishes
beckon ripe berries
into eager fingers

> Turtle on the trail,
> Taking his time and mine,
> Outwaits me in his shell

Chant 37 of "Song"—more of Walt's empathy with the downtrodden, and his identification with all. He is prisoner, mutineer, cholera patient, and beggar: "I project my hat, sit shame-faced, and beg" (55–56). I guess I'm a beggar too, asking the natural world for spiritual handouts.

A cricket in the grass tweedles, katydids in the brush do their stridulating thing, wing on wing, the breeze turns over some leaves. Goldenrod in bloom along the ridge, some wild grapes ripening in several places along the trail. By the log where I sit, the ryegrass is leaning north and east, blond, its tufts of grain intricate, delicate, lovely. The grain crumbles in my fingers.

38

The calendar has officially declared it autumn this week: harvesttime. Headed for climax on the narrative line.

Wet trail today from yesterday's rain; the grass is soaked, and there's still plenty of it long enough on the ridgeline to soak my boots. Some small burrs end up plastered on my shorts—whole green twigs came off with the burrs. Then I do my job of seed distribution by pulling the burrs off me as I walk down the trail.

Walt breaks the somber mood in this section, starting with "Enough! enough! enough!" (56). Enough, I guess, of dwelling on sorrow, or taking it in (which makes him the dwelling, sorrow the inhabitant). Time to remember that "corpses rise, gashes heal," that "The blossoms we wear in our hats [are] the growth of thousands of years." If the poem has descended into grief, now it must reascend.

A sobering thought—every week my hike ends with a descent. And as Maslow points out, peak experiences are fleeting moments. We cannot stay there long.

Ah, but every week I go back up.

Maslow also writes about "plateau-experience," less intense than peak, a "pleasant, continuing, contemplative experience rather than . . . something akin to a climactic explosion which then ends." The plateau experience partakes of the "serene and calm, rather than a poignantly emotional, climactic, autonomic response to the miraculous, the awesome, the sacralized, the Unitive." We reach a plateau not through a single transcendent moment of ecstasy, but through the long process of "maturing, experiencing, living, learning." And the experience "*always* has a noetic and cognitive element, which is not always true for peak-experiences, which can be purely and exclusively emotional."[36]

His plateau sounds like a peaceful place, where we may well find contentment, but still he mentions the plateau almost in passing, in an introduction, while moving on to the apparently more interesting region of the peak, which he dwells on at book length. Personally, I would not want to dwell in the unvariegated terrain of plateau experience. Give me life's ups and downs, the love and pain, the extraordinary as well as the level plain. If there is something to be said for a long road of upward striving, perhaps the peak is the better setting for that, for when we saunter along a plateau we might cease striving. At the same time, I would not want my experience of life to be purely emotional, not any more than I would like it to be purely intellectual. Give me a life of the body as well as the mind.

As it happens, this Appalachian Ridge may be the perfect compromise. It is not a stand-alone pyramidal peak, with only one peaky point. It is more like an A-frame tent, with a long horizontal ridgeline. I ascend, then I follow a high path long enough to afford the opportunity for contemplation. A little bit of peak and a little bit of plateau—that is the nature of the ridge-and-valley country.

Walt ends the chant with an address to his "Eleves"—"Continue your annotations, continue your questionings." Does he mean me? These burrs from Whitman—the lines of his poem—they cling to me. My pen held between fingers, pinched lightly between first knuckles, the tips of these same fingers pick off the burrs—and then I distribute them here in the open field of this page.

39

OCTOBER

Some orange in the east, ascending over clouds. Two whitetails and a wild turkey (heard but not seen) on the way up.

Walt in this section sounds like a cultural anthropologist, wondering about the nature of "The friendly and flowing savage" (56). Like contemporary anthropologists, and unlike most white Americans and

Europeans of his day, he does not automatically disparage other cultures as inferior. Those cultures are suited to their members, adapted to their place. In fact, Walt even wonders if the ways of the "savage" are superior to his (and our) cultural values: "Is he waiting for civilization or past it and mastering it?" Perhaps as a late romantic Whitman is celebrating the primitive now that it no longer poses a threat to his culture, singing the glories of what is now gone. Perhaps we are still in that mode today. But maybe we also see—and maybe Whitman did too—that the "primitive" way of life kept us in touch with nature (and so ourselves as well?) and managed to maintain a culture coexistent with nature, a trick we seem to have been unable to pull off.

And Walt, like Thoreau before him, sees beauty in the "savage" life—"Behavior lawless as snow-flakes, words simple as grass." Walt's "Leaves of Grass" are akin to Thoreau's call in "Walking" for a literature made of words "transplanted to [the] page with earth adhering to their roots."[37]

At its heart, maybe this is the lesson of the mountain, or one of them. At its essence, at its roots, life is simple. You walk, one foot in front of the other—we all know how to do that—and you get where you're going. Then you return. That is how to climb a mountain. How to live a life. It is the path of the hero, departing home and engaging in adventure and then returning home with good tidings, and we are all the hero in the epic of our lives, all writing a song of ourselves.

But some don't write it down, as per Thoreau:

My life has been the poem I would have writ,
But I could not both live and utter it.[38]

I'm reminded of the lessons of my hike of the Appalachian Trail, on trips lasting anywhere from a weekend to three months over a period of twenty years (with many off years) till I'd completed its two-thousand-plus miles. I had started with plenty of apprehension about whether I had the physical or psychological stamina to make it all that way. What I found, to my utter surprise, was how easy it is. Each day, walk your miles, move from Point A to Point B, drink from the streams en route, then do it again the next day. And enjoy the walk—that's what you're there for—not the arrival at Point B (or C or D or E, the End), but the journey itself.

It is on your way up the mountain, maybe, and not necessarily at the top, that you are most apt to have a peak experience. That's when you are most apt to lose yourself on the mountain—and then find yourself again. On top we are often too full of ourselves and our accomplishment to let self-awareness fall away.

In *Zen and the Art of Motorcycle Maintenance*, Robert Pirsig says, "Mountains should be climbed with as little effort as possible and without desire.... You climb the mountain in an equilibrium between restlessness and exhaustion. Then, when you're no longer thinking ahead, each footstep isn't just a means to an end but a unique event in itself. *This* leaf has jagged edges. *This* rock looks loose. From *this* place the snow is less visible, even though closer. These are things you should notice anyway. To live only for some future goal is shallow. It's the sides of the mountain which sustain life, not the top. Here's where things grow."[39] We grow on the upward path because we are still immersed in what is around us, still striving, and not yet arrived at the point of putting all that behind or beneath us.

The point is not to arrive or to accomplish but to become absorbed in the journey itself. At the same time, though, notes Pirsig, "without the top, you can't have any sides. It's the top that *defines* the sides."[40] The summit, too, can become a moment worth noticing. At *this* point, there is no more mountain. It gives way to sky.

40

Cold, in the thirties. A couple of whitetail down below the hemlock stand, a few snowflakes falling now, at the top of the ridge. At Porky Pine, the porky poop has disintegrated into brown soil, loose and thick. It makes me appreciate the exquisite timing of decomposition. One year, with its cycles of moistening, baking, and chilling, some mixing with odd bits of organic detritus, then stirring with breezes, is about what it takes to build soil. Dung, leaves, whole corpses—one cycle of seasons is sufficient to reincorporate all that into the world.

The grasses, the thistle, the mullein—drying in shades of beige, gray, and brown. Definite autumnage.

I, too, am in my autumn. Last weekend, on a field trip to the Delaware Water Gap with my students, I had one of those college-era late night talks with a student named Sara. She was full of wonder at the miracle of starlight and the expansiveness of time, full of queries about how human relationships fit in all the vastness of existence. I admired the passion of her inquiries, and recognized it as something I've become distant from. Sure, I still have my passions, but they are all so guarded now. In your mid-forties you don't fall in love so far or so fast as you did half a lifetime ago. And you don't feel the palpable ache of awe at considering the long path of starlight. So, yes, I feel a little cooler about life these days. And here I am dispensing my leaves—pages, words, the ideas and tidbits from my reading that I distribute in class.

Make no mistake, though, there is still plenty of life here. On Bald Eagle, the goldenrod is still out, and there is a vibrancy to the leaves before they drop. Autumn is about retreat and consolidation, not death, and it all adds up to preparation for the nurture of new life.

Here's another time where it seems Walt must have been reading over my shoulder. Here I am, feeling autumnal, and Walt says, "Flaunt of the sunshine I need not your bask" (57). Here I am, feeling reflective, wondering, at the top of the mountain, and Walt says:

> Earth! you seem to look for something at my hands,
> Say, old top-knot, what do you want?

(The "top-knot," I believe, is a vulture.) Here I am thinking of my words and pages falling like leaves, and Walt says:

> Behold, I do not give lectures or a little charity,
> When I give I give myself.

And I remember a colleague, in a discussion on the art of teaching, saying, "The truth is, we teach ourselves." That's true in a couple of ways. First, we teachers are the ones doing most of the learning, and, second, what we have to teach is our selves, our values, our knowledge, our passion for all those things, red yellow orange drifting swirling settling down.

41

Up here with Jace, gorgeous sunny day, about seventy. Hard to believe I saw snowflakes a few days ago.

Grackles collect in trees by the hemlock stand and below the first stream crossing. Jacy gets the joke about Porky Pine when we stop to examine the poop already recycled into soil. We see a red-tailed hawk right over us on the way up.

Walt says he has "heard what was said of the universe"—that it is good, maybe?—but asks, "is that all?" (58). He compares himself to Kronos, Zeus, Hercules, Osiris, Isis, Brahma, Buddha, Allah, Odin—and sees as much or more in common people going about everyday lives.

In the ladybug settling on my palm, in grackles squawking, in hay-scented fern gone gold in the cool of the past week—in all of these we perceive creation, and it is good. But there is more to it than that. Even more than very good, or great.

Miracles.

And now my son is eager to lead me down the mountain. First he rests by my side, a turkey feather in his breast pocket.

42

A mosquito on my knee—hey, what are you, stupid? It's October.

In this section, Walt reminds us that this is a song, played with "easily written loose-finger'd chords" (59). In the key of G-whiz?

Walt offers a view of eternity that includes the everyday—"politics, wars, markets, newspapers, schools, / The mayor and councils, banks, tariffs, steamships, factories, stocks, stores, real estate and personal estate." He sees in everyone around him "duplicates of myself," and he sees wasted lives, in an apparent critique of capitalism:

> Here and there with dimes on the eyes walking,
> To feed the greed of the belly the brains liberally spooning,
> Tickets buying, taking, selling, but in to the feast never once going,
> Many sweating, ploughing, thrashing, and then the chaff for
>   payment receiving,
> A few idly owning, and they the wheat continually claiming.

But all these minutiae of daily life, including the social critique, are framed in a far view of time and life: "ever the upward and downward sun, ever the air and the ceaseless tides." In the long view, complaints about social injustice and class warfare seem petty. To answer the big

questions—"and what is reason? and what is love? and what is life?"—
Walt always includes nature in his thought process. No, not a "thought
process"—a song.

Nearby now a cricket whirrs. Not chirps—the sound is ongoing.

43

With the kids and my daughter Kira's stuffed cats. Another gorgeous
day. Slow, fun dawdle getting up here, and I'm glad the kids have come
up with me.

Walt ponders religion in this section, accepting it in all its varieties.
Interesting to see how the nature images function. Encapsulating the
origin of religion, he speaks of worshippers "saluting the sun, / Making a fetich of the first rock or stump"—a fetish being "an inanimate
object worshipped by savages, as having inherent magical powers or
being animated by a spirit" (60, 505). So religion begins with a sense of
spirit pulsing through all nature.

Maslow also has interesting things to say about religion, seeing its
organized form as emerging from the "effort to communicate peak-
experience to non-peakers," and terming peak experience as "the model
of the religious revelation or the religious illumination." For him, then,
the peak experience is the origin of religion. But peakers tend to belong
to no organized religion. Maslow theorizes that conventional religion
tends to "dereligionize" life, because "the experience of the holy, the sacred, the divine, of awe, of creatureliness, of surrender, of mystery, of
piety, thanksgiving, gratitude, self-dedication, if they happen at all, tend
to be confined to a single day of the week, to happen under one roof
only of one kind of structure only, under certain triggering circumstances only"—all of which "seems to absolve many (most?) people
from the necessity or desire to feel these experiences at any other time."
Religion can lead to "de-sacralizing much of life . . . dichotomizing life
into the transcendent and the secular-profane and can, therefore, com-
partmentalize and separate them temporally, spatially, conceptually, and
experientially."[41]

In his mystic experiences, then, Walt understands what the priests
are getting at: "I do not despise you priests, all time, the world over." But
he feels no need to become the follower of any one of them, for true re-

ligious experience is found somewhere out of earshot of their cant. He can say, "My faith is the greatest of faiths," because his faith (in nature and in himself) is at the root of religious experience. But his is also "the least of faiths" because it adheres to no settled doctrine.

Later in the section Walt speaks to nonbelievers and skeptics, those floundering in a "sea of torment, doubt, despair and unbelief." Then he picks up the sea metaphor and describes the skeptic as a wounded whale:

> How the flukes splash!
> How they contort rapid as lightning, with spasms and spouts of blood! (61)

This is more, I think, than mere metaphor. Just as Walt's powers of empathy can encompass all, from priests to atheists (who may be equally deluded), so too can he "feel the pain" (to use Bill Clinton's phrase) of even the nonhuman. To capture the pain of a human, he uses the image of a wounded animal. The wounded whale is the vehicle of the metaphor, the image that he takes for granted we will immediately recognize the validity of. Sympathy for the atheist, he knows, from the devout, will come even harder. But in taking for granted empathy with the whale, he makes an even larger claim, a more radical move.

So in natural images in this section we see nature as the starting point of our sense of the sacred; as the source of metaphor, the physical means by which we image truth and understand it; and by implication the ultimate goal of our recognition of spiritual truths—to reestablish our connection with the spirit that runs through all things. Walt refers to himself as "One of that centripetal and centrifugal gang," spiraling outward to touch all things, then absorbing all into what David Reynolds calls "the magnetic 'I' at the heart of his poetry."[42] Outward and in, ebb and flow, inhale exhale.

44

Warm autumn day, trail loud with leaf-fall, up here with environmental writers Tim and Ann, who are staying with me as they visit campus to present slide shows on rivers and wetlands. Nice having friends to hike up here with. Our chatter and the leaf-crunch of our boots in the late fall make the trip more sound-full.

In this chant Walt climbs a mountain, too. It starts, "It is time to explain myself—let us stand up" (61). Walt's climb is perhaps more metaphoric than literal, leading to the issuance of his proclamation on high, essentially a proclamation of here I am, I made it. The section ends, "Now in this spot I stand with my robust soul." Right here, atop Bald Eagle. And to get here:

On every step bunches of ages, and larger bunches between the steps,
All below duly travel'd, and still I mount and mount.

Walt seems to have a sense of geologic time in the perception of ages and ages underlying his steps as he climbs. By my calculations, I cover about 175,000 years per step, figuring approximately 1,800 steps on my way up the mountain and dividing that into 320 million. It was that many years ago, during the geologic period known as the Pennsylvanian, that the continent of Gondwanaland (since broken up into South America, Africa, and much of Asia) rammed into Laurentia (now North America and Europe), thus forming the Ridge-and-Valley region. The usual analogy says to imagine someone kicking a loose carpet, creating rippling folds. Bald Eagle Ridge is the last fold created by that cataclysmic continental kick. Geologically speaking, then, this is a highly significant place, and I am riding the crest of a far-flung, long-rolling sandstone wave set in motion over 300 million years ago.

Of course, the truth is that I'm not really standing on rock from back then. That rock has eroded away. At the same time, there have been further upthrusts of rock from below, and I'm actually standing on Cambrian rock, predating the collision of Gondwanaland. Predating even the dinosaurs.

Walt makes an apparent reference to dinosaurs, "monstrous sauroids," in this section. They may have been in Whitman's consciousness in the mid-1850s, since it was not many years earlier, in 1842, that Sir Richard Owen first used the name "dinosaurs" to describe the creatures that left those large fossilized bones that Englishmen had begun digging up in the previous couple of decades. Then in the Great Exhibition of London in 1854, the Crystal Palace featured Owen's display of life-sized (though inaccurately depicted) dinosaur models. So dinosaurs had been in the news when Whitman was pondering his

"Song," as were the long stretches of geologic time implied by their discovery.

Evolutionary time may also be on his mind when he says, "Immense
have been the preparations for me." Evolution, too, was in the air of the
1850s when Whitman was writing this, culminating at the end of the
decade in Darwin's *Origin of Species,* which introduced not the theory
of evolution itself, but the theory that natural selection was the mechanism by which evolution operates. But notice Walt's placing of the self
at the center of the universe, the epitome of evolution, as if its purpose
has been to lead up to us, or, rather, himself, as the marvelous end point
of creation. That sort of teleological reading of the creation was typical of the mid-nineteenth century. In *Walt Whitman's America,* his study
of the intellectual and cultural currents flowing into and through Whitman's poetry, David Reynolds notes that by the 1850s a "progressive con-
sensus [had] emerged among naturalists and biologists." Accepting the
optimistic view of the creation implicit in the argument from design
(with every detail of life bespeaking God's care), scientists such as
Robert Chambers (*Vestiges of the Natural History of Creation,* 1844) saw
humans as the end point of the progression of species, presuming that
we are the ultimate item of the creation in terms of complexity, intellect, spirit, and self-awareness.[43]

In these post-Darwinian days, of course, we are no longer so san-
guine about our species' position as top leaf on the tree of life. Sitting
here at the apex of Bald Eagle Ridge, I don't imagine that the mountain
exists solely to provide a momentary butt-rest for me, or to serve as the
geologic stepladder (with 1,800 rungs) by which I ascend to self-
actualization. If there is an evolutionary purpose to life, ours included,
it is to fit in well with the environment we are adapted for. Which makes
me wonder about my evolutionary niche here. What role do I play in
the life of the mountain? I can't claim to have done much in the way of
being this ecosystem's top predator. In fact, while I see the need for deer
hunters in the late fall, and I respect their necessary work of thinning
the herd, and I know that this mountain probably remains green space
because the owner likes to hunt, I tend to resent their presence for re-
stricting my walks in the woods to Sundays only. I'd rather encounter

the long-gone wolves and mountain lions that once managed the deer population.

Do I play a role here then? Am I advancing the cause of evolution? The trash cans outside my apartment provide an occasional meal for the local bears, but that's probably diminishing their foraging skills, and the road I live on serves to fragment their habitat. Living where I do encourages certain species that can tolerate people (like opossums) at the expense of others that cannot. On the other hand, my walks serve to heighten the flight responses of the deer and the grouse, keeping them on their toes, or wings, as the case may be. And at times I feel like the sentience of the mountain, that part of its life capable of perceiving its history and its place in the world.

45

NOVEMBER

Dreary, bleak, cold November day. I'm thinking of how often weather is evoked in literature as a barometer of mood and emotion—the overcast sky as objective correlative. But isn't it also true, perhaps more true, that our mood is the product of weather conditions? So believe psychologists who have identified the winter blahs as Seasonal Affective Disorder (SAD). Our mood is the barometer, we are a subjective correlative.

Been battling a cold, ennui, and work responsibilities (meetings, meetings, meetings) the last couple of weeks.

If Walt felt the expansiveness of time, evolutionary and geologic, in the previous section, here he dwells on the expansiveness of space. At first he feels "suffocated" by lovers "Jostling me through streets and public halls" (62). But then he moves out of the city, to a place where lovers call to him "from the rocks of the river," and they are "chirping over my head, / Calling my name from flower-beds, vines, tangled underbrush," issuing "soft balsamic busses." Amid streams, birds, trees, far from feeling suffocated as he had in the city, he now becomes expansive (63). His consciousness ventures out to the stars next, to "far-sprinkled systems," as far as we can see, past the near edge of the next system:

> Wider and wider they spread, separating, always expanding,
> Outward and outward and forever outward.

Time and space, "a few quadrillions of eras, a few octillions of cubic leagues . . . They are but parts, any thing is but a part." Again, the perspective seems one part ecology, one part zen.

Does it diminish our sense of self, I wonder, to become aware of the vastness of time and space? No, says Walt, because we are part of that vastness, integral, and to have a sense of self is to see how expansive and great is this thing, life, that we partake of and are part of. Whitman's perceptions reach out to the stars, or back to the Cretaceous, and they are part of his self, the outstretching fingers of senses, mind, and awareness. Maslow points out that this sort of fluidity in time and space is typical of peak experience, which is characterized by "disorientation in time and space, or even the lack of consciousness of time and space." It is like "experiencing universality and eternity."[44]

The next ridges to the south—Nittany, Tussey—I can see myself there.

And just now, geese yelping, arrowing toward Tussey. I take my place in the V, till the rustle of desiccating leaves still hanging on the nearest oak calls me back, and I am the wind chilling my fingers holding book and pen—let me stir the blond grasses, carry messages across the valley, before I head down the mountain.

46

Another day of coldclear. I surprise two whitetails up on the Ridge Trail, and now that the leaves are down I can follow them further, visually at least. One flashes its tail, bounding ten feet (I don't think I'm exaggerating) over brush, then lightly touches down and prances for thirty feet and stops. And suddenly I can't see—she drops the flashing beacon of her tail and blends in to the woods. But when I step forward again, she moves, on a different angle this time, crossing the trail fifty feet in front of me, then downslope.

So the season of leafdown is a good time for deer watching. I remember reading that Andrew Wyeth liked this time of year because he could better see the land's shape and the skeletal structures of trees.

Walt says, "I know I have the best of time and space" (63). Two possible readings here—either through his powers of empathy and imagination he can connect to the best times and places of the past, or that the here and now, the top of Bald Eagle Ridge just after noon on a November Sunday, is the best place and time.

"I tramp a perpetual journey," he says, "My signs are a rain-proof coat, good shoes, and a staff cut from the woods." Me, I've got fleece, lug soles, and the shaft of an old hockey stick (a Titan). And my journey is not quite perpetual—an hour and a half or so every week. Unless I think of myself as part of the life of the mountain. If Thoreau could see himself as "nature writing," maybe I can be the "mountain climbing"—the mountain climbing itself. Up like the wind and spring sap, down like gravity, autumn leaves, and snow.

This section is full of hiking imagery. Walt says, "each man and each woman of you I lead upon a knoll." Here I am, following your directions, looking for your prints under my boot soles. He speaks of "My right hand pointing to landscapes of continents and the public road" (64). Yes, I see it, now that the leaves are down—Mount Nittany, Tussey, Happy Valley, Beaver Stadium, and the Route 322 bypass.

> Not I, nor any one else can travel that road for you,
> You must travel it for yourself.

We have had that conversation on other high points, and then I was directed here. This path up Bald Eagle is the one I chose to travel this year, searching for my self, but of course one never finds the definitive location of the self. Or if you do—and I think I just got the poem—it's pointing out some road or path further beyond, urging you—me—us—to go there. And it (the self) can't go with you because when you get there, or while you are on your way there, you become another self. So yes, Walt Whitman *is* the self, pointing the way, walking with me, us, there for us to lean on when we turn to him ("rest the chuff of your hand on my hip"), but the steps must be your, our, my own.

In this section Walt speaks of ascending a hill before dawn and looking at far stars and wondering, or his spirit wondering, once we know those distant spaces and can enfold those into our sense of self, then "shall we be fill'd and satisfied?" And the answer is no, because then we'll want to go further, beyond. We never get to the top of this mountain, it seems. Or no, that's not it—we just can't stay there, because there are things to do at home—pick up the kids, remember a friend's birthday

and make a quick call, pay the bills, grade papers and prepare class—
and then other mountains to climb, other journeys to take. Meanwhile,
reminding us of the satisfaction of attending to our physiological needs
and the comfort of being cared for, Walt offers us sustenance:

> Sit a while dear son,
> Here are biscuits to eat and here is milk to drink.

And something worth reading.

47

Up with Jacy, cold day, some snowfall, but also some sun, which has us
looking around for a "snowbow." Couple of deer in the woods on the
way up, a grouse. More snow moving in from the west now, dark over
the Allegheny Front.

My page in "Song of Myself" is marked with a wayward blade of
grass, some sort of grain. A rye gone awry.

This is the section where Walt says, "I teach straying from me" (65).
He addresses one of the concerns any reader of "Song of Myself" ought
to have. What good is his song of myself in our attempt to discover or
sing or scribe our self? Part of the answer, says Walt, is that his song is
our song, and mine, and yours: "It is you talking just as much as myself,
I act as the tongue of you." And I see another connection between
singing the self and nature writing. The problem in nature writing is
how to give voice to the nonhuman, to "speak for the trees," as the Lorax
says, "for the trees have no tongues."[45] The writer always speaks for the
voiceless, or at least the unheard. Most of us have become as detached
from our inner self as we have from the world around us.

To understand him, says Walt, "go to the heights or water-shore." A
good defense of my practice of going to the top of Bald Eagle every
week—that's what he says we should do in order to hear him. His song,
like my pennywhistle, may be too shrill for the indoors: "I swear I will
never translate myself at all, only to him or her who privately stays with
me in the open air." Walt, is that you freezing my fingers? Speak a little
less, would you, in that cold grave voice.

My Appalachian ridge is far from the Long Island dunes and shores
that Whitman was so fond of. But, yes, I can safely say that his song car-

ries here. Why must we be outside to understand him? "The nearest gnat is an explanation, and a drop or motion of waves a key." And Bald Eagle's a Rosetta stone.

48

After a nap, up with Susan. Cold—high twenties, overcast. Monday starts deer season, and we can hear shots in the valley—hunters getting their guns primed. Saw two guys dressed in camouflage on ATVs on the way up.

Walt speaking of body and soul here, neither greater than the other, "And nothing, not God, is greater to one than one's self is" (66). Reminding us, towards the end here, of his thesis. Something about walking, too, in the next line: "And whoever walks a furlong without sympathy walks to his own funeral drest in his shroud." Interesting juxtaposition—after asserting the primacy of the self, he immediately speaks of the need for sympathy, which is a giving of the self to others. So to celebrate the self is not simply to take or to absorb sympathy or any other resource from the world. It is to give and radiate, like a sun.

And yet we do accrue: "I or you pocketless of a dime may purchase the pick of the earth." We may even purchase an entire mountain, one already written up in some deed. Here is my deed: My lug soles gain purchase on the mountain's steepest trail.

Similarly, as we need no title to possess the earth, we need no diploma to live: "to glance with an eye or show a bean in its pod confounds the learning of all times." Walt urges self-reliance, not reliance upon wisdom transmitted by word of God or book. We can "hear and behold God in every object" and "find letters from God dropt in the street." On the mountain those letters arrive in the form of leaves. Heaven-sent, as we say, postmarked from upper branches of oak, hickory, maple. Or they arrive as gusts of snow, no return address.

49

DECEMBER

Clearblue cold day. Four degrees when I got up this morning, in the teens now. Rhododendron leaves curled up vertically, forming green tubes. Their response to freezing temperatures? But it's not something they do right at thirty-two degrees. They must have some mechanism that prevents the moisture within from freezing right away. It seems to take temperatures below twenty to bring about this leaf-curling response.

Snow up to an inch still on the northwest slope on the top few hundred yards, but gone on the southeast-exposed ridgeline and down below.

My first close call today with carnivores on the mountain—dogs. A boxer and a yellow lab ran at me on the ridge trail, fast, and started barking. I yelled, "Hey, Hey!" Then the owners, two women, came up the trail with another yellow lab and boxer. All big. Hard to say, but I think the boxer meant business and wasn't running up just to greet me.

Trails hard packed with recent four-wheeler traffic of hunters, followed by the freeze. Porcupine poop piling up again by Porky Pine. Hesheit evidently made it through the year and moved back in a couple of weeks ago.

In this section Walt accepts death and mortality, and life as "the leavings of many deaths" (67). The language suggests, as Thoreau thought, that Whitman had been reading Eastern ideas about reincarnation. But Whitman denied it. Maybe he was just being sensitive to seasonal cycles. Again, this important insight in the poem is expressed in natural imagery. The corpse is "good manure," giving rise to "roses sweet-scented and growing." The images of "perpetual transfers and promotions" are "stars of heaven . . . suns . . . grass of graves." There are images of a pool in the forest, a "moon that descends the steeps of the soughing twilight," the "moaning gibberish of the dry limbs." All these indicate the movement toward winter. And here I am, here Bald Eagle is, advancing there, too. My kids are already excited about Christmas, that new frame on the old pagan solstice rituals, celebrating, in the darkest season, as we approach the coldest, the turn toward the light and warmth and new life of the seasons ahead.

You don't have to be a student of religion to grasp these deeper meanings of things, or a philosopher or Maslowian psychologist. You just have to pay attention to how nature works. Nature is not just the laboratory of life, it is the experiment itself, and the report where the findings and results are published.

Self-actualization incorporates a kind of placidity born of acceptance—acceptance of life, of things as they are—and the main lesson of nature (the same lesson which the poem started with four seasons ago) is the acceptance of death as part of the cycle. I am perceiving now the circular form of "Song"—not the shape of the mountain, rising to some imagined climax, but maybe the path of my looping route up and around behind the South Knoll, then along the ridge to the Bald Spot, then back down in front of the knoll.

Many critics have sought to explain the structure and plan of "Song of Myself," but most have continued to assume that there is a consistent direction to some unfolding story of self-development. But any such assumption about the story line of the poem must struggle to explain the recurrence of key themes and ideas—like the comments on death in this chant. That sort of repetition and Walt's vacillations of mood do not seem compatible with the usual path of narrative, a linear path, where the hero overcomes one difficulty and proceeds on to meet the next, progressing ever onward in a given direction—the narrative as arrow, as Ursula K. Le Guin terms it. That is the typical hero's story, traveling from here to there, presupposing conflict and an enemy to overcome. Le Guin proposes an alternative shape for narrative, the container, whose purpose is simply to gather things together, available for our perusal.[46]

But haven't I, too, imposed linearity on "Song of Myself" by imposing a plotline with exposition, complications, rising action, and climax? And I've found it, building up to the climax of Whitman's preoccupation, in the latter stages of the poem, with big ideas like evolution, religion, and the meaning of life and death, and his taking long views of time and space. Maybe it's like the laws governing light. Does it behave like a particle or a wave? Whichever you look for. Is "Song of Myself" linear or circular? Whichever you look for. It is large, it contains multitudes.

Same goes for a life, I suppose. Is it linear narrative or container? Whichever you look for.

Those rhododendron leaves—in the spring, or on the next warm day, they will unfurl. I should accept that my life these days—absent a romantic partner—is a kind of furling, with my kids wrapped protectively inside. But there will be an unfurling, a return of warmth.

Not that today is so bad. It's gorgeous. Though it's cold, the sun is sending some warmth, and I'm comfortably wrapped up in hat and gloves and coat.

50

Up with Jace, following tire tracks in the inch-deep snow, tracks accompanied by droplets of blood, presumably from a shot deer hanging off the back of an ATV. Fascinating to try to recreate stories of what happened here from signs left in the snow.

It's still cold today, twenties, but the rhododendron leaves are not furled up. Maybe it's a few degrees warmer than last week? Or do they furl up only in the first cold spell? Have to watch for that next week, or next year.

Last week, on my way down the mountain, I met the two women with the four dogs. One of the boxers had gotten a mouth full of quills—and a toe full. They all came down to my house for pliers. The owner of the boxers works at a veterinary hospital, and she pulled out the quills. The dog was remarkably calm and uncomplaining. It must have hurt, but he seemed to trust that his human friend and caregiver was doing what she could to help.

In this section of *Leaves,* Walt speaks of some mysterious *it* that dwells inside him, "without name . . . a word unsaid / . . . not in any dictionary, utterance, symbol" (67). Maybe only a term as all-embracing as "the life principle" could substitute for *it.* He won't name it because it is vast enough to spill over the denotative boundaries of any conception we can capture in a word or phrase: "It is not chaos or death—it is form, union, plan—it is eternal life—it is Happiness." It is something big as a mountain, as vast and productive and full.

And yes, here, in the course of a year, we can see "form, union, plan," evident in life's patterns—seasonal cycles, the dying preparing for and nurturing the living, making possible the living, summer born of winter, sky defined by mountain. The perception of how it all pieces together—the porcupine and its scat, the deer, the hunter, the blood line in the snow—no, not how it all pieces together, how it is all of one piece—that perception, that apprehension (without apprehensiveness) comes at a moment of ecstasy. It is what *makes* the moment of ecstasy. That is the peak experience, an ecological perspective become spiritual insight.

51

Dreary day, drizzle at the start of my hike, lots of blowdowns from a gusty day, up to sixty-five mph earlier this week. Two downed trees by the hemlock stand. A few inches of wet snow earlier this week, then freezing rain to leave a hard crust, now softening under the drizzle of the last couple of days. Footing at times slippery, at times mushy slogging in thick slush.

Lots of scat pellets spreading out from Porky Pine, sliding downhill in an arc from the entrance to the hollow trunk.

My pattern on these hikes: Get to the logs around the fire circle at Bald Spot, jot down notes of the hike up, then read Walt aloud, ponder, respond. Today I go up the High Knob Trail, over the top of South Knob—didn't want to try the Steep Trail that goes behind the knob and back along the ridge.

The woods seem especially dynamic today with all the blowdowns—mostly finger-diametered, some arm- and calf-thick. A lot has been happening here in the past week. The effect is to make the trails new. And of course the conditions, the weather, the color of the day have that effect as well. Today is silver and gray—dark undersides to the clouds, snow silvered where it has turned to ice or slush. The next ridges look black.

Some seeds scattered on snow on the Knob Trail.

Blowdowns also let me see the truth of "Song"—each death makes way for new life. Where that branch has fallen, sunlight will reach through to nurture a seed that has made its way there, maybe after landing in snow, then being kicked by deer hoof, then sliding down in snowmelt to land just there.

In this section Walt speaks of contradicting himself, which is OK by him: "I am large, I contain multitudes" (68). So, too, is a mountain, does a mountain. Have I become one with this mountain, interchangeable with it? I am getting a little too large myself these days, beginning to pack on winter weight. But I'm not so confident in my absorptive powers as Walt is.

Well, wait—sure I'm multitudinous in my carrying capacity. I contain images of the mountain—clatter of grouse wings, white rump of deer bounding, porcupine pellets in snow, branches encased in ice, rhododendron leaves curled, glider planes whirring, a black tree with gray branches silhouetted against silver sky. And I contain in me lines of a poem about containing multitudes. And love for my kids, yearnings for a partner, regret for ill-considered remarks, remorse over my contributions to the world's sadness, and a fair share of joy.

I have in me images of the life of the mountain, colored by a whole range of emotions. My autumn haiku:

Hay-scented fern gone gold—
one lick
of autumn flame

> By fall, pellets of scat
> from a winter burrow
> are new soil

Ridge after parallel ridge—
crests of slow-moving
Appalachian waves

> V of geese—
> a loud arrow
> aimed south

Leaves furled
in autumn cold—the lesson
of the rhododendron

Walt asks, "Who wishes to walk with me?" Those alliterative *W*s are echoed by the cold wind penetrating my bare fingers clutching this pen and writing one more quick haiku:

Words on a page
like seeds
fallen in snow

52

Denouement: the return of winter. The cycle begins anew. Cold spell
the last couple of weeks, in aughts and teens mostly. Record number
of consecutive December days below freezing—twenty, I think. Today,
maybe ten degrees. Two inches of light powder atop a couple of inches
of crust. Lots of tracks—mostly deer and wild turkey (which look like
dinosaur prints). Almost saw the porcupine—heard him scuttling up
the hollow tree just as I approached. Waited for ten minutes, heard more
scuffling, but his patience exceeded mine. When I rapped on the tree
with my hiking stick, a test to see if that would scare him into action,
he went silent. They're not as dumb as they look.

Rhododendron leaves curled up again, looking crisp, as if they'd
shatter like champagne glass.

Two pages left in the journal notebook to record the last entry—
good timing, or good spacing. I have wondered at times about organizing this chapter in journal form, certainly not the usual mode of literary criticism (if that in fact is what this is—improvisational lit crit,
maybe? stream-of-consciousness scholarship?). But the journal form,
besides being the customary way of conducting an exploration of the
self, also has an honored place in the nature-writing canon—consider
Thoreau's journals, which some critics consider his greatest work, or
Susan Fenimore Cooper's 1850 *Rural Hours*. In fact the next ridge to the
south of here, Brush Mountain (really the same ridge broken by a water
gap) is the subject of Marcia Bonta's seasonal journals *Appalachian
Spring, Appalachian Summer,* and *Appalachian Autumn.*[47] The nature
journal seems to be regarded as a way of presenting an unmediated view
of nature as well as the self—which seems to conflate the two, so that
getting closer to nature is the same as getting in touch with the self.
There is something paradoxical here, too—the way to satisfy the inner
self is to go outside, outside our individual and human selves, to contact the world around us.

That conflation of self and mountain has been my main conceit throughout, and I've been engaged in a sort of self-ascent, progressing up the life zones of psychological needs. But how can I be both the climber and the thing climbed? Let me consider the mountain as mountain for a moment, and Maslow and Whitman two slopes rising to meet at the ridgeline. That's what literary critics do—bring some sort of theory in contact with literature: Maslow's hierarchy, biopoetics, ecopsychology, Freud, flow, touching on *Walden, The Odyssey,* the poems of Pattiann Rogers, John Muir's mountaineering essays, Whitman's "Song of Myself." I have walked those slopes, followed those paths, my boot soles striving for contact (contact!) with "the *solid* earth, the *actual* world," striving for that high point where all meet and merge, fall away and disappear into sky.[48] The slopes of the pyramid are not walls penning us inside, but a series of footholds. And at the top, where slope meets slope and together they come to a point (and here I come to the point), the self ends.

So is it here that I claim to have melded with the absolute, my self now one with the all of existence? Have I reached that point where the mountain, whether it's the physical world or the self, dissolves into nothingness a step beyond its highest point? Where I can simultaneously have my feet on the ground and my head in the clouds?

Right now I'm conscious that the heavens are cold, and they are infiltrating my fingers.

And now I write this last page at my kitchen table—the walk recollected in tranquillity, accompanied by hot coffee. (In between those last sentences, between "now" and "now," insert Bald Eagle Mountain. How can I gloss over the whole mountain of descent, with nothing on the page, not even a space, to mark its mass underfoot? How have I ever pretended to transpose anything of the mountain to the page?)

In this final section, Walt compares himself to a hawk, "not a bit tamed" and "untranslatable" (68). He boasts of sounding his "barbaric yawp over the roofs of the world"—that, too, like the hawk. And what have I been doing the past year but sounding Walt's barbaric yawp over one of the ridged roofs of the world, and trying to translate it to the here and now?

Propinquity: Walt says, "The last scud of day holds back for me." Me, too, the sky pinkening while I was on top, dulling to dusk and dark by the time I walked to my door. Walt bequeaths himself "to the dirt to grow from the grass I love, / If you want me again look for me under your boot-soles." He is snow, settling on the page; he is the sky itself, in the blue of my pen. At times he has been solidly underfoot, at others he has left tracks to follow:

> Missing me one place search another,
> I stop somewhere waiting for you.

I looked for you, Walt, and looked for myself, on Bald Eagle Mountain. And what I found was the mountain.

NOTES

INTRODUCTION

1. Benton MacKaye's vision of an Appalachian Trail was first presented in "An Appalachian Trail: A Project in Regional Planning," *Journal of the American Insitute of Architects* 9 (1921): 325–30. For a collection of MacKaye's statements of philosophy, see *From Geography to Geotechnics*, ed. Paul T. Bryant (Urbana: University of Illinois Press, 1968). My thinking about the Antaean and the Herculean was sparked by Paul Bryant's "Benton MacKaye: The Planner as Antaeus," presented at a conference on "Benton MacKaye and the Appalachian Trail: A 75th Anniversary Celebration of Vision, Planning, and Grass-Roots Mobilization," Albany, N.Y., 22 November 1996.

2. Henry David Thoreau, *The Journal of Henry Thoreau*, ed. Bradford Torrey and Francis H. Allen (New York: Dover, 1962), 10:141–42.

3. Henry David Thoreau, Letter to H. G. O. Blake, 16 November 1857, in *The Correspondence of Henry David Thoreau*, ed. Walter Harding and Carl Bode (New York: New York University Press, 1958), 497.

4. A quick bibliographic check of articles based on Maslow's ideas shows the range and continuing influence of his ideas. In the last few years such articles have appeared in the following journals and magazines beyond the field of psychology: *Management Learning, Psychology and Marketing, Political Psychology, Journal of Socio-Economics, The American Journal of Economics and Sociology, Human Relations, Comparative Drama, Studies in the Literary Imagination, Geophysics, Teaching Exceptional Children, Journal of Adventure Education and Outdoor Leadership, Journal of Professional Nursing, Journal of Staff Development*—to list just a smattering. Recent collections on the pertinence of Maslow's ideas to the business world include Deborah C. Stephens and Gary Heil, eds., *Maslow on Management* (New York: John Wiley, 1998), and Deborah C. Stephens, ed., *The Maslow Business Reader* (New York: John Wiley, 2000). References to Maslow in psychology journals are, of course, widespread and commonplace. For a collection of essays applying Maslow's humanistic or "third force" psychology to literary studies, see Bernard J. Paris, ed. and intro., *Third Force Psychology and the Study of Literature* (Rutherford, N.J.: Fairleigh Dickinson University Press, 1986). Maslow's idea of "peak-experience," important to my thinking, also informs Natalie

Crohn Schmitt's "Ecstasy and Peak-Experience: W. B. Yeats, Margharita Laski, and Abraham Maslow," *Comparative Drama* 28.2 (Summer 1994): 167–81.

5. S. Kitayama and H. R. Markus, "Construal of Self as Cultured Frame: Implications for Internationalising Psychology," Symposium on Internationalism and Higher Education, Ann Arbor Mich., 1992; cited in Matt Jarvis, *Theoretical Approaches to Psychology* (London and Philadelphia: Routledge, 2000), 69. For a good review of criticisms of Maslow's ideas, see Jarvis, *Theoretical Approaches to Psychology,* 68–69, 73–74.

6. Abraham H. Maslow, *Motivation and Personality,* 2nd ed. (New York: Harper and Row, 1970), 164. On "peak-experiences," see also Maslow's *Religions, Values, and Peak-Experiences* (New York: Penguin, 1970).

7. Abraham Maslow, *Toward a Psychology of Being,* 2nd ed. (New York: Van Nostrand Reinhold, 1968), iii–iv. For an introduction to deep ecology, see Bill Devall and George Sessions, *Deep Ecology* (Salt Lake City: Peregrine Smith, 1985); Paul Shepard, *Nature and Madness* (San Francisco: Sierra Club Books, 1982); Chellis Glendinning, *My Name is Chellis and I'm in Recovery from Western Civilization* (Boston: Shambhala, 1994); Ralph Metzner, *Green Psychology: Transforming Our Relationship to the Earth* (Rochester, Vt.: Park Street Press, 1999), 96. Metzner offers a useful review of the other diagnoses I refer to in his chapter, "Psychopathology of the Human-Nature Relationship," 80–97.

8. Theodore Roszak, Mary E. Gomes, and Allen D. Kanner, eds., *Ecopsychology: Restoring the Earth, Healing the Mind* (San Francisco: Sierra Club Books, 1995); Howard John Clinebell, *Ecotherapy: Healing Ourselves, Healing the Earth: A Guide to Ecologically Grounded Personality Theory, Spirituality, Therapy, and Education* (Minneapolis: Fortress Press, 1996); Jean Troy-Smith, *Called to Healing: Reflections on the Power of Earth's Stories in Women's Lives* (Albany: State University of New York Press, 1996); Deborah Du Nann Winter, *Ecological Psychology: Healing the Split between Planet and Self* (New York: HarperCollins, 1996).

9. Rachel Kaplan and Stephen Kaplan, *The Experience of Nature: A Psychological Perspective* (Cambridge, England, and New York: Cambridge University Press, 1989), and *Humanscape: Environments for People* (North Scituate, Mass.: Duxbury Press, 1978). Selected examples of Roger Ulrich's work are as follows: "Biophilia, Biophobia, and Natural Landscapes," in Stephen R. Kellert and Edward O. Wilson, eds., *The Biophilia Hypothesis* (Washington, D.C.: Island Press, 1993), 73–137; "Natural Versus Urban Scenes: Some Psychophysiological Effects," *Environment and Behavior* (1981), 523–56; "View Through a Window May Influence Recovery from Surgery," *Science* 224 (1984): 420–21. See also Nancy Gerlach-Spriggs, Richard Enoch Kaufman, and Sam Bass Warner, Jr., *Restorative Gardens: The Healing Landscape* (New Haven, Conn.: Yale University Press, 1998), especially "Toward a Theory of the Restorative Garden," 35–41. For examples of the application of environmental psychology to land-management practices, see B. L. Driver et al., eds., *Nature and the Human Spirit: Toward an Expanded Land Management Ethic* (State College, Pa.: Venture, 1996).

10. For information on sociobiology and evolutionary psychology, see Edward O. Wilson, *Sociobiology: The New Synthesis* (Cambridge, Mass.: The Belknap Press of Harvard University Press, 1975), *On Human Nature* (Cambridge, Mass.: Harvard University Press, 1978), and *Consilience: The Unity of Knowledge* (New York: Knopf, 1998);

Richard Dawkins, *The Selfish Gene* (Oxford, England, and New York: Oxford University Press, 1976); the essays collected in Jerome Barkow, Leda Cosmides, and John Tooby, eds., *The Adapted Mind: Evolutionary Psychology and the Generation of Culture* (New York: Oxford University Press, 1992); Robert Wright, *The Moral Animal: Why We Are the Way We Are: The New Science of Evolutionary Psychology* (New York: Random House, 1994); Daniel Dennett, *Darwin's Dangerous Idea: Evolution and the Meanings of Life* (New York: Simon and Schuster, 1995); Stephen Pinker, *How the Mind Works* (New York: W. W. Norton, 1997); and David M. Buss, *Evolutionary Psychology: The New Science of the Mind* (Boston: Allyn and Bacon, 1999). For critiques of evolutionary psychology, see Hilary Rose and Steven Rose, eds., *Alas, Poor Darwin: Arguments against Evolutionary Psychology* (New York: Harmony, 2000). On human preference for savannalike settings, see John D. Balling and John H. Falk, "Development of Visual Preference for Natural Environments," *Environment and Behavior* 14 (1982): 5–28, and Jay Appleton, *The Experience of Landscape,* rev. ed. (Chichester, England: Wiley, 1996).

11. On Metzner's references to mythology and story, the relevant chapters in *Green Psychology* are "Sky Gods and Earth Deities" (114–31), "The Black Goddess, the Green God, and the Wild Human" (132–56), and "The Place and the Story" (183–94); Herb Hammond and Stephanie Judy, "Belief, Wholeness, and Experience: Sensitizing Professional Land Managers to Spiritual Values," in Driver et al., eds., *Nature and the Human Spirit,* 377.

12. Scott Slovic, *Seeking Awareness in American Nature Writing: Henry Thoreau, Annie Dillard, Edward Abbey, Wendell Berry, Barry Lopez* (Salt Lake City: University of Utah Press, 1992), 3.

13. Henry D. Thoreau, *Walden,* ed. J. Lyndon Shanley, intro. Joyce Carol Oates (Princeton, N.J.: Princeton University Press, 1989), 3; Walt Whitman, "Song of Myself," in *Complete Poetry and Selected Prose,* ed. James E. Miller (Boston: Houghton Mifflin, 1959), 25; John Elder, *Imagining the Earth: Poetry and the Vision of Nature* (Urbana: University of Illinois Press, 1985), 3. The term "narrative scholarship" was coined by Scott Slovic, "Ecocriticism: Storytelling, Values, Communication, Contact" (Paper delivered at Annual Meeting of the Western Literature Association, Salt Lake City, 5–8 October 1994). For a further defense of "narrative scholarship," see John Tallmadge, "Toward a Natural History of Reading," *ISLE: Interdisciplinary Studies in Literature and Environment* 7.1 (Winter 2000), 33–45, and Ian Marshall, *Story Line: Exploring the Literature of the Appalachian Trail* (Charlottesville: University Press of Virginia, 1998), 7–9. For a fine example of narrative scholarship in practice, I recommend John Elder's *Reading the Mountains of Home* (Cambridge, Mass.: Harvard University Press, 1998). Narrative scholarship is akin to the feminist practice of "autobiographical criticism." See, for example, *The Intimate Critique: Autobiographical Literary Criticism,* ed. Diane P. Freedman, Olivia Frey, and Frances Murphy Zauhar (Durham, N.C.: Duke University Press, 1993).

14. See, for example, the end-piece diagram in Alexander von Humboldt and Aimé Bonpland, *Personal Narrative of Travels to the Equinoctial Regions of the New Continent, During the Years 1799-1804,* vol. 6, trans. Helen Maria Williams (London, 1826).

15. Octavio Paz, *The Other Mexico: Critique of the Pyramid* (N.Y.: Grove Press, 1972), 76–84; Richard Dawkins, *Climbing Mount Improbable* (New York: W. W. Norton, 1996); René Daumal, *Mount Analogue: A Novel of Symbolically Authentic Non-Euclidean Adventures in Mountain Climbing,* trans. Roger Shattuck and Vincent Stuart (New York: Pantheon, 1960; rpt. Boston: Shambhala, 1986, 1992); Kathleen Ferrick Rosenblatt, *René Daumal: The Life and Work of a Mystic Guide* (Albany: State University of New York Press, 1999), 197, 199.

16. My sources on the Psyche myth and other Greek and Roman myths are Michael Grant, *Myths of the Greeks and Romans* (New York: New American Library, 1962), and Edith Hamilton, *Mythology: Timeless Tales of Gods and Heroes* (New York: New American Library, 1940).

1. PHYSIOLOGICAL NEEDS

1. Henry D. Thoreau, *Walden,* ed. J. Lyndon Shanley, intro. Joyce Carol Oates (Princeton, N.J.: Princeton University Press, 1989), 11. Subsequent page references to *Walden,* given parenthetically, are from this edition.

2. Loren Eiseley, "The Flow of the River," in *The Immense Journey* (New York: Random House, 1957), 15.

3. Henry D. Thoreau, "Resistance to Civil Government," in *Walden and Resistance to Civil Government,* Norton Critical Edition, 2nd ed., ed. William Rossi (New York: Norton, 1992), 241.

4. See Jennifer Price, "When Women Were Women, Men Were Men, and Birds Were Hats," *Flight Maps: Adventures with Nature in Modern America* (New York: Basic Books, 1999), 57–109.

5. Frank Lloyd Wright, "Organic Architecture Looks at Modern Architecture," *Frank Lloyd Wright Collected Writings,* ed. Bruce Brooks Pfeiffer (New York: Rizzoli, in association with The Frank Lloyd Wright Foundation, 1995), 49. Wright was actually referring not to coffins but to modern architecture's persistent clinging to the idea of the box—but I couldn't resist the pun. For more on Wright's objections to the idea of the box, see his comments on "The Destruction of the Box: The Freedom of Space," in *Frank Lloyd Wright in the Realm of Ideas,* ed. Bruce Brooks Pfeiffer and Gerald Nordland (Carbondale: Southern Illinois University Press, 1988), 9–27.

6. R. Murray Schafer, "Acoustic Space," in David Seamon and Robert Mugerauer, eds., *Dwelling, Place and Environment: Towards a Phenomenology of Person and World* (Boston: Nijhoff, 1985), 88, 91, 93.

7. Frank Lloyd Wright, "The Natural House," in *Frank Lloyd Wright Collected Writings,* vol. 5, ed. Bruce Brooks Pfeiffer (New York: Rizzoli, in association with The Frank Lloyd Wright Foundation, 1995), 112.

8. John Keats, "La Belle Dame sans Merci: A Ballad," in *The Poems of John Keats,* ed. Jack Stillinger (Cambridge, Mass.: The Belknap Press of Harvard University Press, 1978), 357–59.

9. Robert Frost, "Two Look at Two," in *The Poetry of Robert Frost,* ed. Edward Connery Lathem (New York: Holt, Rinehart and Winston, 1969), 229–30.

2. SAFETY NEEDS

1. Abraham Maslow, *Motivation and Personality,* 2nd ed. (New York: Harper and Row, 1970), 41.

2. Herman Melville, "Bartleby the Scrivener," in *The Piazza Tales and Other Prose Pieces,* ed. Harrison Hayford et al. (Evanston and Chicago: Northwestern University Press and The Newberry Library, 1987), 14.

3. Maslow, *Motivation,* 154.

4. Ibid., 39, n. l.

5. See Viktor Shklovsky, "Art as Technique," in *Russian Formalist Criticsm: Four Essays,* ed. and intro. Lee T. Lemon and Marion J. Reis (Lincoln: University of Nebraska Press, 1965), 3–24.

6. Joseph Bruchac, "Gluscabi and the Game Animals," *Native American Stories* (Golden, Colo.: Fulcrum, 1991), 108–13.

7. The text I carried with me was Albert Cook's translation, *The Odyssey: A New Verse Translation* (New York: W. W. Norton, 1967). The Cyclops episode is in book 9. But since my concerns in this chapter are with the story as story as opposed to its language, all my references to the story are paraphrases or recollected (and not necessarily accurate) quotes. My concern is with the narrative as "diegesis," to use Robert Scholes's terminology, "the events narrated as events," as opposed to the narrative as a text (106). See Robert Scholes, "Decoding Papa: 'A Very Short Story' as Work and Text," in *Semiotics and Interpretation* (New Haven, Conn.: Yale University Press, 1982), 110–26; rpt. in *Literary Criticism: An Introduction to Theory and Practice,* 2n d ed., ed. Charles E. Bressler (Upper Saddle River, N.J.: Prentice Hall, 1999), 104–13.

8. David Abram, *The Spell of the Sensuous: Perception and Language in a More-than-Human World* (New York: Vintage, 1996), 95–96.

9. Edward O. Wilson, "The Arts and Their Interpretation," *Consilience: The Unity of Knowledge* (New York: Alfred A. Knopf, 1998), 210–37. Other important works on bioaesthetics include Ellen Dissanayake, *Homo Aestheticus: Where Art Comes From and Why* (New York: Free Press, 1992); Joseph Carroll, *Evolution and Literary Theory* (Columbia, Mo.: University of Missouri Press, 1995); Robert Storey, *Mimesis and the Human Animal: On the Biogenetic Foundations of Literary Representation* (Evanston, Ill.: Northwestern University Press, 1996); Brett Cooke and Frederick Turner, eds., *Biopoetics: Evolutionary Explorations in the Arts* (New York: Paragon Press, 1999). All these raise provocative ideas about the role evolutionary psychology can play in understanding art and literature, but many, including Wilson's *Consilience,* suffer from a bias against postmodern theory. Their objection is that postmodern theory overemphasizes "unscientific" ideas about cultural relativism. But such ideas seem entirely in keeping with the direction of findings in twentieth-century physics. See my review of *Consilience* in *ISLE: Interdisciplinary Studies in Literature and Environment* 6.1 (1999): 168–70. For the case against the role of postmodern theory in ecocriticism and a review of its incompatibility with science, see Glen Love, "Science, Anti-Science, and Ecocriticism," *ISLE* 6.1 (1999): 65–81.

10. Vladimir Propp, *Morphology of the Folktale,* trans. Laurence Scott, intro. Svatava Pirkova-Jakobson, 2nd ed. revised, ed., and preface Louis A. Wagner, new intro. Alan Dundes (Austin: University of Texas Press, 1968).

11. Wilson, *Consilience,* 223–24.

12. Alfred, Lord Tennyson, "Ulysses," in *Tennyson's Poetry,* sel. and ed. Robert W. Hill, Jr. (New York: W. W. Norton, 1999), 82–84.

13. See, for example, the essays collected in *Alas, Poor Darwin: Arguments against Evolutionary Psychology,* ed. Hilary Rose and Steven Rose (New York: Harmony Books, 2000). The Roses' collection demonstrates the fierce controversy engendered by sociobiology and evolutionary psychology, and the essays collected there identify the excessive claims of evolutionary psychology. To fend off possible attacks, let me clarify that I do not claim that all elements of all literature are somehow adaptive, just as it is clear that not all human behavior is adaptive; nor do I deny the massive and obvious influence of culture on works of literature or claim that all elements of culture can be traced to some genetic or adaptive origin. I do not have some right-wing agenda that I wish to further. (Far from it!) But not even the staunchest critics of evolutionary psychology claim that there is nothing to the idea of some evolutionary basis for the functioning of the human mind. What I wish to do is explore the potential relevance to literature of some of the ideas of evolutionary psychology, assuming that some of our behavior, artistic and otherwise, has a genetic and adaptive basis. I do so out of a sense that literary critics in general have paid little attention to any evolutionary basis for literature, and those that have, it seems, often do have (if not a right-wing bias) an antipathy to postmodern thought which I do not share.

14. Edward O. Wilson, *On Human Nature* (Cambridge, Mass.: Harvard University Press, 1978), 167. Wilson also discusses the "genetic leash" by which cultural vagaries are constrained by our genetic predisposition in *Consilience,* 157–58.

15. A literary work that emerges from the test of time would qualify, then, as a "meme," Richard Dawkins's term for a piece of memorable information that is passed on in a culture, a cultural building block, the equivalent of a successful gene in biological evolution. See Richard Dawkins, *The Selfish Gene* (New York: Oxford University Press, 1976). Daniel C. Dennett also identifies *The Odyssey* as a meme in *Darwin's Dangerous Idea: Evolution and the Meanings of Life* (New York: Simon and Schuster, 1995), 344.

16. Storey, *Mimesis,* 83.

17. William H. Calvin, *The Cerebral Symphony: Seashore Reflections on the Structure of Consciousness* (New York: Bantam, 1990), 23, 24, 83, 270, 297, 308, 322.

18. A. E. Housman, *The Collected Poems of A. E. Housman* (New York: Holt, Rinehart and Winston, 1965), 90.

19. Henry D. Thoreau, *Walden,* ed. J. Lyndon Shanley (Princeton, N.J.: Princeton University Press, 1971), 97.

20. Storey, *Mimesis,* 85.

21. Julie Davis, "The Lion Didn't Eat Us," *Journey to the Fluted Mountain: Stories and Music from the Colorado Trail* (Nederland, Colo.: Winter Wind Music, 1997).

22. Robert Pack, "Afterword: Taking Dominion over the Wilderness," in *Poems for a Small Planet: Contemporary American Nature Poetry,* ed. Robert Pack and Jay Parini (Hanover, N.H.: University Press of New England, 1993), 275.

23. On the shape of the hero's journey, see Joseph Campbell, *The Hero with a Thousand Faces* (Cleveland: World, 1956), and *The Hero's Journey: The World of Joseph*

Campbell: Joseph Campbell on His Life and Work, ed. and intro. Phil Cousineau (San Francisco: Harper and Row, 1990); Jon Krakauer, *Into the Wild* (New York: Villard, 1996), and *Into Thin Air: A Personal Account of the Mount Everest Disaster* (New York: Villard, 1997); Andrea Barrett, *The Voyage of the Narwhal* (New York: W. W. Norton, 1998).

24. Sebastian Junger, *The Perfect Storm: A True Story of Men Against the Sea* (New York: HarperCollins, 1997).

25. Caroline Alexander, *The Endurance: Shackleton's Legendary Antarctic Expedition* (New York: Knopf, in association with the American Museum of Natural History, 1999).

26. Shepard makes a similar point in *Coming Home to the Pleistocene,* contending that in our ancestral past "observational learning" made every animal a "potential teacher" from whom we learned both hunting and survival skills. Further, he suggests that imitations of animal calls and behavior, or "sharing the idea of an animal," may have been the origin of human communication. Paul Shepard, *Coming Home to the Pleistocene,* ed. Florence R. Shepard (Washington, D.C.: Island Press/Shearwater Books, 1998), 31, 54. See also Shepard's *The Others: How Animals Made Us Human* (Washington, D.C.: Island Press, 1995).

27. Wilson, *Consilience,* 127.

28. Ibid., 278. The idea of our evolutionary adaptation to a world we no longer live in echoes Shepard's *Coming Home to the Pleistocene.*

29. Shepard, *Coming Home,* 133.

30. "Petroglyph Trail Guide" (Mesa Verde Museum Association, Inc., for the National Park Service, n.d.), 10.

3. LANDSCAPES OF LOVE AND BELONGING

1. Though I had *Firekeeper: New and Selected Poems* in my pack (Minneapolis: Milkweed Editions, 1994), the publisher has requested that I cite the more recent and complete edition of Rogers's poems, and I am happy to oblige: Pattiann Rogers, *Song of the World Becoming: New and Collected Poems, 1981-2001* (Minneapolis: Milkweed Editions, 2001), 85. Subsequent references to Rogers's poems, given parenthetically, are to this edition. Even when I refer to *Firekeeper* in the text (because that's the book I actually had with me), the citations are to *Song of the World Becoming.*

2. Laura Sewall, *Sight and Sensibility: The Ecopsychology of Perception* (New York: Jeremy P. Tarcher, 1999), 167–68.

3. E. B. White, "Once More to the Lake," in *Essays of E. B. White* (New York: Harper and Row, 1977), 197–202.

4. Gary Paul Nabhan, "Going Truant: The Initiation of Young Naturalists," in Gary Paul Nabhan and Stephen Trimble, *The Geography of Childhood: Why Children Need Wild Places* (Boston: Beacon Press, 1994), 40. Nabhan notes that the numbers are a paraphrase of a Harris poll.

5. Louise Chawla, *In the First Country of Places: Nature, Poetry, and Childhood Identity* (Albany: State University of New York Press, 1994), 11. The study Chawla cites is D. C. Rubin, S. E. Wetzler, and R. D. Nebes, "Autobiographical Memory Across the Lifespan," in *Autobiographical Memory,* ed. David C. Rubin (Cambridge, England, and New York: Cambridge University Press, 1986).

6. Chawla, *In the First Country,* 29–30, 31.

7. Ibid., 26.

8. Henry David Thoreau, "Walking," in *The Natural History Essays,* intro. and notes Robert Sattelmeyer (Salt Lake City: Peregrine Smith, 1980), 99.

9. Chawla, *In the First Country,* 14–15, 26; William Wordsworth, "Preface to *Lyrical Ballads,*" in *The Selected Poetry and Prose of Wordsworth,* ed. and intro. Geoffrey H. Hartman (New York: New American Library, 1970), 423. For an example of Wordsworth's celebration of childhood sensationalism, see "Ode: Intimations of Immortality from Recollections of Early Childhood," 163–68.

10. Pattiann Rogers, *The Dream of the Marsh Wren: Writing as Reciprocal Creation* (Minneapolis: Milkweed Editions, 1999), 13.

11. Aldo Leopold, *Round River: From the Journals of Aldo Leopold,* ed. Luna B. Leopold (Oxford: Oxford University Press, 1993), 146; David Quammen, "Sympathy for the Devil: A More Generous View of the World's Most Despised Animal," *Natural Acts: A Sidelong View of Science and Nature* (New York: Avon, 1985), 27.

12. Rogers, *Dream of the Marsh Wren,* 86, 27.

13. See Edward O. Wilson, *Biophilia* (Cambridge, Mass.: Harvard University Press, 1984); Stephen R. Kellert and Edward O. Wilson, eds., *The Biophilia Hypothesis* (Washington, D.C.: Island Press, 1993).

14. "As flies to wanton boys are we to the gods, / They kill us for their sport"—Shakespeare, *King Lear* 4.1.38–39.

15. The poems I refer to are Richard Wilbur's "Love Calls Us to the Things of This World," William Shakespeare's "Shall I Compare Thee to a Summer's Day," Robert Burns's "Oh, My Love Is Like a Red, Red Rose," Emily Dickinson's "Wild Nights! Wild Nights!," John Donne's "The Flea," and T. S. Eliot's "The Love Song of J. Alfred Prufrock." All are in *An Introduction to Poetry,* 9th ed., ed. X. J. Kennedy and Dana Gioia (New York: Longman, 1998), 86–87, 115–16, 133–34, 364, 403–4, 409–13.

16. Diane Ackerman, *A Natural History of Love* (New York: Vintage, 1995), 12. The other universal themes of love poetry identified by Ackerman are "Love's alchemy, or the power to transform," "Love as enslavement," "Being disabled," and "A secret kept from one's parents" (11–13).

17. Jerry Mander, *Four Arguments for the Elimination of Television* (New York: Quill, 1978), 61, 275–82; Bill McKibben, *The Age of Missing Information* (New York: Plume, 1992), 190–91.

18. Walt Whitman, "Song of Myself," in *Complete Poetry and Selected Prose, by Walt Whitman,* ed. and intro. James E. Miller, Jr. (Boston: Houghton Mifflin, 1959), 26.

19. Ackerman, *Natural History of Love,* 68, 19, xxi, 43, 196.

20. Ibid., 95, 320.

21. Gregory Corso, "Marriage," in *Mindfield* (New York: Thunder's Mouth Press, 1989), 61–64.

22. Mark Twain [Samuel Clemens], "The Diary of Adam and Eve," in *The Complete Short Stories of Mark Twain,* ed. and intro. Charles Neider (New York: Bantam, 1957), 278.

23. James Fenimore Cooper, *The Pioneers, or The Sources of the Susquehanna: a*

Descriptive Tale, ed. James Franklin Beard et al. (Albany: State University of New York Press, 1980), 293.

24. Ralph Waldo Emerson, "The American Scholar," in *Emerson's Prose and Poetry,* ed. Joel Porte and Saundra Morris (New York: W. W. Norton, 2001), 56–69. For nineteenth-century discussions of the landscape as source of America's national literature, see "American Poetry," *The Knickerbocker* (November 1838), 383–88; "The Great Nation of Futurity," *The Democratic Review* 6 (November 1839), 426–30; "Nationality in Literature," *The Democratic Review* 20 (March 1847), 264–72; "Griswold's *The Poets and Poetry of America,*" *The North American Review* 58 (January 1844), 1–29; "Have Great Poets Become Impossible," *Harper's New Monthly Magazine* 1 (August 1850), 340–45. These essays make specific mention of American nature as subject matter for a distinctively American literature, but in almost every essay on the subject of literary nationalism at that time the notion is at least implied. For a sampling of such essays, see Robert Spiller, ed. and intro., *The American Literary Revolution, 1783-1837* (Garden City, N.Y.: Anchor, 1967). The most complete study of the rise of American literary nationalism is Benjamin T. Spencer, *The Quest for Nationality: An American Literary Campaign* (Syracuse: Syracuse University Press, 1957). For specific references to American nature as a source for literary inspiration, see pages 10–14, 47–51, and 164–67.

25. Washington Irving, "Rip Van Winkle," in *The Sketch Book of Geoffrey Crayon, Gent.* (New York: Heritage, 1939), 33.

26. Louis Legrand Noble, *The Life and Works of Thomas Cole,* ed. Elliot S. Vesell (Hensonville, N.Y.: Black Dome Press, 1997), 259.

27. Paul Shepard, *Man in the Landscape: A Historic View of the Esthetics of Nature* (New York: Alfred A. Knopf, 1967), 105; Denis E. Cosgrove, *Social Formation and Symbolic Landscape* (London: Croom Helm, 1984), 20. See also Shepard's *Coming Home to the Pleistocene,* ed. Florence Shepard (Washington, D.C.: Island Press, 1998), 138–42.

28. Cosgrove, *Social Formation,* 176. On the implications of prospect views, see Alan Wallach, "Thomas Cole: Landscape and the Course of American Empire," in William H. Truettner and Alan Wallach, eds., *Thomas Cole: Landscape into History* (New Haven, Conn.: Yale University Press, 1994), 74–75; Carole Fabricant, "The Aesthetics and Politics of Landscape in the Eighteenth Century," in Ralph Cohen, ed., *Studies in Eighteenth-Century British Art and Aesthetics* (Berkeley: University of California Press, 1985), 49–81; James Turner, *The Politics of Landscape: Rural Scenery and Society in English Poetry 1630-1660* (Oxford, England: Basil Blackwell, 1979); John Barrel, "The Public Prospect and the Private View: The Politics of Taste in Eighteenth-Century Britain," in Simon Pugh, ed., *Reading Landscape: Country—City—Capital* (Manchester, England: Manchester University Press, 1990), 19–40.

29. Cosgrove, *Social Formation,* 26.

30. Sewall, *Sight and Sensibility,* 39, 35–36, 138, 36, 54, 59.

31. Ibid., 35.

32. Bruce Wadsworth and the Schenectady Chapter of the Adirondack Mountain Club, *Guide to Catskill Trails,* 2nd ed. (The Adirondack Mountain Club, 1994), 59; Helen Gere Cruickshank, ed., *John and William Bartram's America: Selections from the Writings of the Philadelphia Naturalists* (Greenwich, Conn.: Devin-Adair, 1990), 247.

33. Roger Weingarten, "Incidental Music: The Grotesque, The Romantic, and the Retrenched," *Poetry East,* ed. Richard Jones and Kate Daniels, nos. 20–21 (1986): 177–78; quoted in Rogers, *Dream of the Marsh Wren,* 35.

34. José Emilio Pacheco, "High Treason," in *Don't Ask Me How the Time Goes By: Poems, 1964–1968,* trans. Alastair Reid (New York: Columbia University Press, 1978), 35.

35. Nathaniel Hawthorne, "The Ambitious Guest," in *Twice-Told Tales,* vol. 9 of *The Centenary Edition of the Works of Nathaniel Hawthorne,* ed. William Charvat et al. (Columbus: Ohio State University Press, 1974), 324–33.

36. Rogers, *Dream of the Marsh Wren,* 6.

4. ESTEEM NEEDS

1. Edward Whymper, *Scrambles Amongst the Alps in the Years 1860–1869* (Philadelphia: J. B. Lippincott, 1872); Alexander von Humboldt and Aimé Bonpland, *Personal Narrative of Travels to the Equinoctial Regions of the New Continent, During the Years 1799–1804,* 7 vols., trans. Helen Maria Williams (London, 1826); Joe Simpson, *Touching the Void* (New York: Harper and Row, 1988); Jon Krakauer, *Into Thin Air: A Personal Account of the Mount Everest Disaster* (New York: Circular, 1997).

2. John Muir, "A Near View of the High Sierra," in *John Muir: Mountaineering Essays,* ed. Richard F. Fleck (Salt Lake City: University of Utah Press, 1997), 9, 43.

3. See, for example, Michael P. Cohen, *The Pathless Way: John Muir and American Wilderness* (Madison: University of Wisconsin Press, 1984), especially the section on "Ego and Games," 83–86; Arthur W. Ewart, "John Muir and Vertical Sauntering," in *John Muir: Life and Work,* ed. Sally M. Miller (Albuquerque: University of New Mexico Press, 1993), 42–62; and Richard F. Fleck, "Introduction" to his *John Muir: Mountaineering Essays,* xix.

4. *The Life and Letters of John Muir,* ed. William Frederic Badè, in *John Muir: His Life and Letters and Other Writings,* ed. and intro. Terry Gifford (Seattle: The Mountaineers, 1996), 195.

5. Whymper, *Scrambles,* 43, 152; John Ruskin, *Sesames and Lilies,* vol. 18 of *Modern Painters: The Works of John Ruskin,* ed. E. T. Cook and Alexander Wetterburn, 39 vols. (New York and London: G. Allen and Longman, Green, 1904), 25. Ruskin's most extended commentary on mountain aesthetics, of course, comes in *Of Mountain Beauty,* vol. 4 of his *Works.* For a partial list of mountaineering titles in Muir's library, including accounts from the Himalayas, the Andes, the Canadian Rockies, and Alaska as well as the Alps, see Fleck, "Introduction," *John Muir,* xvi.

6. Michael P. Cohen, *The Pathless Way,* 85.

7. Whymper, *Scrambles,* 161.

8. Muir, "South Dome," in *John Muir Summering in the Sierra,* ed. Robert Engberg (Madison: University of Wisconsin Press, 1984), 149.

9. David Roberts, "Patey Agonistes," in *Moments of Doubt* (Seattle: The Mountaineers, 1986), 189; Heinrich Harrer, *The White Spider: The Classic Account of the Ascent of the Eiger,* trans. Hugh Merrick (New York: Tarcher/Putnam, 1998), 174, 116.

10. James Ramsey Ullman, *The White Tower* (Philadelphia: J. B. Lippincott, 1945); Harrer, *White Spider,* 175.

11. Ewart, "John Muir," 58. Ewart also calls Muir "the best climber of his era."

12. Muir made the comment in a letter to Robert Underwood Johnson, editor of *Century* magazine. See Badè, *John Muir*, 319.

13. John Muir, "A Perilous Night on Shasta's Summit," in Fleck, *John Muir*, 69–70.

14. Ibid., 72.

15. Ibid., 73–75.

16. Muir, "A Near View," 47–48.

17. Whitney qtd. in Francis P. Farquhar, *History of the Sierra Nevada* (Berkeley: University of California Press, 1966), 156; Clarence King, ed., *Systematic Geology: Report of the Fortieth Parallel Survey* (Washington, D.C.: Government Printing Office, 1878), 478. Muir had one thing wrong in his account of glaciation in the Sierras. He assumed there was but one ice age; in fact, there were four.

18. Clarence King, *Mountaineering in the Sierra Nevada* (London, 1872), 272, 275.

19. John Muir, "Ascent of Mount Whitney," in Engberg, *John Muir Summering in the Sierra*, 112, 105.

20. Rachel Kaplan and Stephen Kaplan, *The Experience of Nature: A Psychological Perspective* (Cambridge, England, and New York: Cambridge University Press, 1989), 50–57.

21. Simpson, *Touching the Void*, 120, 138.

22. Krakauer, *Into Thin Air*, 23.

23. Muir, *Our National Parks* (Boston: Houghton Mifflin, 1901), 56.

24. Harrer, *White Spider*, 111.

25. Ibid., 12, 120–21.

26. Ibid., 12, 10.

27. Heinrich Harrer, *Seven Years in Tibet*, trans. Richard Graves (New York: Dutton, 1954).

28. For more on the legends of Shasta, see John Calderazzo's Shasta chapter, "Eighteen Views of a Volcano," in *Where the Earth Begins: Volcanoes and Our Inner Lives* (forthcoming).

29. Henry Thoreau, "Ktaadn," in *Thoreau in the Mountains*, ed. William Howarth (New York: Farrar, Strauss, Giroux, 1982), 150.

30. Harrer, *White Spider*, 131.

31. Muir, "Wind Storm in the Forest," in *The Wilderness World of John Muir*, ed. and intro. Edwin Way Teale (Boston: Houghton Mifflin, 1954), 186–87, 189–90; Thomas J. Lyon, "Part I: A History," in *This Incomperable Lande: A Book of American Nature Writing* (New York: Penguin, 1989), 59; Muir, "The Tuolomne Camp," in Fleck, *John Muir*, 5.

32. Muir, "Wind Storm," in Teale, *The Wilderness World of John Muir*, 189–90.

33. Mihalyi Csikszentmihalyi, *Flow: The Psychology of Optimal Experience* (New York: HarperPerennial, 1991), 49–61. Csikszentmihalyi himself, though he does not refer to Muir, cites mountain climbing on several occasions as an experience that lends itself to the experience of flow.

34. Muir, "A Perilous Night," 76.

35. Ibid., 79–80.

36. Ibid., 83.

37. Michael P. Cohen, *Pathless Way*, 145–46; Muir, "A Perilous Night," 80, 85–86.

38. Muir, "A Perilous Night," 87.

39. Ibid., 85.

40. Ralph Waldo Emerson, "Nature," in *Emerson's Prose and Poetry*, ed. Joel Porte and Saundra Morris (New York: W. W. Norton, 2001), 3; Henry David Thoreau, "Walking," in *The Natural History Essays*, intro. and notes Robert Sattelmeyer (Salt Lake City: Peregrine Smith, 1980), 93.

41. Muir, "Mountain Thoughts," in Fleck, *John Muir*, 99.

42. Qtd. in Michael P. Cohen, *Pathless Way*, 122.

43. Muir, "Mountain Thoughts," 99–100.

44. Ibid., 100.

45. Muir, "An Ascent of Mount Rainier," in Fleck, *John Muir*, 116.

46. Ibid.; "Glenora Peak," in Fleck, *John Muir*, 137.

47. Muir, "Shasta in Winter," in Engberg, *John Muir Summering*, 34.

5. SELF-ACTUALIZATION

1. John Burroughs, "Nature Near Home," in *Birch Browsings: A John Burroughs Reader*, ed. and intro. Bill McKibben (New York: Penguin, 1992), 229; Henry D. Thoreau, *Walden*, ed. J. Lyndon Shanley (Princeton, N.J.: Princeton University Press, 1989), 101; Malcolm Cowley, ed. and intro., *Walt Whitman's Leaves of Grass: The First (1855) Edition* (New York: Penguin, 1959), xxxii–xxxiii, xvi.

2. Maslow, *Motivation and Personality*, 72–74.

3. Abraham Maslow, *Religions, Values, and Peak-Experiences* (New York: Penguin, 1970).

4. Maslow, *Motivation and Personality*, 152.

5. Horace Traubel, *With Walt Whitman in Camden*, vol. 2 (1907; rpt., New York: Rowman and Littlefield, 1961), 175.

6. Walt Whitman, "Song of Myself," in *Complete Poetry and Selected Prose*, ed. and intro. James E. Miller, Jr. (Boston: Houghton Mifflin, 1959), 25. Subsequent references to "Song," given parenthetically, are to this text.

7. Henry D. Thoreau, *Journal 4: 1851-1852*, ed. Leonard N. Neufeldt and Nancy Craig Simmons, in *The Writings of Henry D. Thoreau*, gen. ed. Robert Sattelmeyer (Princeton, N.J.: Princeton University Press, 1992), 28.

8. John Burroughs, *Notes on Walt Whitman, as Poet and Person* (New York: American News Company, 1867; rpt. New York: Haskell House, n.d.), 37–38. For a discussion of Burroughs's nature-based criticism of Whitman, see Jim Warren, "Whitman Land: John Burroughs's Pastoral Criticism," *ISLE: Interdisciplinary Studies in Literature and Environment* 8.1 (Winter 2001), 83–114.

9. Thoreau, Letter to H. G. O. Blake, 7 December 1856, in *Great Short Works of Henry David Thoreau*, ed. and intro. Wendell Glick (New York: HarperPerennial, 1993), 107; Maslow, *Motivation and Personality*, 156, 57–58.

10. Maslow, *Motivation and Personality*, 73.

11. Quotes from Whitman in my parodic verse from "Song of Myself," 28; Herman Melville, *Moby-Dick Or, The Whale*, intro. Andrew Delbanco (New York: Penguin, 1992), 175; Robert Frost, "Design," in *Robert Frost Poetry and Prose*, ed. Edward Con-

nery Lathem and Lawrance Thompson (New York: Owl, 1984), 122; Robert Burns, "Tam O'Shanter," in *Robert Burns: Poems*, ed. Henry W. Meikle and William Beattie (New York: Penguin, 1977), 155.

12. Melville, *Moby-Dick*, 5; Ralph Waldo Emerson, "Nature," in *Emerson's Prose and Poetry*, ed. Joel Porte and Saundra Morris (New York: W. W. Norton, 2001), 35; William Shakespeare, *As You Like It*, 2.1.16–17; Jonathan Edwards, *Images or Shadows of Divine Things*, ed. Perry Miller (New Haven, Conn.: Yale University Press, 1948). For the "Images" pertaining to mountains as theologic metaphor, see numbers 29, 47, 64, 66, 67, 74, 105, 107, 124, 151, 175.

13. That, in fact, is the thesis of Perry Miller's discussion of the influence of Edwards and the practice of typology on the development of transcendentalism in his essay "From Edwards to Emerson," in *Errand into the Wilderness* (Cambridge, Mass.: The Belknap Press of Harvard University Press, 1956), 184–203.

14. Maslow, *Religions, Values, and Peak-Experiences*, 63.

15. Annie Dillard, *Pilgrim at Tinker Creek* (New York: HarperPerennial, 1988), 65.

16. Maslow, *Religions, Values, and Peak-Experiences*, 59.

17. Matthew Arnold, "Dover Beach," *The Norton Anthology of Poetry*, 3rd ed., ed. Alexander Wilson et al. (New York: W. W. Norton, 1983), 794; Melville, *Moby-Dick*, 349; Nathaniel Hawthorne, "Ethan Brand," in *The Snow-Image and Uncollected Tales*, vol. 11 of *The Centenary Edition of the Works of Nathaniel Hawthorne*, ed. William Charvat et al. (Columbus: Ohio State University Press, 1974), 83–102; E. M. Forster, *Howards End*, ed. Alistair M. Duckworth (Boston: Bedford Books, 1997), 21.

18. Maslow, *Religions, Values, and Peak-Experiences*, 62.

19. Ibid., 66.

20. See, for example, the section on "Logging" in Gary Snyder, *Myths and Texts* (New York: Totem, 1960); Robinson Jeffers, "Boats in a Fog," in *Selected Poems* (New York: Vintage, 1963), 37.

21. Maslow, *Religions, Values, and Peak-Experiences*, 60.

22. Ibid., 61, 65–66.

23. Gary Snyder, "Axe-Handles," in *No Nature: New and Selected Poems* (New York: Pantheon, 1992), 266.

24. Maslow, *Religions, Values, and Peak-Experiences*, 62.

25. Henry David Thoreau, "Walking," in *The Natural History Essays*, intro. and notes Robert Sattelmeyer (Salt Lake City: Peregrine Smith, 1980), 99.

26. David S. Reynolds, *Walt Whitman's America: A Cultural Biography* (New York: Vintage, 1995), 240.

27. Allen Ginsberg, "Footnote to Howl," in *Collected Poems 1947-1980* (New York: Harper and Row, 1984), 134.

28. Emily Dickinson, "Wild Nights! Wild Nights!" in *The Poems of Emily Dickinson*, vol. 1, ed. Thomas H. Johnson (Cambridge, Mass.: The Belknap Press of Harvard University Press, 1963), 179.

29. Maslow, *Religions, Values, and Peak-Experiences*, x.

30. Ibid., 22.

31. Ibid., 78.

32. Maslow, *Motivation and Personality,* 154.

33. Rogers, *Song of the World Becoming,* 160.

34. Laura Sewall, *Sight and Sensibility: The Ecopsychology of Perception* (New York: Jeremy P. Tarcher, 1999).

35. Walt Whitman, "Out of the Cradle, Endlessly Rocking," in *Complete Poetry,* 184.

36. Maslow, *Religions, Values, and Peak-Experiences,* xv, xiv, xvi, xiv.

37. Thoreau, "Walking," 120.

38. Henry D. Thoreau, *A Week on the Concord and Merrimack Rivers,* ed. Carl F. Hovde, William L. Howarth, and Elizabeth Hall Witherell; intro. Linck C. Johnson, *The Writings of Henry D. Thoreau* (Princeton, N.J.: Princeton University Press, 1980), 343.

39. Robert Pirsig, *Zen and the Art of Motorcycle Maintenance* (New York: Bantam, 1984), 183.

40. Ibid.

41. Maslow, *Religions, Values, and Peak-Experiences,* 24, 26, 30–31, 33.

42. Reynolds, *Walt Whitman's America,* 275. Reynolds notes that Whitman's references to centrifugal and centripetal forces are derived from the Harmonialist movement of the day, perhaps also a source for Whitman's optimism, mysticism, and nature worship. The centripetal-centrifugal idea, says Reynolds, helps Whitman resolve in his poetry "the increasing conflict between the individual and the mass" in American culture (274).

43. Ibid., 242–43.

44. Maslow, *Religions, Values, and Peak-Experiences,* 63.

45. Dr. Seuss [Theodore Geisel], *The Lorax,* in *Six by Seuss* (New York: Random House, 1991), 307.

46. Ursula K. Le Guin, "The Carrier Bag Theory of Fiction," in *The Ecocriticism Reader: Landmarks in Literary Ecology,* ed. Cheryll Glotfelty and Harold Fromm (Athens: University of Georgia Press, 1996), 152–53.

47. On Thoreau's journal as his masterpiece, see Sharon Cameron, *Writing Nature: Henry Thoreau's Journal* (Oxford, England, and New York: Oxford University Press, 1985); Susan Fenimore Cooper, *Rural Hours,* ed. Rochelle Johnson and Daniel Patterson (Athens: University of Georgia Press, 1998); Marcia Bonta, *Appalachian Spring* (Pittsburgh: University of Pittsburgh Press, 1991), *Appalachian Summer* (Pittsburgh: University of Pittsburgh Press, 1999), *Appalachian Autumn* (Pittsburgh: University of Pittsburgh Press, 1994).

48. Henry David Thoreau, "Ktaadn," in *Thoreau in the Mountains,* ed. with commentary by William Howarth (New York: Farrar, Strauss, Giroux, 1982), 150.

INDEX

UNDER THE SIGN OF NATURE
Explorations in Ecocriticism